The Flame of Eternity

The Flame of Eternity

An Interpretation of Nietzsche's Thought

Krzysztof Michalski

Translated from the Polish by Benjamin Paloff

Princeton University Press

Princeton and Oxford

© 2007 Krzysztof Michalski
English translation copyright © 2012 by Princeton University Press

Published by Princeton University Press, 41 William Street,
Princeton, New Jersey 08540
In the United Kingdom: Princeton University Press,
6 Oxford Street, Woodstock, Oxfordshire OX20 1TW
press.princeton.edu

Library of Congress Cataloging-in-Publication Data
Michalski, Krzysztof, 1948–
  [Plomien wiecznosci. English]
  The flame of eternity : an interpretation of Nietzsche's thought / Krzysztof
Michalski ; translated from the Polish by Benjamin Paloff.
    p. cm.
  Includes bibliographical references (p.   ) and index.
  ISBN 978-0-691-14346-0 (alk. paper)
  1. Nietzsche, Friedrich Wilhelm, 1844-1900.   2. Eternal
return.   3. Eternity.   I. Title.
  B3318.E88M5313 2012
  193—dc23   2011025268

British Library Cataloging-in-Publication Data is available

The translation of this publication has been subsidized by Instytut Książki—the
©POLAND Translation Programme

©POLAND

This book has been composed in Adobe Caslon Pro

Printed on acid-free paper. ∞

Printed in the United States of America

10 9 8 7 6 5 4 3 2 1

Contents

Preface

THE SUBJECT OF THIS book is eternity, the concept of eternity. The point of departure is Nietzsche. I contend that Nietzsche's thought can be organized into a consistent whole through precisely his concept of eternity. Both original and at the same time deeply rooted in tradition, Nietzsche's concept remains as thought-provoking for us as it had been among his contemporaries.

In Nietzsche's books and notes, eternity emerges under the name "the eternal return of the same." But we find the notion of eternity not only where we hear of eternal return: it is present in nearly everything Nietzsche wrote, from his first sketches to his last pages before he succumbed to madness. Nietzsche's intellectual work is, from beginning to end, a reflection on human life—how it passes, how it gives rise to new things—and therefore on time. And time, Nietzsche believes, cannot be understood without eternity; without reference to eternity one cannot understand how it flows, what we mean when we say that it destroys or creates.

In my reading of Nietzsche eternity is a dimension of time, the core of time, its essence, its engine. Not its infinite continuation, not its refutation; eternity is neither a diamond nor the rock of which "time does not partake." The concept of eternity answers the question of why "today" transforms into "yesterday"; eternity comes to the fore precisely in the flow of time.

Eternity, for Nietzsche, is thus a physiological notion; the concept that succinctly expresses the temporality of our lives is that of "the body." If eternity comes to the fore in time, then it is precisely our bodily presence in the world, "the body," that must be its expression.

The body: hair falls out, muscles get flabby, memory fades. But that's not all. The concept of "the body," Nietzsche contends, points to something more than this falling out, this loss of tone, this fading. To something more than disintegration. The confrontation with death demonstrates this. As does love.

In the face of death, all known concepts, all words, lose their meaning, are no longer useful. What good, then, are such notions as "more" or "less"? What's "broken" here? Death is not the next step in life; when I am dying, I am not "more" ill. Death is a step into the abyss, a radical interruption of continuity. Death does not fit what I know; our confrontation with death places us before a wall of incomprehension. Before a mystery.

Isn't it for precisely this reason that love is as "strong as death"—because, like death, love demolishes everything it had seemed we understood and interrupts the course of the life we have lived till now?

The body: our physical, fragile, inevitably mutable presence, inexorably slipping away, is also a—what? a sign? a symbol? a reaching-out?—for a mystery that evades words and concepts, a mystery hidden in a loved one's smile, in the terror-inflected hope that confronts the inevitably approaching end of everything I see, feel, and think. Death and love reveal the fundamental discontinuity of our bodily presence in the world. The fact is that in every moment of our lives all meaning may become suspended, and (here's Nietzsche) "the clock of my life"—the clock that measures the rhythm of events: yesterday a seminar, today shopping, tomorrow travel—"[draws] a breath."[1] In this interval, briefer than any moment one can measure, in this crack, this fissure, this tear—in the *blink of an eye*—everything is left to question, and a chance for a new beginning arises. This is "eternity." Because of it, the seemingly ever-present network of meanings—the world—"passes," "becomes," but "is" not.

"Eternity" is therefore a concept that characterizes our lives in their physical, material, corporeal reality—day in, day out. It is a concept that refers to the impossibility of uniting any moment of life into one, content-filled totality, into the totality of some content. Eternity is the internal diversification of our lives, the difference between what is or could be known and that "more" which escapes all knowledge.

"Eternal life," Nietzsche notes, "is no other life: it's the very life you are living."[2]

It may be that only in life so conceived—life that cannot be consolidated into a totality, fractured life, marked with the irremediable fissure of eternity—perhaps only in such a life one may find a place for God.

From the perspective of life as a sequence of interlinked moments—from birth to death, from breakfast to dinner—this interval, this fracture, this momentary breathlessness is naturally a threat, a sickness, a pathology. We're sick with eternity: its chronic state is time, its crisis—love and death. But, on the other hand, isn't it also pathological that we see sickness in the very thing that constitutes the meaning of life, that determines what it means to live? That we take the essential discontinuity of our lives—the fact that life "passes away," "becomes," "flows"—for a sickness to be treated? That we try to fill this gap with concepts, to patch the fracture of every moment with some piece of knowledge, to remove that internal diversification of life with the help of some truth underlying it, and thus to render our lives consistent and comprehensible?

It is precisely this pathology that Nietzsche calls "nihilism."

He recognizes it in many phenomena of modern culture: in history as science, in science in general. In morality, insofar as it attempts to construct a totalizing account of good and evil. In religion, particularly in Christianity, insofar as it takes "God" for "truth," knowledge of which (if only at some other time, in some "other world") allows one to resolve all (or at least the most important) problems and find unshakeable certainty.

Can such *nihilism* be overcome?

Of course not. At least, not in the same way that my organism overcomes the flu or bronchitis. Isn't life of necessity an effort to connect "today" with "yesterday" and "tomorrow," an effort to construct some continuity, to unite what is different? Can life therefore dispense with the instrument of this effort—the truth—along with its claims to universality? Nihilism is a disease whose symptom is man as he is: human life.

But at the same time, yes, nihilism can be overcome. Each moment of my life provides yet another chance to do just that; insofar as it conceals within itself the possibility of breaking free from the continuity of "yesterday" and "tomorrow," the possibility of liberation, the chance at a new beginning. We see this in the confrontation with death, in love, in "eternal love." But we cannot overcome nihilism in this way once and for all, not even for the moment: today in nihilism, tomorrow not. Life is a constant overcoming of nihilism, unwavering tension between the effort to establish continuity and the effort to break free from it.

The concept to which Nietzsche often refers in analyzing this tension is "innocence." To be innocent is to be "beyond good and evil," like Adam and Eve in Paradise, like lovers who forget the external world, the guilt and obligations of the past, future plans. Like a newborn child. Innocence is the breaking of the continuity between one moment and the next. Innocence, thus understood, is located beyond my memory's reach: it is not "yesterday" or the "day before yesterday"; I will not find it by going further down the trail of successive moments. And it is beyond the reach of my will: I will not find it "tomorrow" or "the day after," if I look for it in the opposite direction. In this sense, innocence is something inhuman, something superhuman—Nietzsche also uses the term "overman" in this context—and yet this possibility, this chance, hidden from sight in everyday life, to break free of rules, principles, views, considerations, commandments, concepts, the chance to be reborn, to overcome oneself, ever anew: this, too, is human life.

The attempt to break free in this way—the attempt to return to an unattainable innocence, the attempt to reach a new beginning—is, Nietzsche writes, "art." Art: not an occupation of the few but the subcutaneous current of our lives, the countermovement to nihilism.

If this is the case, then *overcoming nihilism* cannot be a program of action; "beyond good and evil" is not a slogan that points out where humanity is supposed to go. Nietzsche does not exhort us toward immorality, nor does he propagate some ideal of man or society. *Overcoming nihilism* is the meaning of our lives, life as a constant, unlimited—and in this sense one that potentially exceeds all that is human—effort to begin anew. The effort to return to one's innocence, which was never a real state in our lives. The effort to break free from time. The effort to transform our lives into limitless possibility.

Nihilism and its *overcoming*; the continuity between one moment and the next—and its constant severance, starting everything anew, eternity, *the blink of an eye*; life united in a biography, a history, some kind of sense—and life that is sick with eternity, open to the unknown, permeated by mystery: all these are thus intelligible only in relation to each other. In relation to each other but not as a conceptual unity. No logic, not even a "dialectical" one, can link one pole with the other. The tension between them is not that of logical negation. It does not come to the fore in concepts. Or, rather, not in concepts alone. Nihilism cannot be understood in abstraction from the resistance to it, from rage at the burden of concepts, at the burden of what is (for I am always something more); overcoming it cannot be understood without the pain it causes (for doesn't it hurt to leave it all behind?) and the joy of liberation. This rage, this pain, this joy: in Nietzsche's view, these are the conditions for reflection on life, on the human condition, on eternity and time. Without them, these concepts are empty.

Nietzsche's reflections on human life—both on its time as well as on the eternity that both interrupts it and makes it possible—is therefore, if I understand it correctly, first of all an analysis of concepts, an analysis of our knowledge. It attempts to demonstrate that our concepts—our effort to know, our effort to gather the diversity of our lives into a kind of unity—are necessary but always inadequate, that the attempt to unite them is inevitable but also futile. That we cannot do without concepts but that they cannot be arranged into a consistent totality either. Which is also a chance, an infinite chance, a chance that exceeds everything that we can know about ourselves: a chance for creativity, for eternal love, for hope in death.

The term "life"—similar to the terms Nietzsche uses to explain life, *overman, will to power,* and *eternal return of the same*—refers to this very impossibility of totality, to the vanity of the necessary effort to find or form it. As well as to this chance.

We should not be surprised, therefore, that Nietzsche so frequently reaches for metaphors; it's not (only) because of the need to illustrate but is first of all a result of his belief that knowledge, inherently incomplete, cannot do without them. His central metaphor is, I believe, the metaphor of fire, the ancient metaphor of the eternally living fire, the metaphor of the flame of eternity: in Nietzsche's eyes, this is an image of the link between knowledge and life, between successive moments and the *blink of an eye,* which interrupts that succession; it is an image of this tension, impossible to resolve, of this game without rules, which makes our concepts hurt—scorch—and break apart as they open us to the unknown. In one of his earliest works, left unpublished in his lifetime, Nietzsche writes:

> In this world only play, play as artists and children engage in it, exhibits coming-to-be and passing away, structuring and destroying, without any moral additive, in forever equal innocence. And as children and artists play, so plays the ever-living fire. It constructs and destroys, all in innocence. Such is the game that the *aeon* [eternity, though also time] plays with itself.[3]

• • •

The book before you consists of nine essays dedicated to various aspects of my main subject: the concept of eternity. In them you will find attempts at interpreting what I take to be Nietzsche's main concepts, culminating in a discussion of the concept that organizes them all: the concept of *the eternal return of the same*. In my interpretation of Nietzsche, I have tried to contextualize him in his own time, seeking out not only actual historical links but also intellectual affinities with the philosophers, poets, and authors near him in time: Hegel, Kafka, Kierkegaard, D. H. Lawrence, Marx, Rilke, and Stanisław Brzozowski foremost among them. I have also tried to situate Nietzsche in a tradition of philosophical and religious thought.

Why does the context of religious thought strike me as essential? Because it is not without reason that we may call Nietzsche's work a "struggle with God." The book that Nietzsche cites most frequently (though most of his citations are hidden) is Luther's translation of the Bible. That Nietzsche was a harsh critic of Christianity we all know. His best-known sentence is most likely "God is dead." But perhaps—I for one am convinced—the radical critique to which Nietzsche subjects our concepts, our knowledge, also opens the door to an understanding of religion that may also prove convincing to a mind living among a multitude of incompatible meanings, a diversity of cultures, in a modernity permeated by science.

I have of course also made frequent use of what others have written about Nietzsche, though I have undoubtedly succeeded in reading only a small fraction of it. Foremost among these are Martin Heidegger, Hans-Georg Gadamer, Gilles Deleuze, Emmanuel Levinas, Paul Ricoeur, and E. M. Cioran. From Gadamer I learned that to understand a given thinker requires one to presuppose that he is right. This is why I have tried to discern in Nietzsche's concepts and metaphors arguments that can convince, to recognize their power, and to allow the reader to feel it as well.

But my greatest debt of gratitude belongs to two Polish thinkers: Leszek Kołakowski, who has been teaching me to read and think since I was a student, and Józef Tischner, who in the course of our many years of friend-ship taught me how to understand ideas as well as people.

In preparing the English translation of this book, the translator and I have relied on the editions of Nietzsche that are most readily available and that strike us as truest to his exceptional qualities as a prose stylist.

The Flame of Eternity

I

Nihilism

CURIOSITY ABOUT THE WORLD, as we know, sometimes leads to philosophy. It can happen when that curiosity cannot be satisfied by knowledge of
one or another event, by knowledge of one or another contingency, or by
discovering the causes behind one or another phenomenon. It happens
when we are not satisfied with the information we have about particular
events or relations, or with a discovery of their causes. When, in short, we
are curious to understand the world, and not just a fragment thereof.

It is only then—when we understand what the world is like, when we
discover the universal and eternal order of things—that this kind of curiosity about the world will be satisfied. Philosophy born of this kind of
curiosity, philosophy that endeavors to satisfy it, is an attempt to find the
immutable and universal structures that allow us to understand the world
as it is, an attempt at a universal theory.

Of course, this is hardly the only motivation toward philosophy that we
can think of. Others include anger and pain, the rejection of the world as
it is. The world—not this or that fragment of the world, this or that situation or institution, this or that fact as it is—hurts and outrages us, it chafes.
Bringing some piece of reality to order—controlling the river that has,
until now, regularly flooded the neighborhood, or freeing oneself from
political oppression, or finding a treatment for a heretofore untreatable illness—does nothing to relieve this kind of pain. Only a new, universal
order of things could free us from this pain, quiet our rage, and reconcile
us to the world.

A philosophy motivated by a rejection of the world around us is an attempt to find a treatment or therapy, an attempt to find a way out of crisis,
an attempt at liberation. Its goal is the creation of the new: change, not
description. It is, above all else, a program of action, not a theory.

Wouldn't it be better to call these two activities, so disparately motivated, by different names, since the one attempts to discover the eternal
and universal order of things, whereas the other attempts to change a
world that causes us pain and outrage? Does it make sense to call them
both "philosophy"?

I believe that it does, and I think that there is a very good rationale for
doing so. For in both cases, as we have already seen, we are speaking of

"the whole," of "the world," and not of "a fragment" of the world. In philosophy as theory, we are talking about understanding "the world"; in philosophy as a program of action, about how to change it. This universal character allows us, I believe, to call both kinds of activity "philosophy."

All the more so because what distinguishes one from the other is itself different from what differentiates the work of the cobbler from that of the tailor. These are not two kinds of activity dealing with different things and, accordingly, calling on us to separate them, at least in principle. In its universality, philosophy in both senses knows no limits; it cannot tend its own garden without peeking at the neighbor's. To put it another way, these definitions of "philosophy" do not complement one another but compete. From the perspective of philosophy as theory, "changing the world," no matter how much we wish it, demands a prior understanding of that world, and at the same time, from the point of view of philosophy as an outgrowth of rejection, it is the very pain that "the world" causes us that assures our knowledge of the world. And so our rejection of the world and our understanding of it are not two separate activities but one and the same.

2

Nietzsche understood philosophy primarily in the second of these two meanings. Humanity, he maintained, is sick; the world in which we live is sick. The task of philosophy should be the liberation of humanity and the world from the grips of this sickness.

What is wrong with the world in which we live, according to Nietzsche? What is the basis of this pathology? And is this pathology treatable? And, if so, what should this treatment (read: philosophy) look like? The answer to both questions requires us to refer to the concept of *nihilism*.

Nietzsche writes, "What does nihilism mean? *That the highest values devaluate themselves.*"[1]

What is a *value*? Let's start with the following general, formal definition: *values* are norms, principles, and rules that determine the order of our lives in all arenas, the experiential order, as well as the material or physical order, as well as the moral order, as well as the weather. The order of the world around us is determined by a set of rules. Following Nietzsche, we will call these rules values, deferring for now an answer to the question of why we do so.

Values, Nietzsche maintains, not only establish order but are also themselves ordered. This is why we can speak of "higher" or "lower" values (those that are subordinate to the "higher" ones), and especially of the *highest* values, those to which all others are subordinated.

What does it mean that "values devaluate themselves"? This happens when they no longer serve to establish order, when they no longer impose obligations upon us, when reality slips away from them, resists them, contradicts them. We are dealing with *nihilism*, Nietzsche asserts in the aforementioned passage, when this happens to the *highest* values, that is, when the basic principles organizing our reality no longer organize or order our lives.

If this is the case, then what Nietzsche calls nihilism is not an outlook, or at least it is not principally an outlook. Specifically, the nihilism he speaks of is not the view that everything is meaningless, that there's not really any point to anything we do, that what seems to us to be "everything" is really "nothing." The nihilism that Nietzsche has in mind is first of all something that happens and not something that we, correctly or incorrectly, think about reality. Nihilism is therefore an event, or a chain of events, a historical process—and only secondarily, if at all, an attitude, outlook, or position.

Consequently, *overcoming nihilism* cannot depend on discovering the falsehood or moral error of "nihilistic" attitudes or views and convincing their proponents of other, non-nihilistic ones. Overcoming nihilism must mean, first of all, the modification of reality, the modification of what happens, and not of one's outlook.

3

Why must we call what is happening around us "nihilism"? How is it that the historical process, that history itself, has assumed such a meaning?

God is dead, Nietzsche tells us: that's what happened. The death of God is the highest—really, the only—essential "event," and it is this that imparts meaning to all other things. What does this mean? What does it mean for God to be dead?

First, let's try to deal with what it might mean for God to be "alive." When does God "live"? One can surely say that "God is alive" when belief in God organizes human coexistence and determines the meaning of human activities and, consequently, of the world to which those activities refer. But that's not all. Even as Christianity (for Nietzsche is primarily concerned with the Christian God) is losing its power—and still people continue to organize their world around some ultimate purpose (though it is no longer God but "progress," "social justice," or something else) when they seek a single, all-encompassing totality—even then, Nietzsche maintains, God "lives."

Thus when Nietzsche is talking about the "life" or "death" of God he does not mean the existence or nonexistence of some supernatural or otherworldly being. Accordingly, the death of God is not something that happened to such a being and is not, in this sense, an "event." Rather, Nietzsche is concerned with the order we strive to impose on the world around us, even when we no longer believe in God's existence, even when the Churches have lost their social significance. "God lives" when we seek an ultimate meaning or some kind of all-encompassing totality in the world around us, when that search organizes our world into a teleological, comprehensive order.

But this search is in vain. For the world in which we live, Nietzsche asserts, does not lend itself to being organized toward some ultimate goal. Nor do things, people, events, or thoughts lend themselves to being arranged into a single, all-encompassing totality. Successive attempts, successive projects to order the world in this way—in the guise of "Christianity" or "faith in progress" or "socialism"—inevitably fail. In the world we live in, no form is ultimate—"becoming aims at *nothing* and achieves *nothing*," Nietzsche says—and the diversity of forms cannot be reduced to a common denominator.[2] The world around us is a world of constant change and irreducible diversity: it is a world of *becoming*.

But what if the world around us is not the real world? What if it's only an illusion? What if this world of ceaseless change, this world of irreducible diversity, this world of *becoming*, is only a mirage that conceals the real world? What if it is only in this hidden real world that the search for an ultimate goal and an all-encompassing unity can reach a successful conclusion? What if we have been looking for our ultimate goal or all-encompassing totality in the wrong place? What if God is alive but not here, in the world of appearances, of change and difference, but beyond it, in the world as it truly is?

And yet there is no other world than the one around us, the *world of becoming*, the world in which we live. This, according to Nietzsche, is the only real world. Looking for a real world "beyond" the world around us, the world of change, is just as pointless as looking for an ultimate goal within it, or a totality that encompasses all of it. Sooner or later, Nietzsche argues, we will inevitably realize that the "ideal world," the "truth in itself" of philosophy, religion, or science, is the very same dream, humanity's dream, as "the ultimate goal" or the "all-encompassing totality." *The world of becoming* is the only real world.

God is dead.

And so, Nietzsche argues, we cannot deny the reality of the world as we know it, the world of infinite change (because there is nothing, no "real world," hidden beyond it)—and at the same time all attempts at bringing order to the world, with the help of such categories as "goal" and "totality," end in failure. The "death of God" places us in an impossible situation. On the one hand, it confronts us with the irrefutable reality of a world of constant change and irreducible difference, and on the other, it deprives us of the tools we have used till now to bring that world to order and, by the same token, to give it meaning and value.

It is an impossible situation, an untenable situation, a situation of crisis, of the ultimate exacerbation of our sickness. But also of its potential turning point, as the impossibility of accepting the status quo forces us to look for a remedy, for new means by which to bring the world of our lives to order, for new values.

Nietzsche writes:

> Having reached this standpoint, one grants the reality of becoming as the *only* reality, forbids oneself every kind of clandestine access to afterworlds and false divinities—but *cannot endure this world though one does not want to deny it.*
>
> What has happened, at bottom? The feeling of valuelessness was reached with the realization that the overall character of existence may not be interpreted by means of the concept of "aim," the concept of "unity," or the concept of "truth." Existence has no goal or end; any comprehensive unity in the plurality of events is lacking [. . .]. One simply lacks any reason for convincing oneself that there is a *true* world. Briefly: the categories "aim," "unity," "being" which we used to project some value into the world—we *pull out* again; so the world looks *valueless.*[3]

Unless we forget all of this and disregard the crisis we have found ourselves in. Nietzsche, again:

> *The ways of self-narcotization.*— Deep down: not knowing whither. *Emptiness.* Attempt to get over it by intoxication: intoxication as music [. . .]; intoxication as blind enthusiasm for single human beings or ages [. . .].— Attempt to work blindly as an instrument of science: opening one's eyes to many small enjoyments; e.g. also in the quest of knowledge [. . .]; art "for its own sake" (*le fait*) and "pure knowledge" as narcotic states of disgust with oneself; some kind or other of continual work, or of some stupid little fanaticism [. . .].[4]

Art, science, ideologies—the occupations of our times: Nietzsche tells us that these are intoxicants, drugs we use to escape having to confront the "death of God," the need to order our world anew.

God is dead, and the values we have held till now no longer order the world in which we live. We cannot stand it, and yet we cannot deny it. What is to be done? To sleep, so as not to know, hear, or understand (and

Nietzsche maintains that contemporary European culture puts a vast range of sedatives at our disposal). Or else to create new values, a new world order: *to reevaluate values.*

What, then, is nihilism?

Nihilism (in Nietzsche's use of the word) is first of all a situation in which the world appears to be without value, the world after "the death of God." There is no escape from the reality of the world, and at the same time there is no way to reconcile oneself to it because all known means have utterly failed. This is a dilemma, an untenable situation, a state of powerlessness that we cannot possibly endure.

It is precisely this situation, this nihilism, that is the source of philosophy as Nietzsche understands it: philosophy that responds to the pain the world causes by trying to change it.

But, Nietzsche demonstrates, theoretically we can also call the process that has led us to this situation "nihilism." For the world appears to be without value precisely because the values we have invested in the world are failing: they no longer perform their ordering or organizing function. The project (*investment*) of these very values—*the ultimate goal, the all-encompassing totality, truth in itself*—is therefore the beginning of nihilism. The sickness whose culmination is the critical situation in which we find ourselves today derives from the attempt to order the world in which we live according to these values. We cannot therefore liberate ourselves from this nihilism if we resume living in accordance with them and seeing the world through their prism. On the contrary, doing so sets us on a path that leads necessarily to nihilism, in the aforementioned sense of historical crisis. Nihilism is a pathology not of outlooks or attitudes but of their historical motivations, a pathology of life—but the attempt to reorganize life according to the patterns from which we have departed when we fell into the crisis of nihilism does not lead to our liberation from it. On the contrary, the values whose abandonment the word "nihilism" signifies cannot save us from it because they are in fact its root cause.

Nihilism is a critical, unbearable situation in which the world appears to be without values; it is a sickness, the pathological history that leads to it; finally, it is the infection from which all of this began: the attempt to order life in a way that it cannot be ordered. The attempt to order life according to values that are antithetical to it.

4

In what sense, however, can we speak here of the "necessity" that leads us from the project of a certain system of values to the nihilistic crisis that, in Nietzsche's view, troubles us today? On what basis can I say that this crisis is an *untenable* situation and that it therefore leads to a project of new values, to *the revaluation of all values?* What is the fundamental "logic" linking the elements in the sequence presented above—the search for an ultimate goal and an all-encompassing totality, the failure of that search, the attempt to escape from a world of constant change—the project of the "real world" hidden behind the illusion of a mutable reality, the subsequent failure, the crisis that places us before the necessity of *revaluating values?*

Let's make the question more precise. This is not simply a matter of stringing together some chain of historical events. The aforementioned analysis of nihilism is not only a critique of culture, of modern European culture in Nietzsche's own time. It is also something more. In the nihilism of the historical situation in which he finds himself, Nietzsche wants to uncover the nihilism of the human condition, what is in his view the necessary link between nihilism and its overcoming. In this sense the question of the "necessity" of this linkage is a question concerning the historical process itself, entirely different from a question about, say, the causes of the Second World War. At issue here is why a given stage of human life is followed by another at all, why any fact follows another. It is not a matter of why capitalism replaced feudalism, or why democracy replaced totalitarianism, but of why anything follows anything else. What drives historical change, the change we call "time"? What causes it to take place at all?

Or, to put it still another way: we will understand "historical necessity" in the above sense only when we succeed in understanding the here-and-now, the moment in which we now find ourselves, as laden with the future, when we succeed in understanding the future (any future) as an inherent element of this moment.

We will not find this "logic of history," thus understood, by referring to a logic we know from other sources, independently of historical experience. (I take this argument from Leszek Kołakowski's essay on the understanding of the historical event.)[5] The answer to our question cannot be the discovery of a "logic in history," the application of otherwise known criteria, criteria of understanding, to historical process. For by doing so we would be reducing history to logic, thereby removing the very object of the question: the "historicity" of the historical process, the simple though quite perplexing fact that history "flows," that anything changes at all. If we "understand" the transition from one historical situation to another in the same way as we understand the link between the two terms of a syllogism (or any other rule of logic), history will lose for us (the subject of this "understanding") its specific character and will become a sequence of arguments rather than a sequence of events.

At any rate, in Nietzsche's opinion, a logic independent of historical experience is a complete fantasy. We can therefore understand history and its logic, the historicity of history, only by referring to history itself. The "ahistorical" perspective, the point of view "from beyond" history that would aid us in this understanding, is nonsense. There is no such thing. "History," in this context, is yet another name for the world in which we live: the world of becoming, the world of constant change and irreducible diversity. Attempts at discovering a goal, a totality, a "truth" beyond it, attempts at discovering the "transcendent meaning" of the world in which we live, or else at understanding in reference to some "external" system of reference—all these end, as we have already seen, in utter failure. Everything we know is comprehensible only in the context of our irreducibly diverse, infinitely mutable lives.

An understanding of history, of its "logic," and not merely of this or that sequence of events, of this versus that historical process—an understanding of history as such, of history in its historicity—is, for Nietzsche, possible only "from within" and thus only from the perspective of a participant. We are the ones who, through what we do, through the acts that compose our lives, give history its meaning and make it comprehensible as history: we arrange it in some sequence of events, we "project some value" into it. Let us recall what Nietzsche says above: "the categories 'aim,' 'unity,' 'being' which we used to project some value into the world—we *pull out* again; so the world looks *valueless*."

So it is only for us, only from the perspective of an active subject (a subject who *projects values* into the world and *pulls them out* of it), that it might be comprehensible why the categories we have established are then *pulled out* and why a world that seems to lack values is impossible (i.e., impossible to bear) and thus forces us to *revaluate all values*, why, in short, history goes on. The "necessity" that connects one stage to the next is not the necessity of logical deduction but necessity comprehensible only from the perspective of a subject who shapes history: it is the necessity of our lives.

The future-laden present, the current moment necessarily leading to the next, assumes an active subject. Without him, the historicity of history—and thus the fact that the future follows the present—would be incomprehensible. In other words, history is real only as *our* history, only for the subject taking part in it. Not for the observer: history is not a process that flows forward independently of us; it is not like rain, which one can escape under a roof. History goes on only insofar as it concerns us.

5

History as we know it *is* nihilism, a sickness that leads us to today's turning point, which forces us to *revaluate all values* and, by the same token, *to overcome nihilism*. Let's try to understand what this "overcoming of nihilism," this "revaluation of all values," may mean.

Let us consider, first of all, the values that, according to Nietzsche, lead us to nihilism. Why is it that using these values to bring order to the world ends—and this is inevitable—in failure?

The answer demands that we consider an even more fundamental problem: how can values be justified at all?

We can try to do so by referring to "truth in itself," "the world of ideas," or "God" and thus to a reality that transcends the constantly mutable world of our lives. In this regard, something can be true or false, good or bad, independently of what we do, what we want, what we say, or what happens to us (and it's all the same whether it's because of God's will or because these things are ultimately controlled by ideal—and thus timeless—laws). In other words, values, thus understood, are independent from our lives, and this independence is part of their meaning. Nothing, it seems, could be closer to common sense. The laws of nature, after all, apply regardless of what happens in our lives, and logic determines the validity of our thoughts regardless of whether our lives go this way or that way.

But then what are we to do with the fact that (in Nietzsche's opinion), as we have seen, the concepts of "truth in itself," "the world of ideas," and "God" have no meaning when isolated from the constantly changing, irreducibly diverse world of our lives? If this is the case, then the claim that values can be independent of this world is absurd. Where are they supposed to have come from, if not from the world we live in?

In this regard, the question of how to justify our values becomes a matter of how our lives create the values that organize it.

The only possible way to justify values, according to Nietzsche, is therefore to refer to the life from which they are derived. The question of justification leads necessarily to the genesis of a given phenomenon. In order to understand and justify the system of values by which our lives are organized—even, as in the case of nihilism, incompletely and with awful consequences—we have to discover its genesis (i.e., to answer the question of how life produced just such a system). A philosopher, insofar as he strives to understand values, to discover their basis, must be a "historian," a "geneticist," a "genealogist," an "archaeologist." We can find a similar argument in Marx and, later, in Husserl. For Marx, understanding modern science requires us to refer to its (social) genesis, and for Husserl, understanding geometry requires us to discover the history of human activities, of which geometry is a product.

The above argument can also be formulated as follows: the attempt to justify (discover) values independent of life is, we can say, an attempt to evaluate the world as a whole, to discover the values of the world as such. This is possible only insofar as we assume a frame of reference with regard to which the world as a totality can be evaluated. Only by referring to such a frame of reference—to another, "real" world—can we offer a positive or negative evaluation of life as a whole, can we affirm or negate it. And yet there is no such frame, no such standard, Nietzsche argues, no "real," "other" world: there is only the constantly changing, diverse world in which we live. Consequently, then, the world as a totality "has no value at all, for anything against which to measure it, and in relation to which the word 'value' would have meaning, is lacking. The total value of the world cannot be evaluated [. . .]."[6]

Life as we live it is the only possible measure of value. It is our life that creates the order that organizes its diverse and ever-changing forms, but it cannot be appraised in itself: its value is the same in each individual moment, and the sum of values produced by it always remains the same. This is the core of nihilism, the answer to the question of what's wrong with the values that give birth to nihilism: it is their claim to assess, to evaluate, the world as such, life as such.

Thus while the project of traditional values, or nihilism, is a negation of our life as it is, the *revaluation of all values* is not an affirmation of life as it is. Life finds no values, no order independent of it, to which it could correspond or not; it creates its own values. This does not mean that each of us is free to create our own rules. Rather, Nietzsche suggests that such rules cannot be formed until we begin to act; they are not prior to our life. The affirmation of life is therefore not a supplemental, reflexive act of assessment but is life itself. To "revaluate values" does not mean to replace one set of values, one list of rules (which negate life and are therefore nihilistic), with another (which affirm life). We do not to replace "God" (after His "death") with something else (whether "man," "nature," or "life"). The *revaluation of values* Nietzsche has in mind is an attempt to justify them differently: values (the order of the world) must, in this perspective (in the perspective of revaluation), originate in life liberated from nihilistic fictions (the ultimate goal, the all-encompassing totality, the truth-in-itself).

The *revaluation of all values* occurs only when our lives cast off the burden of the illusions that weigh them down and order themselves around new organizing principles, when these principles—these "values"—are the product of a life that depends only on itself, not on dictates "from outside." Which means: insofar as life becomes unimpeded creation and is no longer a response to challenges imposed "from outside." The revaluation of values should liberate life rather than try—in vain—to bring it under control.

Which means: if fundamental values are to undergo a radical revaluation, it will not be enough to understand them differently: one must live differently. The "revaluation of values" is possible only if it is a possibility of your life or mine. It is not an intellectual operation. Philosophy can cure the world's sickness and point the way out of crisis only insofar as the "life" in the phrase "philosophy of life" is not just the object but the subject as well—only insofar as a "life philosophy" is itself life and not just a theory of life. Which also means that one cannot first understand it in order to apply it to life later. Here, the action of understanding and the action of application cannot be separated from one another.

At the beginning, I defined values as the rules of some order, any order. It has now become clear, I hope, why Nietzsche calls such organizing principles "values." We now know that no order can be imposed on the world "from outside," for there is no "outside." We also know, therefore, that every order is created in our lives through what we do, through our actions and lack thereof. The order that life falls under is created together with it, in its course. It is in this sense that its rules can be called "values": they are evaluations of how and to what extent something is valuable for the life in which they are made. They open certain opportunities, certain possibilities for a particular life (and no other). This is why Nietzsche calls values "conditions of life": they are the conditions of its development, the conditions that make it go this way and not that way.

6

Is "truth" also merely a value, a condition of life? For Nietzsche, the answer is clearly yes: it is only in the context of a certain life, only by virtue of its significance, the "weight" it bears for a given life, that knowledge means anything. Knowledge, cognition, cannot be separated from the self-affirmation of life. Which means—if we take into account that the affirmation of life is not, as we have seen, a secondary act, the acceptance of something that already is, but an act of life itself—that knowledge cannot be separated from action. If our cognition communicates something essential about the world to us, this happens only because we are living this way, not some other way. Knowledge removed from this element, from life—consciousness or thought left to itself—would be utterly stupid, disoriented, blind. It is life that opens the world and gives us knowledge. The pathology of life is, at the same time, the pathology of knowledge: a kind of stupidity.

"We can comprehend only a world which we ourselves have made," Nietzsche writes.[7]

The conviction that knowledge, especially true knowledge, depends on the situation from which it arises (a conviction that Nietzsche shares with Husserl and Heidegger) is by no means equivalent to relativism. It would be relativism to claim that different situations define different truths, hence there is no one truth. Such a claim presupposes a point of view external to every situation that allows us to define situations as different and, at the same time, equivalent, one no better than the next. This is precisely the premise that Nietzsche questions: a point of view external to every life situation is nonsense; any life other than mine, any claim to truth, must always be seen from the perspective of my own life and is always better or worse (and never equivalent) and only in this sense different. Indeed, truth is always my truth and has meaning only in the context of the life I can call my own. But it would be futile to try to represent that life from outside, like one of the butterfly species displayed in a museum case.

Nietzsche sometimes defines his position as *perspectivism*: the world in which we live, he notes, "has no meaning behind it, but countless meanings."[8] We always see the world from the perspective of the situation we find ourselves in. But this perspectivism of Nietzsche's is not in opposition to "absolutism," to the view that it is possible to have knowledge independent of the situation in which the subject finds himself. Nietzsche's perspectivism is rather an attempt to formulate the conditions according to which a view makes sense. "Absolutism," much like "relativism," does not meet these conditions. It is, for Nietzsche, nonsense.

Concepts-in-themselves are therefore stupid. Consciousness and conceptual knowledge are derivative; they reach only as far as they are taken by the life from which they originate. The world is revealed to us only as it is interpreted by our actions, only in their perspective, only as a set of values born in the course of living: only from the point of view of a participant, not that of an observer. Every attempt at understanding the world as such (i.e., independent of the concrete life of the subject) creates a fiction that damages the life from which it is drawn. This is nihilism and—one follows the other—stupidity.

If this is so, saying that "the world around us is a world of constant change and irreducible diversity, a world of becoming," and that it is not, accordingly, a universal whole and does not move toward any goal, Nietzsche is not opposing one (true) thesis about the world to another (false) one. He's after something more. This is an attempt at altering our sensibility, an attempt to free the potential that Nietzsche believes is hidden within each of our lives: an attempt at overcoming nihilism, at revaluating all values.

7

The *revaluation of all values*, I have said, is the necessity that Nietzsche believes we face as a result of the crisis in which we live. The source of this crisis is ultimately the negation of life contained within the project of values that leads to it. This negation, and consequently our nihilistic history and our nihilistic crisis today, which arise from that negation—*nihilism* in general—thus also has, we might say, a positive, creative significance, much like a health crisis: it is a condition for the possibility of self-overcoming, for the *revaluation of all values*. Nihilism, as a historical process, is therefore not only the history of the twilight of the gods (values that negate life) but also the path toward liberation from them, a liberation that is not otherwise possible.

Does this not mean, however, that, following Nietzsche, we have ultimately nevertheless introduced some ultimate goal into history by a back-door, a goal that organizes history's entire process up till now? That, against our initial intent, we have hitched the negation of life to the tread-mill of history, so that it would work toward the achievement of its positive ends (the revaluation of all values) and, accordingly, toward its self-negation?

No, not at all. Here's what Nietzsche has to say on the subject of negativity:

> Waste, decay, elimination need not be condemned: they are neces-sary consequences of life, of the growth of life. The phenomenon of decadence is as necessary as any increase and advance of life: one is in no position to abolish it. Reason demands, on the contrary, that we do justice to it.
>
> It is a disgrace for all socialist systematizers that they suppose there could be circumstances—social combinations—in which vice, disease, prostitution, distress would no longer grow.—But that means condemning life.—A society is not free to remain young. [. . .]—Age is not abolished by means of institutions. Nei-ther is disease. Nor vice.[9]

To put it another way, Nietzsche asserts that negativity requires no ad-ditional justification: we do not need to justify the negative phenomena of our lives by referring to their future function. Negativity is not a mecha-nism that produces positive results in the future or a means of achieving a future goal. Decline, degeneration, aggression, and destruction are all, in degree and kind, as positive phenomena of life as growth and bloom. The *revaluation of all values* and, consequently, the *overcoming of nihilism* are not the negation of negation; they do not require us to remove negativity from the world. Negativity—and so nihilism as well—is an irremediable aspect of this world.

Nietzsche writes in *The Gay Science*:

> He that is richest in the fullness of life [. . .] cannot only afford the sight of the terrible and questionable but even the terrible deed

and any luxury of destruction, decomposition, and negation. In his case, what is evil, absurd, and ugly seems, as it were, permissible, owing to an excess of procreating, fertilizing energies that can still turn any desert into lush farmland.[10]

It is this conviction of Nietzsche's that, according to Stanisław Brzozowski, assures him a place in the pantheon of philosophy:

> To this day it is not regarded as a loss, as a crime, as a disaster, that we will not have this or that other crumb of human soul, for, after all, other than this one, this one alone, man has nothing. And for this revolt, for this holy rage for man, for the love of everything there is within him, for understanding that the entire content of human life is precious, that it is the only precious thing, the source of everything else, Nietzsche will remain forever in philosophy, he will remain as a great innovator, a creator of moral energy.[11]

We can formulate this position still another way: life—mutable, diverse, endlessly ongoing—must be comprehensible in each individual instant. Understanding life does not require us to refer to something "outside" of the given moment, such as, for instance, a future goal—a reference that would allow us to distinguish between what we should hold onto in this moment and what we should cast aside. "Comprehension" is therefore an affirmation of the moment that life itself is, an affirmation that also encompasses aggression, destruction, and negativity. It does not claim to be an adequate description, a "true" theory (for such a thing establishes what we have already seen to be dangerous fictions, such as "truth-in-itself"), but an affirmative creation. It is a creation rooted in a constant liberation from the fictions that bind life, from the pathologies that threaten it, from the concepts that negate it. It is rooted in the constant overcoming of one's own nihilism.

Where are the limits of such creation? What is at stake in this game, in this confrontation with nihilism? Nietzsche: "We are conducting an experiment with truth! Perhaps mankind will perish because of it! Fine!"[12]

8

To sum up: Nietzsche's philosophy arises from rejection, from outrage at the world, from the pain that the world causes. It is only when we learn to deal with this pain, when we discover its power, that we will understand the world as it is. This demands that we confront nihilism—not only nihilistic attitudes or positions but most of all the nihilism of what happens, the nihilism of our lives. For our lives are nihilistic through and through: the negation of life is one of its inherent features, hidden within the project of values that arrange the world into a rational whole. We cannot blame life for this, nor are history and its (ostensibly) ironclad laws to blame; life and history do not go on independently of our participation, like a carousel you can ride or jump off of at will. History is real only as our history: it is only in what we do that history happens. As such, nihilism itself is the sickness of our actions, a pathology of the force expressed in them. Fictions like "God" or "truth-in-itself" are symptoms of this pathology, fictions that bind our thoughts as well as our hands, so long as we do not discover their genesis. Discovering their genesis, revealing life and its sickness, power and its pathology, which it hides behind the kind of concepts we use to take hold of our lives—this, Nietzsche says, is the task of philosophy. For concepts as such are empty and therefore stupid; if they say anything, if we understand anything through them, it is only thanks to the sensibility of the lives we live. Philosophy, in exposing the genesis of concepts from life, leads to the *overcoming of nihilism* and therefore to the rise of a new life and a new sensibility. To the liberation of the freedom hidden within our lives, which have been distorted by nihilism. To affirmative creation.

But doesn't overcoming nihilism also mean overcoming humanity, that "skin disease" suffered by the world, as Nietzsche says?[13] That is another story.

II

Time Flows, the Child Plays

ON THE FIRST PAGE of his essay "On the Uses and Disadvantages of History for Life," Nietzsche writes: "Consider the cattle, grazing as they pass you by: they do not know what is meant by yesterday or today, they leap about, eat, rest [. . .], fettered to the moment and its pleasure or displeasure."[1]

What is the point of this image?

Where there is no difference between yesterday and today, between the past and the present, there is no room for memory: there is nothing to remember. A herd of animals doesn't remember anything, not because it forgets something that has happened to it earlier but because anything that can happen to it happens "in this moment," which for the grazing herd has no "earlier." The *moment* in which the herd of cows live is not, therefore, "the present moment," "right now," situated between what was and what will be, the moment preceded by one thing and followed by something else. According to Nietzsche, this moment "is a matter for wonder: [. . .] nothing before it came, again nothing after it has gone."[2]

For the herd of cows, time as the succession of past, present, and future does not exist. And because time as the succession of past, present, and future is the basis of memory, cows remember nothing.

Which makes them happy. Because remembering what has been is a *burden*, a *chain*, a *phantom*: memory impedes our living in the moment by summoning things that no longer are; in this way, memory makes room within that moment for nostalgia and satiety, for pain and conflict, and as a result does not allow for our carefree immersion in what there actually is in that moment. A cow lives unflaggingly in what is happening right now. Thus it does not buckle (as we do) beneath the *invisible and dark* burden of yesterday; it does not have to (as we do) pull at the chain that binds it to what was; it is not terrified (as we are) by the phantom of the past.

This is why we look enviously at the grazing herd.

2

But maybe cows are happy simply because they're stupid. Maybe their happiness is simply the flip side of their stupidity, the simple, undisturbed peace of the moment in which they live. Is this the simplicity of the moron?

This would undoubtedly be the case if we were to establish that the point of view of the one observing the grazing herd of cows corresponds to objective reality, whereas the cows' point of view does not; in other words, that this observer sees the world as it is, whereas cows see only a distorted form of the world that has been subjectively simplified and is therefore without an objective ground. Therefore, that temporal succession—the difference between the past, present, and future—exists objectively, and only stupid (i.e., forgetful) cows fail to perceive it (which makes them happy).

Is this how things really are? Is the perspective of a person observing a grazing herd of cows the perspective of "objective knowledge," while the herd's perspective constitutes "subjective distortion"?

3

Let's take a closer look at the "herd's perspective." First of all, for Nietzsche it is not just cows that do not know the difference between "yesterday" and "today"; children don't either. A child plays "in blissful blindness between the hedges of past and future" and is therefore permanently immersed in the moment he is now living.[3] The sight of a child at play confronts us with something that is both foreign and familiar at the same time. When I look at a child, I become aware that that happiness of the grazing herd, the happiness of forgetting the world, is also something close to me, something my own, something that I once had and then lost, perhaps of necessity, and certainly irretrievably. It's like seeing a forever-lost paradise. E. M. Cioran uses still another metaphor to express what I take to be the same idea:

> The regret of not being plants brings us closer to paradise than any religion. One *is* in paradise only as a plant. But we left that stage a long time ago: we would have to destroy so much to recover paradise! Sin is the impossibility of forgetfulness. The fall—emblem of our human condition—is a nervous exacerbation of consciousness. Thus a human being can only be *next* to God, whereas plants sleep *in* him the sleep of eternal forgetfulness. The more awake we are, the greater the nostalgia that sends us in quest of paradise, the sharper the pangs of remorse that reunite us with the vegetable world.[4]

Later, in his narrative of Zarathustra, Nietzsche writes the following about a child at play: "The child is innocence and forgetting, a new beginning, a game, a self-propelled wheel, a first movement, a sacred 'Yes.'"[5] A child does not know what the past is and thus does not know what guilt is, not because he has never done anything wrong but because, for someone who has no past, the concept of guilt makes no sense. This is why in child's play each move is the first, each move is the beginning and the end at the same time, like each point on a circle. Play is thus complete and perfect in every moment of its duration; it lacks nothing, it has no goal, it strives toward nothing. It's like a wheel that keeps turning despite the fact that no one is spinning it, and that goes nowhere. The movement of such a wheel is comprehensible only in itself and not in reference to something else. It is for precisely this reason that the child's play is an affirmation, the "sacred 'Yes.'" The point here is not simply that children like to play. The "affirmation" that Nietzsche describes is not an evaluation that requires a distancing from its object, the kind of appraisal I make, for example, in saying that I like playing tag but that I don't like playing hide-and-seek. The child "affirms" his play by playing: playing—complete, perfect, and self-sufficient in each of its moments—is already the affirmation Nietzsche has in mind.

4

This childish play, Nietzsche asserts (returning now to *Untimely Meditations*), "must be disturbed; all too soon it will be called out of its state of forgetfulness. Then it will learn to understand the phrase 'it was': that password which gives conflict, suffering and satiety access to man so as to remind him what his existence fundamentally is—an imperfect tense that can never become a perfect one."[6]

Let us imagine a mother calling her child, who is playing in the yard, to come in for lunch. For the child absorbed in his play ("Eeny, meeny, miny, moe, catch a tiger by the toe," and so on, and again, ad infinitum) this will always come *too soon*, but he realizes it only when his mother calls him and interrupts his game. So it is only then, when the play is interrupted, that temporal definitions make any sense, only then that "too soon" or "later" (not yet! please!), "it was" (the game, which has suddenly—what a shame!—become the past) and "now it's time" (that horrible lunch!), have any meaning. As long as the game goes on, these words are empty and meaningless.

Nietzsche writes that, sooner or later, this child's play "*must* be disturbed" (my emphasis). And thus *disturbing* this play is no accident, no mistake that can be corrected. In other words, *play* and its *disturbance* are necessarily interlinked. Without being disturbed, play would be incomprehensible. And vice versa: the difference between "was," "is," and "will be," temporal differentiation, is precisely the *disturbance* of the initially undifferentiated *moment*; without this moment, therefore, the difference cannot be grasped. In this sense, the "moment" is the "origin" or "basis" of time; without it, time (the difference between past, present, and future) would be incomprehensible.

It is only here, with this *disturbance*, that human life begins: temporal differentiation is a condition for the possibility of memory and, consequently, of the *conflict, suffering*, and *satiety* of which the child and the cow, unaware of the difference between "was" and "will be" and thus deprived of memory, are incapable. We manage to struggle and suffer only when we understand the word "was." And only someone who is capable of struggling and suffering can be a human being, for it is only in conflict and suffering that the essence of our humanity—the unfinished, temporal character of man's existence (*the unending time of the past imperfect*)—comes to the fore. The loss of the paradise of child's play—immersed in the moment, carefree, happy—is a condition of possibility, the beginning of human life, which is marked by suffering and satiety, nostalgia and struggle.

If this is so, then *conflict, suffering*, and *satiety* will never end, at least not as long as we are alive. Life, human life, always has some past and therefore some future as well—and accordingly the undisturbed happiness of the child at play is inaccessible to it.

5

What could it mean to say that the atemporal *moment* in which the playful child and the grazing cows live is the "origin" or "basis" of the time of human life, stretching between past and future?

Let's return to the image of the child at play: in what sense is the happiness of the child immersed in the lived moment unattainable to me? Is it unattainable in the same way that, for me, a twenty-meter long jump is unattainable? No, this is not the point. After all, the sight of the child at play moves me; what I am seeing is not completely alien to me; it is the paradise I have known, though it is a paradise lost.

Does this mean, therefore, that the play of the child living in the moment is, for me, today, a past tense, though one I recall with nostalgia and emotion, the happiness of my own, long-past childhood? No, this cannot be the point either: the moment undifferentiated in time, the moment represented by the metaphor of the child at play, is not, of course, an event in time, one "moment" of many, of all those "yesterdays," "way-back-whens," "tomorrows," or "laters." The assertion that the *moment* precedes temporal succession (as may be suggested by our earlier recourse to a comparison between the *moment* and the origin of time, between the happiness of the child's play enclosed within that moment and paradise lost, or between the disturbance of the timeless moment and the impatient mother's calling the child in for lunch) wouldn't make sense. The play of the child immersed in the lived moment and the life of an adult, filled with conflict and suffering, are not simply events that follow one after the other.

If this is so, then what connects the *moment* (in which the child is absorbed in play) to a human life pitched between past and future cannot also be, in any respect, a causal link. Thus what Nietzsche has in mind here is not that man is a child until he grows up, that being a child is connected with certain pleasures (important for our future development), which as adults we will recall nostalgically, aware that our capacity for experiencing them has been irretrievably lost. Nor is he arguing that a cow (or a plant) is a stage of evolution prior to that of the human being, the traces of which are visible in later stages.

Here we are dealing, rather, with a different kind of linkage. The *moment* does not pass; in order to be capable of "passing," it would have to be a fragment of time, a "now" or "then," whereas it is temporally undifferentiated. This is similar to how, for a Christian, Paradise and its loss are present in every moment of life, imparting to it its only possible meaning: so, too, is the *moment* present in every instant of time. Without this presence, without this constantly gushing source, the future would not follow the past, and human life would therefore be impossible. The temporally undifferentiated moment, writes Nietzsche, "is like an atmosphere within which alone life can germinate, and with the destruction of which it must vanish."[7]

The child at play, absorbed in the lived moment and, in this sense, *unhistorical*, is for me—burdened with the past and memory, and in this sense a *historical* person—the image of another, inhuman, and in this sense unattainable reality. But it is not the other, alien reality of a Martian or of an ant: the child at play is not an image of a different kind of creature but rather a metaphor for the inalienable dimension of my own life, of that side of life without which its specific, human character—the fact that I remember the past and can thus suffer and struggle—would be impossible.

6

Nietzsche formulates this idea in yet another way: memory, he argues, is possible only insofar as it is delimited; absolute memory is nonsense. In remembering everything, I would seal off the only source from which memory flows; I would undermine the fundamental condition of its possibility. Nietzsche writes:

> Imagine the extremest possible example of a man who did not possess the power of forgetting at all and who was thus con-

demned to see everywhere a state of becoming: such a man would no longer believe in his own being, would no longer believe in himself, would see everything flowing asunder in moving points and would lose himself in this stream of becoming.[8]

Total recall of everything would be an accurate repetition of what was. Or, more precisely, it would be identical to what was. The life of a person who remembers everything would be identical to that which he remembers, and this would therefore be a life in which there is no room for what is now and will be later. Absolute memory would leave no room for someone who remembers "today" what was "yesterday" and would thus undermine the very possibility of life and, by the same token, of memory itself.

Therefore, although a human being can be distinguished from a cow, plant, or child (metaphorically speaking) because of this capacity for memory, and thus in the final tally, thanks to his skill in differentiating the past from the future, an opposing skill—the capacity to block memory, the skill of hindering one's singling out the past—is equally indispensable. Without the latter, the former would be unthinkable. For a human being, it is necessary—in fact, essential—to be capable of *non-historical feeling* and, in this sense, of "forgetting." This is not forgetting in the current sense; the point is not that once-remembered events or names sometimes slip away from our memory against our will. This is rather a question of having a capacity for feeling reality as temporally undifferentiated, of a sensibility for which the term "was" makes no sense. Of the sensibility represented metaphorically by the image of the child at play or the grazing herd of cows. This essential obliviousness to life, an obliviousness without which memory would be impossible, is the return to the lost paradise of child's play.

My memory—my consciousness of the difference between past and future, my awareness of time—thus reaches farther than what can be remembered, reaches beyond itself, to its "beginning," to its "source," which I can no longer remember the way I remember yesterday's storm or the kitchen smells of my childhood home. Or, to put it differently: my memory is necessarily lined with oblivion; it is imperfect, necessarily sick; necessarily, because without this oblivion, without this sickness, the difference between "was" and "will be," and with it the memory of anything, would be impossible.

Let's note that Nietzsche writes of this oblivion as a *capacity* or *skill*: it is a power and not simply its lack (the weakness of memory, for example); it is something we do rather than something that happens to us, activity rather than passivity. It is a positive rather than a negative term. This obliviousness, Nietzsche will later write in *On the Genealogy of Morals*, is "no mere *vis inertiae* [force of inertia]" but is "rather an active and in the strictest sense positive faculty of repression."[9]

7

But in what way does memory connect with oblivion, skill in differentiating past from future with the capacity to erase the difference between them, time with the timeless moment? Where are we to look for the principles of their unity, the measure or degree of their connection? Nietzsche writes:

> To determine this degree, and therewith the boundary at which the past has to be forgotten if it is not to become the gravedigger of the present, one would have to know exactly how great the plastic power of a man, a people, a culture is: I mean by plastic power the capacity to develop out of oneself in one's own way, to transform and incorporate into oneself what is past and foreign, to heal wounds, to replace what has been lost, to recreate broken moulds.[10]

Or, to put it briefly: the synthesis of memory and oblivion, of time and the temporally undifferentiated moment, occurs in the life of every human being (or of every nation or culture), each time anew. It is this life and no other, with its particular intensity, its particular *force*, that decides how much we remember and how much we will remember.

Let us examine the fragment from *Untimely Meditations* whose beginning I have already cited:

> The unhistorical [the temporally undifferentiated moment] is like an atmosphere within which alone life can germinate, and with the destruction of which it must vanish. It is true that only by imposing limits on this unhistorical element by thinking, reflecting, comparing, distinguishing, drawing conclusions, only through the appearance within that encompassing cloud of a vivid flash of light—thus only through the power of employing the past for the purposes of life and of again introducing into history that which has been done and is gone—did man become a man: [. . .] but without that envelope of the unhistorical [man] would never have begun or dared to begin.[11]

The temporally undifferentiated *moment*, that "time" of child's play that knows no difference between past and future, is a condition of the possibility of human life: the *atmosphere* that surrounds it. But human life begins only with the *disturbance* of child's play, only when the undifferentiated moment (the *element* that surrounds us) is *delimited*. Of course, this does not mean that with the beginning of human life the limits of the element surrounding it are fixed, that this element, the *atmosphere* that surrounds human life, has reached only a certain point and no further. Instead, we are dealing here with *imposing limits* in the very same sense as a wave "limits" the sea or a geometric figure space—with internal differentiation. Man becomes man when the past, present, and future hatch from the undifferentiated *moment*.

This differentiation is the *flash of light*—only now, with the appearance of difference, is something like the object of knowledge possible—in an undifferentiated atmosphere; in the *cloud*, all cows are black. And it is only now, only after this burst of light, that the *atmosphere* that protects human life can be called a *cloud;* only now does it turn out that this atmosphere is opaque, that we can see nothing within it; this characteristic would have made no sense before. When there is no light, nothing is yet dark, nothing is transparent or opaque. Likewise, the child at play has no idea that he doesn't remember, for he is ignorant of his own ignorance.

Read in this way, the *flash of light* cannot be gradual; either there is differentiation, or there isn't. Even minimal difference is still difference, just as with the utterance of an initial word or the birth of a child: in that instant the world begins anew, suddenly, in a single, indivisible moment, in one stroke. Like lightning.

How does this differentiation occur? In what way does the *past* hatch from the cloud of the undifferentiated moment? It arises only when the past is *employed for the purposes of life* and *what is gone* is reintroduced *into history*. So it is human life which, thanks to its limited ability to remember, leads the *past* out of the darkness of the undifferentiated *moment*. Only from the perspective of human life, from the perspective of limited human memory, is there room for what is now and what will be later, and thus also for the "future" and the "present." It is only from this perspective, in other words, that the division of "past," "present," and "future" makes sense. And thus it is only from this perspective that history "lives": it goes on, it happens, which is to say that it has some kind of future. Otherwise, history stops; it ceases to be history.

The past is something that I remember or am supposed to remember, the *chain* that delimits my possibilities, the *burden* of the obligations I have assumed, the *phantom* of the sins I have committed. Understood in this way, the past is a part of living history, the other side of which, though inextricably linked to it, is the future: all those duties, possibilities, obligations, everything left to atone for. The past and the future are, in this sense, the dimensions of human life, this *imperfect past tense*.

Living—that is, *thinking, pondering, comparing, performing, associating*—man opens some kind of future and, in so doing, some kind of past. This sudden flash of light that leads what will be and what has already been out from the darkness is human life. It is human life that introduces the difference between the future and the past into the *unhistorical moment* and, in this way, *delimits* it, "diversifies" it into the "moments" that are "yester-day," "today," and "tomorrow." Time does not flow out of itself; it is human life that makes the past differ from the future. Or, rather, the past differs from the future in what we do, and it is only here, in human life, that the difference between past and future has meaning. Time absent its reference to human life is an empty concept—and, on the other hand, human life in fact depends on separating the past from the future: human life is essentially time. The force of oblivion and memory that constitutes human life is, at the same time, the force that distinguishes past and future.

Human life, according to Nietzsche, is essentially the power to open the past and the future.

8

This is, therefore, what I see when I gaze at a grazing herd: creatures ignorant of the difference between "was" and "will be" and in this similar to children at play, utterly absorbed as they are in the moment (which is not, from this point of view, the "now" squeezed between past and future) and consequently deprived of memory—and happy. Seeing all of this, I realize who I, the observer of the grazing herd, am: a creature who transcends the given moment and crosses into the past and the future, a creature burdened with memory of what has been and therefore no longer happy but suffering, struggling, satiated. What I see is not alien to me—that's why when I gaze at the grazing herd and imagine a child at play I am both envious and moved.

For Nietzsche, this sight—the sight of the grazing herd or the child at play—is thus a metaphor for the fundamental dimension of my own—human—existence. For the past, memory, and therefore also the suffering, conflict, and satiety that determine my humanity, would not be possible without this other kind of sensibility, without the sensibility that erases the difference between "was" and "will be." This sensibility—this *unhistorical feeling*—is in this sense the "source," the "origin," of time as a succession of "was," "is," and "will be" and, at the same time, the "basis" of what is human.

Time is not, therefore, a "river," it is not a "stream" I can enter or leave at any moment and that flows regardless of what happens to me. It is the human being who, through the force of his life, tears the past from the future; it is the force of human life that tears up the undifferentiated moment, thereby creating "past," "present," and "future." This force of human life is the ability to remember, and thus also to suffer and struggle and, at the same time, the ability to forget and to be happy.

If this is so, then there naturally cannot be any talk of the happy cow from our initial discussion, the cow that has forgotten itself in the lived moment, being a metaphor for stupidity, and of its point of view differing from that of the person observing it in the same way as falsehood differs from truth or a "subjective" point of view from an "objective" one. It is in no way true that temporal succession is an "objective" reality that adults can recognize, whereas stupid cows and children, as yet mentally undeveloped, cannot. On the other hand, the fact that I have good reason to long for the simple happiness of a child, and thus for an irretrievably lost paradise, does not also mean that as a child I saw the world as it is, maybe even better and more fully than I see it as an adult—nor, for that matter, that a cow is so wise. The happiness of the child or the cow and the suffering of the adult, child's play and the conflicts of adult life, the *bliss* of oblivion and the *phantom*, *burden*, and *chain* of memory—these are two sides of the same thing, two dimensions of the *conditio humana*.

9

Let's have a look at some consequences of this perspective. As we have seen, the opposition between "subjective" and "objective" does not help us understand the Nietzschean metaphor of a man looking enviously and affectionately at grazing cattle or a child at play. Furthermore, from the point of view opened by this metaphor (inasmuch as I understand it) such an opposition takes on a completely different meaning from what we are used to. If the past is real only in its difference from the future—a difference introduced into the world by human life; in other words, if the term "past," like "present" and "future," means nothing without its relation to human life—then it follows that knowledge of the past must seek out such a relation and not try to eliminate it. At the same time, it is precisely the elimination of any connection to one's own life—an elimination that is called "objectivity"—that is, in Nietzsche's opinion, the ideal of knowledge in the age in which we live, an ideal instilled in this age by science, particularly by the science we call history.

Objectivity, Nietzsche says, "means a condition in the historian which permits him to observe an event in all its motivations and consequences so purely that it has no effect at all on his own subjectivity."[12] Achieving such a state requires us to excise all feelings, emotions, and personal interests regarding the phenomenon under study, so that the researcher will become entirely indifferent to it. The historian must forget himself and everything "subjective"; he must, as Michel Foucault writes, "mimic death in order to enter the kingdom of the dead."[13]

In other words, the historian who strives to achieve "objectivity" understands history only insofar as it is dead. Nietzsche writes:

> A historical phenomenon, known clearly and completely, and resolved into a phenomenon of knowledge, is, for him who has perceived it, dead: for he has recognized in it the delusion, the injustice, the blind passion, and in general the whole earthly and darkening horizon of this phenomenon, and has thereby also understood its power in history. This power has now lost its hold over him insofar as he is a man of knowledge.[14]

Delusion, injustice, and *blind passion* determine the historical power of a given phenomenon—insofar as they concern the one who wishes to understand, insofar as they are his affair, insofar as they have an effect on him. Once rendered objects of knowledge ("objectively" described), they are deprived of this effect and are thus excluded—much like the subject striving to understand them—from the *Wirkungszusammenhang*—or chain of interactions, interdependence (in Hans-Georg Gadamer's formulation)—that is living history.

I understand the past (Nietzsche argues) insofar as I am connected to it, insofar as I manage to include it within the horizon of my life, insofar as it has an effect on me. This is why the past cannot become exclusively an "object" of cognition, or knowledge of the past an "objective" science.

10

From this point of view, the question of whether knowledge of the past is "true" or "false" loses its dramatic quality. This does not mean that it is no longer important, but it undoubtedly stops being the most important thing. If "truth" is a quality of cognition and requires "objectivity" and, accordingly, removal from the context of the mutual interactions between the course of things and the actions of man, and if it is therefore a *cold, ineffectual knowledge*, then the question of whether or not something is true must be complemented with an additional deliberation over what comes of it, with an evaluation of its significance, which objective knowledge is in no state to achieve. To put it another way, the question of whether "truth" is important for us cannot be settled by "objective knowledge" alone: we have to look somewhere else as well.

Of course, this doesn't mean that the concept of "objective truth" is entirely useless, nor that "truth" of this kind cannot turn out to be, under certain conditions, quite essential. It means only that if the precondition for the search for truth, for objective knowledge, is my own life, then only with this life, with an evaluation in terms of it, can the significance and thus the meaning of such knowledge be disclosed. Science, particularly historical science in its striving toward objectivity, "requires superintendence and supervision and control: a *hygiene of life* belongs close beside science."[15]

Only when it is inscribed in life does "objective truth" take on any meaning. Only then does it become a truth that one can enjoy or die for. Removed from this context, truth becomes indifferent, nothing comes of it, and a human being, who has succeeded in this operation, loses, as a result, his own humanity. Nietzsche writes: "There are very many truths that are a matter of complete indifference: there are problems whose just solution does not demand even an effort, let alone a sacrifice. In this region of indifference and absence of danger man may well succeed in becoming a cold demon of knowledge."[16]

In other words, if the past, just like the present and the future, is not an infinite road onto which man steps at some point only to leave farther on, if the past opens each time anew in the actions of every person, if—to put it succinctly—it is impossible to separate the past (time) from human life, then "objective" knowledge of the past is a squared circle. More precisely, objective knowledge of the past is abstract knowledge, removed from the context of life, derivative knowledge (which, under certain conditions, does not mean it is useless). For "life" and "time" are not independent of each other; to think of their relation as one of subjectivity versus objectivity is an illusion. "For how," Nietzsche asks, "are human actions and the course of things to be distinguished from one another?"[17]

11

Nietzsche shares this position with authors otherwise as different (from him, as well as from each other) as Marx and Husserl. Marx also believed that "objective truth" acquires meaning only in the context of human life (which, in his opinion, depends on the constant, collective transformation of the world we encounter); seeking out this meaning, we must therefore avail ourselves of tools other than a science that strives for objectivity. Husserl, the author of *Cartesian Meditations* and *The Crisis of the European Sciences*, was equally convinced that understanding the claim to objective truth (an understanding constitutive of science in its modern form) requires us to examine the motivations that lead to it and, therefore, a genealogical analysis that science, and especially history, are unable to substitute. But unlike Marx and Husserl, Nietzsche believes that this understanding is itself lived, is itself a part of life, a life that is always "mine"—and therefore that seeking a point of view that transcends this life in any way is doomed from the very beginning. There is no "subject," no "consciousness," the meaning of which would not be produced in my life, each time anew: such a subject is neither the universal consciousness of the human species, hidden in the class consciousness of the proletariat (as Marx had it), nor the pure, transcendental consciousness that phenomenological analysis claims to find in the various acts of our understanding (as Husserl had it). Consciousness is a function of my life and is meaningless when removed from it. A consciousness whose identity is independent of someone's life is therefore impossible. What I do and what I neglect to do ultimately determine who I am and what the world is; only in this way is the meaning of the past and of the search for its truth determined.

Life, Nietzsche asserts, is the "dark, driving power that insatiably thirsts for itself."[18] *Dark*, because this life is the condition of any knowledge and therefore cannot wholly become its object. A *driving power*, since life is not a static structure, not a system in reference to which we can understand something; I can understand life only in living; only in what I do, in what I neglect, is life real (and in this it is never ready-made, never completely defined). It *insatiably thirsts for itself* because life cannot be understood "from outside," because any perspective "external" to it, any order that transcends it, is an illusion: life aspires to nothing, its dynamics are not an effort to achieve anything that isn't there. Life is not fulfilled with the achievement of any goal different from itself.

To put it differently, it is life that marks the boundaries of what we can understand. A necessary condition of our understanding anything is its inclusion in our own lives, its incorporation, its assimilation. In Nietzsche's language, it is a question of effect, a question of *force*, and not of argument. My actions, force, and the intensity of my life open first a space for argument; they are the element in which arguments can become significant and convincing.

If this is true, then it is a false hope (fed, no doubt, by both Marx and Husserl) that stepping beyond the horizon of my life, the assimilation or inclusion of something heretofore alien into my life, is, in the final tally, a conceptual assimilation, an act of reason. Universal reason, which could justify such a hope, is a fiction. A claim of truth does not create a common space in which we may achieve an understanding of what is other. It is not understanding, not the discovery of a common ground, that allows me to assimilate the otherness of another, alien life, but the other way around: it is only my assimilation of this otherness that allows me to understand it. Assimilation of something other is, therefore, first of all a matter of domination or submission, a question of power and not of argument. Domination or subordination condition, and therefore also limit, the understanding of what has been alien until now. The confrontation of the heretofore familiar with the foreign and new—a confrontation whose result is the horizon that maps out our potential for understanding, the horizon in which each of our lives plays out—is an existential, not an intellectual, confrontation: a confrontation in which life, and not just concepts, is at stake.

12

But don't these arguments ultimately lead to the apotheosis of power and the triumph of fact? No, not at all, Nietzsche tells us:

> But he who has once learned to bend his back and bow his head before the "power of history" at last nods "Yes" like a Chinese mechanical doll to every power, whether it is a government or public opinion or a numerical majority, and moves his limbs to the precise rhythm at which any "power" whatever pulls the strings. [. . .] In that way you become Devil's advocates: you make success, the factual, into your idol, while in reality the factual is always stupid and has at all times resembled a calf rather than a god.[19]

"Fact" is an abstract concept: "facticity," "the past," "what has happened"—these are what they are, after all, only from the perspective of my life; it is this—life—that determines their meaning in the end. And it is continuously doing so anew, for life is necessarily open to the future, it *becomes* rather than *is*, and thus its other dimension, facticity, the past, is never closed, never finished. History is therefore not a natural process, the necessity of which could be established once and for all. Every life is a chance at a new beginning; every life can initiate a new history, impart to it a new meaning, and redefine its internal rules, the criteria by which the success achieved therein is measured.

If human life creates time, if it is only here that the past is distinguished from the future, then history cannot be an "objective" process, independent of human life, a process toward whose ironclad laws man is supposed to relate and in which it is clear from the beginning what it means to "win" and what it means to "lose."

I am not indifferent to "facts" and the "past," whether I am aware of them or not. They appear only on the horizon of what I find relevant, only in the perspective of what I find useful. Furthermore, what I find relevant and necessary cannot be defined in advance, once and for all. If only my life can provide an answer to the question of who I am, if it is only here, in my life, that the question of what it means to be a Pole, a European, or a human being can be decided; if there is no subject whose meaning can be determined independently of my life, then it naturally makes no sense to speak of the universal "needs" of the human species or of what is important or unimportant for man at large. Life means establishing priorities and deciding what is important or not, always anew, always from the beginning; "facts" are what they are only in this perspective, so that every "fact" has a certain weight for me, it is a *burden*, *phantom*, or *chain*, and each one concerns me in some way, though I will never be able to learn completely how or why.

If this is so, then isn't the deification of fact and success just stupid? And, accordingly, is it possible to imagine a more idiotic point of view than relativism? For Nietzsche, it is the modern ideal of objectivity, and not his belief that objective knowledge presupposes life, that leads to relativism, since the viewpoint of an objective, universal reason elides the differences between what is important in my life and what might be important in someone else's. "[E]very age is different," Nietzsche describes the message of scientific objectivism, "it does not matter what you are like."[20]

The *force* that enables a life to assimilate something different or foreign, something other—the domination that first opens a space for argument—is, therefore, not blind, factual, natural. It always already means something to me, it always makes some kind of sense. It is the force of my life, and thus it makes no sense to speak of it as removed from my life. It is a force that cannot be measured from outside, the way one can measure the physical strength of a person or animal. And because my life is always essentially open to the future, because my life, as we have seen, tears the past from the future in each of its actions, always anew and always in a new way, the meaning of this force of life can always undergo even a radical revision. It is for precisely this reason that each new life is a chance at a new beginning, at a new answer to the question of who I am and what the world is in which we live.

13

Let's sum up. The grazing cows, the child at play, and the person observing them with envy and emotion are supposed to confront us—this is, I believe, Nietzsche's intention in the second of his *Untimely Meditations*—with human life, concentrated in the lived moment and simultaneously—in fact, because of this—tearing the past from the future. It is life stretched out from "yesterday" to "tomorrow" and thereby burdened with memory and guilt—and at the same time innocent and oblivious, growing out of time in its every instant: the connection between time and its sickness, eternity.

Such a concept of the human condition carries far-reaching consequences. Since the "past" is a dimension of human life, it cannot be merely an "object" to be grasped, requiring us to tear it free from the context of its "subjective," real-life entanglements. On the contrary, Nietzsche asserts that such an "objectivization" would deny us the only possibility of understanding what has been: the "past" can be understood only insofar as it influences what is happening now, the very life that I am living. And not just the past: objective truth in general becomes comprehensible, in Nietzsche's opinion, only when it is included in someone's life, only as someone's truth, only when someone assumes responsibility for it. There is no authority, however, that could take this responsibility from me: "transcendental consciousness," "the essence of the human species," and similar ideas are, for Nietzsche, dangerous illusions. I cannot defer to any such authority when I want to understand that which is alien to me, different from me, or new. I rely only on the capacity of my life to assimilate, on its *force*.

There are differences—we can formulate Nietzsche's thought this way as well—that cannot be overcome through mutual understanding, differences whose overcoming signifies domination or subordination. Thus the concepts and images that organize my thoughts, my understanding of the world, conceal within them a strategy for struggle, various tactics for confrontation, plans for the exercise of power. They must therefore be regarded cautiously, with suspicion: they do not always mean what they appear to mean. But, on the other hand, this force of my life is not blind; being "mine," it always already means something to me, it always has some kind of meaning, though, for the very same reason, that meaning cannot be settled once and for all. Each moment of life, opening new possibilities of meaning and significance, is a chance at settling things anew, at a new answer to the question of what the force of my life means—and what its consequences may be.

III

Good and Evil, Joy and Pain

THOUGH THERE is a lot that we know, we are least knowledgeable about ourselves. This is what Nietzsche says in the opening passage of *On the Genealogy of Morals*. We do not know who we really are.

Descartes famously argues just the opposite: who we are is the only thing we know for sure. We may be mistaken about the rest of the world (mistaking a bush for a person approaching in the darkness, or adding incorrectly, or misjudging someone else's motives), but we cannot be mistaken with regard to ourselves, or at least with regard to that which constitutes us fundamentally, that is, to our thoughts, our wishes, our desires. In this we know how things really are. And while we often mislead others—sometimes deliberately, sometimes inadvertently—we can't mislead ourselves.

What naïveté! Nietzsche responds. People are just as mistaken about themselves as about others or other things, and they are mistaken not only every so often but as a rule: we (as well as the world in which we live) are, as a rule, different from what we seem to be to ourselves. We are mistaken especially often as to the motives and the meaning of our actions.

The Cartesian position—that we know ourselves better and more thoroughly than we know the world—is based, according to Nietzsche, on a series of illusions. Foremost among these is the illusion of the very idea of the "subject," of a consciousness that is what it is independently of what happens beyond it—independently, for example, of my foot itching or rain falling—and that, in this regard, can be an object of knowledge free of the doubt and uncertainty that come with our engagement with the world. For in reality, Nietzsche tries to convince us, we are who we are dependent on what we do. Our identity is a constantly changing result of our wishes and aspirations (whether conscious or concealed), shifts, habits, success (or lack thereof) in the digestive process, of our infatuations, desires, and runny noses—of our engagements with the world. We are what the lives we live make us. Consciousness, Nietzsche maintains, is merely one among this life's functions, an instrument that life sometimes (and not always) avails itself of. It is therefore absurd to imagine that we can know our thoughts, wishes, and desires independently of our lives, with which they are inextricably intertwined.

In relation to the vastness and multiplicity of collaboration and mutual opposition encountered in the life of every organism, the *conscious* world of feelings, intentions, and valuations is a small section. [. . .] The fundamental mistake is simply that, instead of understanding consciousness as a tool and particular aspect of the common life, we posit it as the standard and the condition of life that is of supreme value.[1]

Consciousness is merely a non-autonomous part of the totality of my life, and not an always identical subject, the foundation of my identity, the meaning of the term "I." The "subject," in the sense of a consciousness that may be comprehensible independently of my life, is an illusion.

It is not just "consciousness" that cannot be understood when removed from the life we live: the identity of any given thing, Nietzsche asserts, is created only in the course of what happens to it. The assumption that things—some, at least—simply are, that they do not merely become what they are, is yet another illusion concealed within the Cartesian thesis, perhaps even more deeply than the first one. There is nothing that exists independently of what happens to it in life. Nothing can be as it is, once and for all. Nietzsche is not concerned here only with the fact that trees rot and people die. It is not only the identity of objects but also the identity of concepts that endow these objects with meaning, that, in his opinion, are created in the course of the lives we live. In other words, life is not just the process of the constant change of things but also the process of the constant change of their meaning. Decay can turn into growth, death into new birth, depending on the system of reference we apply to what happens. And this frame of reference—and not only what happens within it—submits to constant change as well. Or to put it yet another way: history—life as we live it—is change not only in the sense that within it one phase is followed by another, youth followed by maturity and, if we are lucky, old age. And not only in the sense that I myself am changing in the course of history, that I, its subject, become wiser and balder. The meaning of the history I am now living also changes. The question of what's really happening—what is this history, anyway—will never have an ultimate answer.

Thus if we wish to understand the meaning of something (for example, of a moral imperative, or of someone else's conduct), it does not suffice, in Nietzsche's view, to refer to its *source*, to its *cause* or its *function*. For the source, cause, or function can also submit to change; the source of a given moral imperative can cease being essential for it, its primary cause can become entirely irrelevant for its consequences today, and the function it once had may be entirely different from the one it has now. Nietzsche writes in *On the Genealogy of Morals*:

> [T]here is for historiography of any kind no more important proposition than [... that] whatever exists, having somehow come into being, is again and again reinterpreted to new ends, taken over, transformed, and redirected by some power superior to it; [. . .] and the entire history of a "thing," an organ, a custom can in this way be a continuous sign-chain of ever new interpretations and adaptations whose causes do not even have to be related to one another but, on the contrary, in some cases succeed and alternate with one another in a purely chance fashion. [. . .] The form is fluid, but the meaning is even more so.[2]

Let us note that if the above argument is valid, then not only can we not accept as absolute the division of things into mutable (like the weather) and immutable (like a triangle), but we likewise cannot accept the totality of life or of history as the realization of some otherwise comprehensible ideal, as the aspiration, albeit unrealized, toward an otherwise known goal, and so forth. In other words, what is happening to us—history—has no subject: nothing—no ideal, goal, cause, or function—stands outside it (the phrase "outside of history" makes no sense at all); all identity is created in the course of history, and none is independent of it.

And thus it is naïve to believe, as Descartes and his followers do, that our consciousness observes the life going on around us from outside and, therefore, that the doubt and risk of that life don't concern it. Just as a rainbow is an integral part of a landscape, consciousness is an irremovable element of life and cannot be understood in isolation from it. It is also naïve to think that any kind of meaning can be understood in isolation from the life that is that meaning's context: all meaning is constituted only in the course of life. It is naïve, in other words, to believe in a frame of reference independent from life as we live it, a frame of reference that would impart some ultimate meaning to things and their relations, to people and their actions. It is therefore nonsense to think that we know ourselves better than we know the structure of the atom or the motives of our adversaries. It is equally nonsensical to think that we can understand ourselves, the structure of the atom, or the motives of our friends—or anything, really—once and for all.

In fact, Nietzsche tells us, Cartesian naïveté reaches further still, for naïveté is not only the (illusory) belief that we can understand ourselves better than we can understand the rest of the world and, furthermore, that we can, at least in principle, do so completely. Naïveté is also the conviction that we want to understand ourselves at all, that we actually want to know who we really are. The belief that the will to truth determines our self-understanding is based on an illusion. This is not the case. Our lack of knowledge of ourselves, Nietzsche asserts, is not simple ignorance (which can be remedied or not). We are unknown to ourselves because we lead ourselves astray.

The notion of the independent subject looking at the world, the notion of identity independent of the process of its becoming, and finally our unlimited confidence in ourselves—these are the three illusions that Nietzsche reveals as presuppositions of the belief, common since Descartes' time, that we know who we really are.

2

Why exactly do we deceive ourselves? How is this even possible? Nietzsche writes in *The Gay Science*:

> "[W]ill to truth" does *not* mean "I will not allow myself to be deceived" but—there is no alternative—"I will not deceive, not even myself"; *and with that we stand on moral ground.* For you have only to ask yourself carefully, "Why do you not want to deceive?" especially if it should seem—and it does seem!—as if life aimed at semblance, meaning error, deception, simulation, delusion, self-delusion [. . .]. Charitably interpreted, such a resolve [will to truth] might perhaps be a quixotism, a minor slightly mad enthusiasm; but it might also be something more serious, namely, a principle that is hostile to life and destructive. [. . .]
>
> Thus the question "Why science?" leads back to the moral problem: *Why have morality at all* when life, nature, and history are "not moral"? No doubt, those who are truthful in that audacious and ultimate sense that is presupposed by the faith in science *thus affirm another world* than the world of life, nature, and history; and insofar as they affirm this "other world"—look, must they not by the same token negate its counterpart, this world, *our* world?[3]

As we have seen, the hidden premise of the will to truth, the premise of any claim to truth, is, for Nietzsche, morality: a set of rules and criteria that are alien to life as we live it, that negate it. Consequently, in Nietzsche's eyes all knowledge has a moral character, whether it is visible or not. "All experiences are moral experiences," Nietzsche writes in *The Gay Science*, "even in the realm of sense perception."[4] The task Nietzsche sets himself is to bring this premise to light. The path he intends to take is to be a genealogy of morals.

It is to be the history of (our) self-deception, the history of the creation and general acceptance of the mechanisms of concealment, of the institutionalization of pretense, the history of the birth and rise of the social instruments of mendacity—a history without which, Nietzsche asserts, we cannot understand European culture as we know it and, consequently, the human condition as it is here brought to light.

This is hardly a history in the usual sense: this *genealogy* cannot be merely an illustration of some thesis otherwise known, nor can it be merely a narrative about how humanity arrived at this or that otherwise comprehensible end. The end is incomprehensible without the genealogy; since not only the identity of things but also the identity of concepts through which those things are interpreted are constituted in the course of our lives and only there, putting things and concepts into the context of their genesis, relating them to the manner in which they arise and grow in our lives—*genealogy*—is the sole path to understanding them.

The mechanisms that lead contemporary man to self-deception—the mechanisms of mendacity—fall into a certain system, according to Nietzsche. This system is organized around the difference between *good* and *evil*. This is what we know as *morality*.

Like any other meaning, the difference between good and evil is not, in Nietzsche's opinion, simply given, is not simply found in the world by every child that is born. We therefore cannot understand and justify it relative to some immutable frame of reference, whether an extra-historical *source* (God, for example), a *function* that imparts meaning to human history (utility, for example), or a *cause* that sets history in motion (for example, human nature, rotten or good). To understand this difference we must first learn how it is created.

And it is created, Nietzsche tells us, in relations among people. The problem we now face should thus be phrased: what does the social genesis of the difference between good and evil look like? The history in which morality, in which the genealogy of morals is born, is in no way, according to Nietzsche, the history of the relationship of man and God, or man and nature: it is the history of interhuman relations.

Nietzsche proposes that we imagine a world without a difference between good and evil, a world in which people are divided not into good and evil but *good* and *worse*. This second difference has little in common with the first. Nietzsche writes in *On the Genealogy of Morals*:

> [T]he judgement "good" did *not* originate with those to whom "goodness" was shown! Rather it was the "good" themselves [. . .] who felt and established themselves and their actions as good, that is, of the first rank, in contradistinction to all the low, low-minded, common and plebeian. [. . .] The reverse is the case with the noble mode of valuation: it acts and grows spontaneously, [. . .] its negative concept "low," "common," "bad" is only a subsequently-

invented pale, contrasting image in relation to its positive basic concept—"we noble ones, we good, beautiful, happy ones!"[5]

The origin of the term "good" (as opposed to "worse" and not to "evil") is therefore, Nietzsche argues, the spontaneous acceptance of oneself, self-affirmation, limitless consent to what one is. Someone who is not as I am is, from this perspective, *worse;* consenting to what I am—not because I have no other option, not because I accept the necessity, not through comparison with others, not as a result of tallying pluses and minuses, but spontaneously and immediately—I establish my life as the standard others will or will not achieve. If they do not, they are not like me—they're *worse*. *Good*, in this usage, is, as we see, a designation applied not to others but to myself; it is a positive, not a negative, determination. Accordingly, one who is *good* in this sense is also necessarily active, not passive: he sets the standard of *goodness* that he has accepted himself; he does not need to let someone else do it for him. Ultimately, the good person finds joy and happiness in what he does—not with an eye to the outcome, not because his activity brings money, fame, or the respect of others. No—others are less important here, for joy resides simply in what I do—if I'm *good*. I am *good* if I am happy living the way I live, regardless of the consequences. For the *good* person (in this sense), happiness cannot be divorced from activity.

The distinction between *good* and *evil*, according to Nietzsche, results from flipping this perspective upside down. This new point of view is motivated not by a boundless and spontaneous acceptance of one's own life but by a rejection, a negation of the rest of the world, and above all a negation of other people. From this perspective, I am *good* because I am not *evil* like others, in relation to whom I am negatively defined (as the "one honest man" among liars and thieves, the "pinnacle of morality" in a thoroughly corrupted world, etc.). My *goodness* is thus a product (albeit a negative one) of my relation to others, an indirect result of the negation of something that is not me, the fruit of the dialectic that plays out between myself and others, and not, as before, the outcome of a spontaneous affirmation of myself. This is a negative, not a positive, definition. Recognizing someone as *good* is, in this regard, a reaction against the evil of others and not a spontaneous construction of one's own measure; in this sense, *goodness* is passive and not—as *goodness* had been in the former sense—active. Ultimately, here we find no trace of the joy of what is done; in the new, inverse perspective, what had formerly been an inseparable happiness vanishes from action. Happiness and action, joy and life, here part ways; life brings joy (since it brings with it rewards rather than punishments: health, money, success, the misfortune of others) or not, action leads to happiness or not, but happiness is now no longer the same thing as action, or joy the same thing as life.

Which naturally means that these words—"happiness," "joy"—now, from this point of view, utterly change their meaning: life without happiness and joy becomes a *burden*, a *chain*, a *weight*, a "fate, narcotic, drug, rest, peace, 'sabbath,' slackening of tension and relaxing of limbs."[6]

Here one might say that we are dealing with two life strategies: with the strategy of calculation, where happiness and joy are the consequence, the reward for the successful settling of a certain (moral) account; and with a strategy wherein no account is considered, and no calculation is relevant, for happiness and joy are an overabundance, an excess, an overflow of life itself.

Where does this inversion of perspectives come from? For Nietzsche, it results from the *revolt of the slaves*. *Slaves* are those who are *worse*, and therefore those who are unsuccessful in imparting their own measure of things to others and to the world; those who are unsuccessful in adapting the world to their own mold; in brief, those who are unsuccessful at being *good*. As a result, these *worse* people try to be *good* in another way: by changing the rules of the game. Because they have lost at the game as it has been played till now, they attempt to replace it with another, namely, with the kind that will allow them to win—or, rather, that will make it impossible for them to lose. With this goal, they build a "workshop where ideals are manufactured," where "[w]eakness is being lied into something *meritorious*, [. . .] and impotence which does not requite into 'goodness of heart'; anxious lowliness into 'humility'; subjection to those one hates into 'obedience.'"[7]

The *revolt of the slaves* ends successfully when the weak, the spiteful, and the worse actually succeed in opening a new perspective on the world, when they actually succeed in imparting new meanings to things, when they manufacture new ideals, when they succeed in creating new rules for the game—we will recall that Nietzsche calls such rules *values*—and inclining people to arrange their thoughts and things according to those rules. This new game, proposed by the worse, the weak (for they have lost the game as it has been played till now), the common, the spiteful—this new game, as a consequence of which things take on another meaning—is what Nietzsche calls *morals*.

Morals are therefore, in Nietzsche's view, the order of interhuman relations whose source is the incapacity for effective action, a life that cannot succeed, weakness that cannot be remedied. Morals, thus conceived, result from a substitutive reaction (Nietzsche calls it *ressentiment*), a notional reaction. Since I cannot manage to live spontaneously, actively, with a life that seethes with happiness and joy, I reach imaginatively for substitutive means, which allow me not to see my own weakness, my own failure.

3

It would appear that Nietzsche presents us with a picture of paradise lost: a primitive, spontaneous, joyful world in which people once lived happily, only then to endure the progressive degeneration called culture, which increasingly erodes their capacity for the true, full, joyful life, and which puts more and more new goals and needs in its place, goals and needs that have nothing to do with this life. Painting this picture, Nietzsche would call on us—and at least at first glance it seems he is doing just that—to cast away our rotten contemporary culture ("But enough! enough! I can't take any more! Bad air! Bad air!" he writes in a strong reaction to this culture in *On the Genealogy of Morals*) and to return to an ancient, healthy lifestyle.[8] The "splendid *blond beast* prowling about avidly in search of spoil," slumbering in each of us, in every bourgeois mediocrity reading newspapers in the café, must return, Nietzsche seems to say, to its natural element, to the real world, to the wilderness, where one no longer finds roads, benches, or sausage.[9]

If Nietzsche had really had this in mind, he would be situated in the long tradition sometimes called Romantic and conservative, next to Rousseau, full of awe for the "noble savage," and Heidegger, wandering dirt roads far from the bustle of civilization.

But this is off the mark. What Nietzsche calls the *blond beast* is not the brutal blond from the dreams of Hitler and Goebbels. Nietzsche does not tell us a nostalgic tale of the good old days, which are supposed to become reality once again. He has something else in mind. Morals, he claims—the rules of our good and evil behavior—are comprehensible only in the context of behavior, which has little in common with the opposition of good and evil: we can understand the difference between *good* and *evil* only in its tension with the difference between *good* and *worse*, only in the context of that difference.

Nietzsche's genealogy of morals is not, therefore, a relation among stages of development that follow one after another, like day and night or savagery and civilization. The "prehistoric" world of *the good* and *the evil*, where the history of our morals originates, is an ever-present prehistory, a constantly present possibility. We are not, therefore, dealing with the simple opposition of happiness (in which the *blond beast* lives) and the lack thereof (into which we are thrust by a "degenerate" culture). The world of the *blond beast*, a world in which the difference between *good* and *evil* is not the dominant principle of human action, is not a paradise in the sense of a state of attained satisfaction, of complete fullness, of ultimate satiety. True, the *blond beast* lives in happiness, but this happiness is not a "narcotic, drug, rest, peace, 'sabbath,' slackening of tension and relaxing of limbs."[10] Such happiness, or at least the dream of it, is the share of people whose lives lead to "happiness" (satisfaction with one's success, pleasure in having attained one's goal) or not, but are not this "happiness" in themselves. The metaphor of the *blond beast* reveals to us a different form of happiness, a happiness that is simply life as it is lived, as it is, without being valued "from outside" (for there is no "outside"). It is spontaneous action, and consequently absolute acceptance of what that is, an acceptance expressed by the very act of living and in no way similar to the acceptance of a proposition we have accepted after weighing all the pros and cons, though we may just as easily reject it.

4

This being the case, the happiness I am now describing does not exclude pain, suffering, conflict, or death. On the contrary, Nietzsche asserts that, discovering this form of happiness, which is unknown to us in everyday life, we discover at the same time the terror that is inseparably bound up with it. For our world, in Nietzsche's eyes, is terrifying: pain, suffering, conflict, and death cannot be removed from it. Pain, suffering, conflict, and death are irreducible elements of the human condition. Man cannot be understood without them, just as color cannot be conceived without space.

Just as there can be happiness without planning and calculation, happiness and joy that are not a reward or the fruits of success—the opposition between *good* and *worse* is supposed to show us this hidden layer of our lives—so too do our lives contain (as the same opposition is supposed to demonstrate) pain, suffering, and conflict, which are neither punishment nor the product of defeat: pain, suffering, and conflict, in the face of which there is no point in asking, "Why?"

Nietzsche draws far-reaching conclusions from this conviction. If this is so, he maintains, then any intellectual or emotional interpretive strategy that is supposed to help us deal with our terror of the world (or, to put it another way, with our weakness) is a lie, an illusion, which leads us astray. Any theodicy that justifies our pain after the death of a friend with the good of an ultimate goal, any dialectic that persuades us to understand a defeat endured today by discovering its place in the logic of things, is an anesthetic, a narcotic, which induces sleep, ignorance, and flight from the terror of life. It is an ideal manufactured from weakness, making the world a comfortable place where one can sit back and read the newspaper; these are the "sweet" ideals, which cover the world in a layer of sticky, sugary mildness. At the same time, life as it is has a bitter taste; suffering, pain, and death are inextricably intermingled with its joys.

Any religion or philosophy that promises solace is, according to Nietzsche, a (sweet) lie.

5

A lie, a negation of life—of its immanent joy, of its suffering—but not without positive results. Morals (that flight, motivated by weakness, from the terrors and joys of life, in pursuit of *good* and *evil*) are not a common deviation, a correctable loss of one's way, a flu that can be treated without further consequence. Rather, according to Nietzsche, *morality* is a sickness, or at least a condition, in the same sense that pregnancy is a "condition." For *morality*, like pregnancy, enriches the organism that lives through it, and is therefore not merely destructive but also creative and productive. Covering the world in "sweet" appearance (and thereby rendering it habitable for the weak and defeated), stripping things of their names and furnishing them with others (remember that *weakness* becomes *merit*, impotence—*goodness of heart*, lowliness—*humility*, etc.), *morals* add another dimension to reality, complicate it, and thus create the need for a reason capable of interpretation, the need for spirit. Nietzsche writes:

> [I]t was on the soil of this *essentially dangerous* form of human existence, the priestly form, that man first became *an interesting animal*, that only here did the human soul in a higher sense acquire *depth* and become *evil*—and these are the two basic respects in which man has hitherto been superior to other beasts![11]

For someone who doesn't worry about what others do and think, who takes things as they seem to be from his perspective, who acts spontaneously and without regard for potential benefits and losses—for such a person the ability to penetrate to the heart of the matter and bring to light initially invisible motives and consequences—in short, *spirit*—is inessential. Only the weak and the defeated need calculation, reason, and spirit: "Human history would be altogether too stupid a thing without the spirit that the impotent have introduced into it."[12]

The difference between *good* and *worse*—and that between *good* and *evil*; life seething with excess and self-affirmation—and its negation (*morals*), which produces webs of concepts and rules that bind it: these are not two separate social institutions or consecutive stages of our moral evolution. Rather, they are two inextricable aspects of human life.

6

What does all of this mean for an understanding of Nietzsche's genealogy of morals?

The genealogy of morals is not, it turns out, a narrative of a chain of events, similar to a narrative about the Peloponnesian War. It is particularly not the tale of a golden age preceding the gray reality of contemporary Europe, or of a Garden of Eden from which we have been banished, now to live in the desert of modernity. It is not the opposition of some "truth" (life as it is lived by the *good*, the *noble*, the *powerful*) and some "falsehood" (life as it is distorted by *morals* and lived by the *worse*, the *spiteful*, the *weak*). In general, it is not an opposition between two mutually independent states of things. The genealogy of morals is an attempt to show the dynamic hidden behind our moral concepts, the intractable tension that arises from the fact that these concepts are an expression of life and, accordingly, that each one of them is also a kind of *power* that can injure or destroy, as well as aid or liberate. This genealogy of morals is an account of human life as it is, here and now, of the terror that lurks in its depths, as well as of our flight from it, if only, as today, into the pleasant slumber of contemporary culture; of the power of human life, which introduces into the world the only kind of meaning one can find there, and of its irremediable weakness, which adds falsehood and deception to the world and thereby makes it both habitable and interesting.

Moral concepts, the genealogical analysis of morals suggests, are thus necessarily partisan, are instruments in some conflict, serve some cause—but the outcome of these conflicts, the determination of a winner, of the just cause, cannot be based on the solid foundations of a completely objective knowledge. What is right or wrong, true or false, good or not good—even what is success, what failure—cannot be settled by referring to some frame of reference independent of the conflict currently under way, to some meaning just waiting to be discovered: "power" and "weakness," Nietzsche writes in *The Gay Science*, are relative terms. No: legitimacy, truth, good, and success are decided by the dispute in which we are engaged. This is a game in which everything is at stake, including the rules of the game itself. Life, our lives, is a constant confrontation with others, which cannot be completely transformed into an impartial search for the right resolution, the common good, or a truth we all share.

Yes indeed, morality is universal, Nietzsche argues—but not because moral imperatives and punishments have a universal validity. What would this even mean? Morality is universal because all concepts have some kind of moral content, sometimes hidden: every concept is a weapon in some conflict. Every moral concept conceals within itself someone's claim that things should be this way and not another—a claim that can only be measured against the claims of others. Each is accordingly subject to the influence of others and is therefore problematic and, at the same time, fragile.

Nietzsche, too—and for that matter, the genealogy of morals—cannot just tell the truth and shame the devil. The words, arguments, and metaphors that Nietzsche uses to tell us his genealogy of morals cannot be understood outside of the context of agreement or disagreement irreducible to a difference of opinion. They want to hurt us or arouse our admiration, provoke our objection or our solidarity, for Nietzsche maintains that only words capable of hurting us or arousing our admiration can be understood. The sole means of convincing us is, Nietzsche believes, to draw us into an argument that concerns us directly, or rather, to prove to us that, whether we like it or not, whether we know it or not, we have already been engaged in such a dispute for a long time, a dispute in which the very meaning of the culture in which we live and the very meaning of humanity are at stake.

7

The conviction that morals as we know them are always to a large degree problematic, that our knowledge of what is good and evil is not and cannot be based on unshakeable foundations, that even our good will may be an illusion to our very selves—this is a motif that appears frequently in religious texts. The absolute that cannot be grasped in concepts and escapes all knowledge is, in several threads of religious thought, like a harsh light that exposes the fragility and relativity of all concepts, of everything that can be known, of all our behavior: an "absolute" that, like light, can itself be exposed in only this way. The result of the confrontation with the absolute, so conceived, is the terror that is inseparable from the human condition, as well as from the weak and horrified man's flight from it, if only into oblivion. But joy, happiness, and sweetness—or at least the hope for them—which can bring us rescue or "redemption," are likewise comprehensible only against this background.

I know no better witness to this vision of the world than Pascal. Our concepts, he writes, are utterly useless against a reality that constantly slips away from them: "However much we may inflate our conceptions beyond these imaginable spaces, we give birth only to atoms with respect to the reality of things."[13] Similarly, the concept of some natural order, some solid, stable nature that might completely ground our thoughts and behaviors, is empty: "Fathers fear that their children's natural love may be erased. What, then, is this nature that can be erased?"[14] "There is nothing that cannot be made natural. There is nothing natural that cannot be lost."[15] Based on flexible, mutable human decisions, conventions, and forces of habit, the ostensibly "admirable rules of policy, morality, and justice" conceal within themselves the "vile foundation of man, this *evil component* [*figmentum malum*—Gen. 8:21]," and thus the inconstancy, the fragility of the human condition, "only covered up, not removed" by all these laws.[16]

Which is really horrifying: horrifying is the feebleness of my concepts, horrifying is the lack of any ground, my suspension in nothingness—and, finally, the nothingness itself, from which it would seem there is no escape: "The final act is bloody, however fine the rest of the play. In the end they throw some earth over our head, and that is it forever."[17]

How are we to deal with this situation? Chase after the hare, split hairs by resolving a difficult mathematical problem: "How does it happen that [a man who has suffered misfortune] is not sad at this moment and is so visibly free from all these painful and disquieting thoughts? We should not be surprised: he has just had a ball served to him and he must return it to his fellow player."[18] To flee into ignorance, into oblivion. But such a flight does not bring lasting solace. ("For among humanity there is 'still a little light,'" wrote Saint Augustine, Pascal's intellectual forebear. "May they walk, may they indeed walk, 'so that the darkness does not capture them' [John 12:35].")[19] Only faith in God can console us. But are we capable of it?

How kindred this worldview is to that of Nietzsche! But how very different it is at the same time. As much as Pascal believes that "trust in God" is based on a conviction of the existence of a truth about us that is also hidden to us, that the wretchedness and terror of the human condition can be understood from a point of view that stands well above it, that there exists a perspective in which the life of every person always turns out to be the same, endlessly repeated tragedy, an oscillation between the poles of damnation and salvation, which are designated not by him but for him, between wretchedness and eternal happiness, the tragedy of searching and the flight from redemption—as much as Pascal believes that the mutability and variety of human destinies are rooted in a history that is hidden from us and written by someone else, ever the same history of Paradise, guilt, expulsion, and the chance of return—*the wretchedness of man* is then the truth about us that comes to light against the background of our understanding of the *greatness* of God. "There is nothing on earth," Pascal writes, "that does not show either man's wretchedness or God's mercy."[20]

To put it briefly, if Pascal had been of the opinion that the order of our lives and our ideas depended on some "truth"—on a perspective through which we see the world as it is—then in this regard his vision of the world differs radically from Nietzsche's. Truth, as we have come to know from Nietzsche, is not the ultimate frame of reference, a scale that allows me to understand my life. The search for truth, *the will to truth*, contains within itself moral motives that bind us in one way or another with other people, and as a consequence every truth is also a greater or lesser *force*, a threat to or chance at another. This constantly changing system of forces, this continuous battle, confrontation, dispute, cannot be resolved into some immutable pattern; it is impossible to discover within it any laws or ironclad rules that are independent of it. If "God" signifies such a pattern, such laws and rules, then *God is dead*. As a result, in Nietzsche's eyes—and not so much in Pascal's—the fate of man is not a "tragedy," not a constant repetition of the same history. Each of our lives, Nietzsche argues, is continuously writing everything anew. It not only chooses between the always ready-made options (salvation and damnation) but also creates its own options, always different, new each time. The terror of human life, much like the joy inscribed within it, cannot be explained with concepts that are independent of that life. Human wretchedness—the fragility of our concepts, the risk of our activities—does not arise from the fact that we do not live up to the standards that have been thrust upon us. Human greatness arises not from passing the examination of a stern judge. Man is what he himself makes of himself, and it is here that, in Nietzsche's view, we find the horror of our existence: in the risk of every step, in the irremediable and infinite uncertainty that it can bring. Horror and happiness at the same time, one inseparable from the other, for Nietzsche thinks that happiness, too, is drawn from the same source as terror—from risk, uncertainty, and thus from the creative nature of what we do.

IV

Reason, Which Hurts

Zarathustra says: "What returns, what finally comes home to me, is my own self and what of myself has long been in strange lands and scattered among all things and accidents."[1]

One way of interpreting this: chance is something alien. But nothing I encounter on the road of my life, in the course of my experience, is entirely alien to me. Everything I encounter is, to a certain degree, familiar. It is familiar insofar as its meaning—the meaning of what I live through, of what I experience, of mountains, triangles, betrayal, responsibility—relates to me, insofar as it is a fragment of my world. When I understand this, when I understand that everything that might cross my path—the world—is a whole with regard to me and is, in this regard, my world—then chance loses its raison d'être. Things that had seemed devoid of any relevance to me, alien, and in this sense accidental, will *return home*, will turn out to be elements of my identity. Again, Zarathustra: "For me—how should there be any outside-myself? There is no outside."[2]

Of course, this does not mean that the world that comes to the fore in my life is familiar in the sense of tamed, not wild, that it contains no threats or dangers, that it does not resist me, is dependent on my will, bends to my intentions. No, this is hardly the case. And yet everything I encounter—those mountains, terrifying and resistant and in this sense "alien," those (as yet) incomprehensible formulas and hidden mysteries; those who are close to me, though sometimes, all of a sudden, so alien—one way or another, everything relates (Zarathustra teaches us) to my presence (even if it is merely potential).

Which also means that my soul, my identity, is unthinkable without all these mountains and triangles, betrayals and loves, without this resistance, without these mysteries and dangers, which I encounter over the course of my life, and all of which I call "the world." Zarathustra: "To every soul there belongs another world."[3]

Through my presence, my identity, the "I" glues things together into a totality, the whole of my world, but at the same time this "I," this identity of mine, is an incomprehensible, hollow sound—if I try to understand it beyond the world, beyond this pile of things I have glued together into a whole.

2

Sometimes, however, Zarathustra speaks of chance in another, and at first glance seemingly opposite, sense: "'By Chance'—that is the most ancient nobility of the world, and this I restored to all things: I delivered them from their bondage under Purpose. [. . .] I taught: 'In everything one thing is impossible: rationality.'"[4]

In this instance, the term "chance" no longer refers to the opposition of *familiar* and *alien*; here we are dealing with the opposition between *rational* and *irrational*. "As little reason as possible: this, politely, is chance," Nietzsche notes at one point.[5] *Chance* is, in this context, everything that falls outside of rational comprehension, that falls beyond understanding in reference to something that it is not, with regard to something else (*bondage under purpose*). Or, to put it another way: chance is everything that cannot be understood as a part of some totality.

And Zarathustra tells us that there are many such things. Or, put yet another way, rationality is not all-encompassing: by its very nature, something is always left out. There is no such thing as a totality that encompasses everything, a totality without remainder: the world is no such totality. Or, yet another way: the world is incurably diverse, there are differences within it that cannot be eliminated, differences with no common denominator, with no common point of departure. Differences that fall outside of reason, differences about which we cannot reach an understanding.

It is difficult to come to terms with this. We are so invested in the notion that all differences can ultimately be understood—and that, as a result, "rational" understanding knows no bounds. How very tempting is our vision of the world as a well-ordered cosmos, like a garden where everything has its own place! But the world-as-garden is not reality; it is merely an illusion summoned by words. "[W]here there is chattering," Zarathustra says, "there the world lies before me like a garden. How lovely it is that there are words and sounds! Are not words and sounds rainbows and illusive bridges between things which are eternally apart?"[6]

Zarathustra instructs us that beyond the *rainbows* and *bridges* of *words and sounds* are hidden differences that cannot be reduced to something else, eliminated, or removed by understanding: differences that are, in this sense, eternal, *forever*.

Let's take a closer look at these differences.

We are not dealing here with differences like those between men and women, cat and dog, my neighbor and myself. These, of course, can be understood, at least potentially. If I call the difference between men and women a difference that is "forever," I have in mind certain traits that I recognize in each and that I believe cannot be reconciled, like a square and a triangle, or warm and cold. I know what differs here: people, animals, geometric figures, temperatures. These differences—the kinds of differences I perceive, the kinds of differences that can be an object of cognition—assume a *tertium comparationis* and can be grasped, understood, with regard to some common frame of reference. Furthermore, such differences assume an "external," "objective" point of view, an observer capable of confirming such a difference "objectively," of understanding it by referring to a system, in light of which the elements of this difference differ from each other, allowing the observer to find their common denominator. In other words, these differences assume an observer who is not immediately touched by the difference he has discerned, just as the difference between two exotic butterflies does not concern me when I am looking at them under glass at a museum of natural history.

The differences that Zarathustra speaks of are, on the other hand, incomprehensible in principle, not only because I am momentarily unable to comprehend them—and perhaps will tomorrow, once I've slept on it, or maybe my more intelligent friend will. These are differences with no *tertium comparationis*, with no common denominator, with no frame of reference through which to understand them; these are differences that cannot be described from some "external" or "objective" perspective, by an attentive and impartial observer leaning over a display case. Such a perspective is not, and cannot be, all-encompassing: no observer can look down on all things, on the world itself. There is no all-encompassing point of view, Zarathustra tells us: such a notion is nonsense. And because of this, every order that we discover or create has boundaries, has another, unknown, dark side, and the difference between our order and the rest, between the garden we have arranged and what is beyond the fence, is an entirely different kind of difference from that between blue and white, a triangle and a square, you and me.

It is only this version of the world's diversity that is incurable and will not go away, no matter how deep or far our understanding of the world penetrates. For as long and skillfully as we may search, we will not discover any universal common denominator within it.

It is to these kinds of differences—differences that cannot be assimilated, grasped, and thus dismissed, differences that arise from the insurmountable otherness of the world—it is to these differences that the concept of *chance* now refers.

If, however, the diversity of things that I am now discussing cannot be grasped, if it is unrecognizable and in this sense accidental, then how am I aware of it? How does one inquire about it?

I am aware of it—so I would imagine Nietzsche's answer to these questions—insofar as things wound me (though I know not why), insofar as they resist me (incomprehensibly), insofar as they place incalculable danger in my path—or else insofar as they summon from within me an unforeseen power or open unexpected horizons before me. Only in this way do I "learn" the irreducible diversity of the world. I write "learn" because this is not, after all, knowledge, enclosed within concepts, of things and their structure. The "knowledge" I mean here, knowledge of the irremediable diversity of the world, is hidden in pain, in anxiety, in liberation, in the experience of one's collision with the otherness of the world, which can never be completely grasped in concepts. It is only in this way, only in our collisions with that which is incomprehensibly other, that the world as it is, the world in all its diversity, comes to light.

Accordingly, these differences—insofar as they are not framed within a universal reason or universal rationality—are dangerous. The world, insofar as it is incurably diverse, is dangerous. If an all-encompassing reason is an illusion, then there is no guarantee that all things will arrange themselves (sometime, anytime) in neat rows, without interfering with each other; there is no certainty that the world as I have constructed it—my world—will join the harmony of all things. Conflict—and this is unlimited conflict, and hence the kind whose end we cannot know—can never be eliminated once and for all. In other words: *war*—limitless conflict—is inescapable. And not only as inescapable evil but also, or even primarily, as an irremediable element of life—or as the very basis of life. "Faith in [the possibility of general] agreement and the possibility of eliminating discord is a fundamental error," Nietzsche notes. "It would mean death!"[7]

In this context, *war* is another way of describing differences in the face of which our reason is helpless. This is why Zarathustra teaches us that wisdom "is a woman and always loves only a warrior."[8]

Let me be clear: I do not think that Zarathustra means to praise war, for example, because we might say that war helps develop virtues necessary to the human species, such as courage, willingness to take risks, solidarity in the face of danger, and so forth. Nor is the point here to praise "just war." No: the *war* intended here cannot be an object of praise or something to be justified. For there is no point of view that would allow us to evaluate it from outside. *War* here means a perspective on what is radically other and thus new, unforeseeable, mysterious, and consequently infinitely dangerous: "You say it is the good cause that hallows even war? I say unto you: it is the good war that hallows any cause."[9]

If the term "war" refers to an incomprehensible, and therefore potentially dangerous, difference between the world as we have arranged it and this insurmountable otherness that is always confronting us anew, then naturally *war* in itself cannot be defined, determined, or evaluated in any sense, whether to condemn it or to hallow it. Morality and reason cannot be applied to it. On the contrary: all of our concepts, all of our values, are comprehensible only in the context of *war*, only when we uncover their function in the confrontation between my world and that other ("at war"), which waits around every corner. Only when we confront our concepts and our values with something that is radically different from them will we know what they are worth.

"Good and evil, and rich and poor, and high and low, and all the names of values—arms shall they be."[10] Arms in a battle, in a confrontation, with the other, the unknown, the alien.

Thus this confrontation—this *war*—is not in itself "just" or "unjust," good or evil, for it is beyond good and evil. But it can be "beautiful": "[S]truggle and inequality are present even in beauty, and also war for power and more power [. . .]. [W]ith such assurance and beauty let us be enemies too, my friends! Let us strive against one another like gods."[11] We differ *beautifully* when we do not hide differences under concepts ostensibly independent from them, when we do not attempt to understand them and, in so doing, assimilate them, imposing moral categories that are independent from them. ("'Enemy,' you shall say, but not 'villain.'")[12] We differ from each other *beautifully* when we differ *like gods*, who create the meaning of their differences themselves, who do not borrow it from somewhere else. We differ *beautifully* when we are prepared to confront the diversity, difference, and otherness of the world—when we are, in this sense, *brave*. ("'What is good?' you ask. To be brave is good.")[13] We differ from each other beautifully when, at any given moment, we are prepared to expose our habits, rights, and concepts—our world itself—to the risk of confrontation, which knows no end of defeat. I manage to differ *beautifully* when I understand that "[m]y enemies too are part of my bliss."[14]

And therefore, Zarathustra teaches us, it is not evil intentions (from which one can sometimes be freed) or individual or social pathologies (which one may cure) that make the world we live in dangerous. It is not evil introduced into the world "from elsewhere" that is the source of our danger. It is life itself that is dangerous, for it is incurably open to something new and unexpected, for it is the constant confrontation with something other, something alien—and thus it can never remain what it is. It is only in the course of this irreducibly diverse life, in the course of the *war* of life, that things gain this and no other meaning, and that I become what I am.

No, the world does not lie before us like a landscape still in fog, waiting to be discovered. No, reason is not a gentle light that disperses the darkness of ignorance and, with it, the specters and terrors of superstition. No, wisdom is not knowledge of the harmony of things, hidden to the everyday. Zarathustra tells his contemporaries, who, he believes, have been deprived of true wisdom:

> You know only the spark of the spirit, but you do not see the anvil
> it is, nor the cruelty of its hammer. [. . .] In all things [. . .] you act

too familiarly with the spirit [. . .]. [. . .] You are no eagles: hence you have never experienced the happiness that is the terror of the spirit.[15]

Perhaps Heraclitus had something similar in mind when he said, "War is father of all, and king of all. He renders some gods, others men; he makes some slaves, others free."[16]

This being the case, my identity—the sense of that little word, "I"—is not something given, ready-made, the same thing at my life's every step. No, at every step—in the confrontation with the unknown, which demands courage, and in the pain of separating from what has been dear till now—this sense is created anew. Everything I know about myself, everything that is familiar and my own, is in each successive moment placed under a question mark. My identity must therefore entail a readiness to jettison everything I think and feel: "[H]ow else would you want to climb upward? On your own head and away over your own heart."[17] It must entail a readiness to abstract itself from itself: "One must learn to *look away* from oneself in order to see *much*."[18] From myself as I am at this very moment.

Like a snake, I have to be ready to shed my skin in order to remain myself. I have to be ready to burn my own house down, to distance myself from what is dear, to ignore what has been important till now. Not only in order to find a new home, new loved ones, new values, but to go even further, ever farther, without the illusory hope of ever attaining once and for all a safe haven, peace, warmth, or domicile. Everything that sustains this hope—all concepts, all moral sanctions in light of which some situation, some state of things, appears as the end of the road, an ultimately safe shelter, a home that never need be abandoned again—these are false gods.

> Truthful I call him who goes into godless deserts, having broken his revering heart. In the yellow sands, burned by the sun, he squints thirstily at the islands abounding in wells, where living things rest under dark trees. Yet his thirst does not persuade him to become like these, dwelling in comfort; for where there are oases there are also idols.[19]

Life is incurably diverse and, because of this, dangerous at its core, for it is a continuous confrontation with something that is radically new, inconceivable, and alien. With *chance*. More precisely, I shouldn't write "life is" this way or that, one way or the other, since life, open to the new and the other, never "is." Because it "must overcome itself again and again."[20]

No, Zarathustra does not want to convince us that this is easy. He does not suggest that if we listen to him we will be able to abandon everything that has been near and dear to us till now, like a runway model changing her outfit between forays onto the catwalk. Maybe a snake can painlessly shed what had been its skin. Not us. It hurts us. It hurts to throw away one's world, to throw away everything that is familiar and beloved, to toss away our habits, including those I can't get by without, to throw away everything I know. This isn't merely an outfit, not merely a mask, behind which there's the real me: it *is* me, me as I really am, my own skin, an integral part of my body. Stripping it off hurts. But no one is forcing me; there is no alien and evil power. It is my life, my constantly self-overcoming life that leads me, painfully, from each place I have made my home. In this way, as long as I live, I remain open to the new, the other, and the unexpected. To the world, in its irreducible diversity. In this way—through my life, and not through my concepts—I understand the world around me.

"Spirit," Zarathustra teaches us, "is the life that itself cuts into life: with its own agony it increases its own knowledge."[21] Thanks only to this, thanks only to the injuries it inflicts on itself, does life gain sensitivity to the world that surrounds it. Only a life thus torn apart opens itself to the world, only then does the world come to the fore within it. Through Zarathustra's lips, Nietzsche complains:

> The audacious daring, the long mistrust, the cruel No, the disgust, the cutting into the living—how rarely does all this come together! But from such seed is truth begotten.[22]

3

But is it possible to reconcile this notion of chance with our previous one? Is everything I experience in life essentially my own, mine, though it may not seem so at first glance, so that chance, something absolutely alien to me, is, as I wrote at the beginning, impossible? Or is it rather the other way around, that the world cannot be assimilated and my life is a continuous confrontation with the alien, the new, the unexpected, so that chance, something that is incomprehensible, is the central category of my life?

This is only an apparent contradiction. It arises only when I assume that I know, or at least that I can know, who I am. That my identity can be, at least in theory, completely defined. That I am or can become—even if attaining this goal might be infinitely far away—something completely determined, whether this or that—for example, a creature entirely free or infinitely reasonable, someone who is happy, and so on. In such a case, if everything I experience is—at least potentially—mine, and in this sense familiar (and so if chance in the first sense is an illusion), then, indeed, there is no room for chance in the second sense, that of incomprehensible otherness.

My identity, however, is not after all a stable and immobile unity, not even one deeply hidden in the flux of everyday life and thus infinitely distant. In every moment of my life—to the extent that it is open to something heretofore alien, to something other, to a situation in which my concepts up to that point will fail me, as will my ability to assimilate what I encounter—my identity is once again placed under a question mark: each moment forces me into a new self-definition. My identity is becoming, is constantly overcoming itself; no state of identity, Nietzsche maintains, is final. In other words, not only am I never completely one thing or the other, not only is there no description or concept that characterizes or encompasses me completely—nor am I becoming this thing or another: I am not on my way to realizing any concept, any essence, any ideal. Which means that the confrontation with the alien, the new, and the unexpected is a vital element of my own identity. Thanks to it, I am becoming what I am, always and anew.

The world, Zarathustra tries to convince his audience, is not a self-contained whole: what an absurd, unjustifiable proposition! The world becomes a whole only when it is glued together by what I do, in my life, such that this whole, my world, is therefore like a clay pot, fragile, easy to break. The world, my world, is constantly undermined. In order to understand it, one must sense the dynamite hidden beneath its surface, the dynamite that is the possibility of encountering something radically new, other, alien—something that places a question mark over the world as I know it and demands its radical revision. The world conceived without this hidden dynamite, without the possibility of explosion, disintegration, or shattering, is an abstraction. But it is only in this way—only abstractly, only as an (at least potentially) ready-made, solid structure—that the world can be grasped at all. Otherwise, the world cannot be grasped, and so it will always slip out from the web of concepts in which we would wish to catch it.

And thus it is true that there is no *chance*: everything I encounter is, in some sense, mine; it concerns me in some way. But this does not preclude *chance* in the other meaning, that of something completely other, alien, not encompassed by any criteria I have applied until now. Such *chance* lies in wait around the corner, at my every step, at every moment of my life, bringing to the fore the irremediably temporary, transitory, and thus also dangerous nature of my life. Demonstrating that my life is not only this or that but also, above all else, constantly overcoming itself.

We are not concerned here with the simple fact that we always settle into knowledge we have already managed to acquire, that we grow accustomed to concepts and differences that are already familiar, and yet, unexpectedly and by chance, some new, as yet unfamiliar concepts are always showing up, some Martians, certain differences we had had no inkling of, which then broaden our knowledge. Rather, we are concerned with the difference that puts a question mark not only over this or that fragment of my knowledge, this or that superstition or habit, but over my very identity ("Krzysztof Michalski") up until this point and, at the same time, over the order of the world I live in. That *chance* in this sense therefore concerns me most deeply, most intimately, as only it can—that without it I would not be who I am, and my world would not be what it is. In other words, that this *chance*, this question mark, co-creates my identity, the meaning of my "I." The world is mine, but at the same time, and by the same token, it is open to the new, the alien: it is incoherent and mysterious.

In this way, both concepts of chance are connected.

4

Consequently, the concept of necessity also acquires a new meaning. If the concept of universal rationality is an illusion, then the concept of a universal necessity that orders the world is equally meaningless. The "necessary and universal laws of nature," the "iron laws of history"—these are fiction. "Let us beware the notion," Nietzsche notes, "that there is some law [. . .] that applies everywhere in *the universe* and is its eternal property."[23]

Can one still speak of "necessity" in such a situation? Sure, if I understand Nietzsche correctly, insofar as "necessity" is not then something found, something waiting to be discovered and understood. "Necessity" is now a certain possibility standing before me, a state I can attain: a unity of will, a merging of everything I do into a whole. If I succeed in doing so, "necessity" of another kind will disappear, "necessity" in the sense of need, of the trouble I have found myself in, "necessity" imposed from outside. Unity, the necessity of will, is impossible so long as compulsion—need dictated by external factors—so long as "necessity" imposed by the resistance of things remains unconquered. "O thou my will!" Zarathustra calls out to himself. "Thou cessation of all need, my *own* necessity!"[24]

Necessity, thus understood, is therefore also the opposite of *chance*, is the assimilation of each successive situation, of every state in which I may find myself, insofar as that state of things seems "accidental" to me, imposed from outside, not my own. "[Chance] came to me domineeringly," Zarathustra says, "but my will spoke to it still more domineeringly—and immediately it lay imploringly on its knees."[25]

Chance: the world that does not concern me, the world that is not my own, therefore exists only for him who does not succeed in assimilating the situation he finds himself in, for him who succumbs to the pressure of his surroundings, who allows some situation he has encountered to completely define who he is. For someone who is weak: "'Chance' is what the weak call it. But I say to you: what could happen to me that my burden has not forced and taken on itself? [. . .] [When it happens] chance becomes for me 'my will and my destiny.'"[26]

5

The world, Zarathustra tells us, is like the heavens over my head: "O heaven above me, pure and deep! You abyss of light! [. . .] O heaven over me, pure and high! That is what your purity is to me now, that there is no eternal spider or spider web of reason."[27]

The heavens above me: the world around me. This world is as *pure* as the heavens, for no definition, no feature, no quality conceivable to us takes it on. The world cannot be sad, rainy, sunny, mountainous. Or rather, sure, it is these things, too, but not completely, for there is always something more, always that undefined, evasive "more." As if all these definitions didn't really have anything to do with it. In this same sense the world is also *deep*. When it seems to me that I have reached it, that I have finally understood how it is, that I can at last see bottom, it turns out to be an appearance, that in front of me, beneath me, and above me there is that same depth as before. The world, like the heavens, is infinite; the world is an *abyss*, for the world is, after all, a whole glued together by what I myself do—but a whole open to something radically new and alien, mined with the dynamite of the incomprehensible future: the unreachable horizon of my continuously self-overcoming life.

But don't think, Zarathustra warns us, that the world, not being "something," therefore becomes "nothing": "your nothing too is a spider web and a spider, which lives on the blood of the future."[28] Such a concept of nothingness, just like the notion of the world as a totality, is also the product of an ostensibly universal rationality; the negation of the world as a totality, Nietzsche believes, is the same kind of myth, illusion, and lie as its affirmation. The world around me is not empty; it is always already some kind of world, it is always already filled with some content by your life or mine, whose horizon it is, though that content is never finished, will never be ready-made, and always remains open to future change, revision, and revolution.

The concept of the world as an all-encompassing totality and its opposite, the concept of nothingness—these concepts have no designata. If they have any, perhaps hidden, meaning, some subcutaneous pulse, it flows (like all meaning) from life that is open to the new, the unexpected, the alien, the very life these concepts negate. From a life that no project of rationality can encompass. It therefore makes no difference, Nietzsche tries to convince us, whether you imagine that the world around you is an ordered cosmos (even if this cosmos is supposed to be an infinitely complicated order, inaccessible to us now or even tomorrow, and maybe forever) or that it is nothing, a lack of order—chaos. Both notions are absurdities that negate life—life as it is, life in its irreducible and infinite diversity. They deform and degenerate life, like a blood-sucking spider.

The negation of universal reason is not an affirmation of nothingness or assent to (in this sense) nihilism.

But does this mean that, contrary to my declarations, I am here following Zarathustra into a description of the "world as it is," as opposed to other, competing descriptions? Am I not asserting something about its structure, namely, that its meaning is always slipping out from comprehension, that it is consequently as "deep" and "pure" as the heavens?

No, I am not. "Height," "depth," and "purity" are not characteristics of the kind of object I can look at. The world is not such an object. The high, deep, and pure heavens above me are not a metaphor for such an object. "To throw myself into your height [O heaven!], that is *my* depth. To hide in your purity, that is *my* innocence."[29] And thus we are not interested here in a description of the world, better and more correct than others. The pure heavens above me are rather a challenge directed toward me, toward the life I am living: they are an appeal to the force slumbering within me, which leads me out of every situation I find myself in, to the potential hidden within, which can never be expended.

"Seeing you [O heaven!], I tremble with godlike desires."[30] This invocation of a (high, deep, infinite) heaven from Zarathustra's lips is at the same time a testimony about the human condition. The sight of heaven arouses my godlike desires, dormant, perhaps, in everyday life. *Godlike* because they are infinite, because they cannot be satisfied. Faced with the pure, infinitely high heavens, my life turns out to be something still other than merely a search for happiness or fame, the realization of moral imperatives or the fulfillment of obligations: it turns out to be the overcoming of itself, without end, a constant tossing away of everything I have gathered together as my own—*a godlike longing*.

A description of the world as it is is thus also an articulation—this, I believe, is what Zarathustra and Nietzsche wish to make us understand—an expression of a will to its overcoming, to a triumph over every form of the world I might come upon. Reason without practical effort is an abstraction, just like the notion of a world I can look upon as I would a butterfly under glass in a museum. Every form of the world that I can encounter is comprehensible only in the context of my effort to overcome it, which is at the same time an effort to overcome myself, whoever I happen to be.

6

This kind of understanding therefore also means acceptance, says Zarathustra: "I have become one who blesses and says Yes."[31]

Of course, for such a blessing—for the acceptance of the world as incurably diverse, the acceptance of differences as such—words alone do not suffice. It is not enough to say "yes" (to difference) where one has said "no" till now (searching for the unity hidden in difference). For aren't words like "rainbows and illusive bridges"?[32] Knowledge—the recognition that the world is "good" or "the best of all possible," that it is adequately understood, that it will bring happiness—cannot be the basis for such an affirmation. For aren't concepts always too short to reveal the world as it is? Deeds, and not words, are called for here; we are dealing with life, not just knowledge. This is a question of my openness to the unexpected novelty of the world, to an otherness that exceeds all concepts held until now, to its resistance, which I have not yet known. I *bless* things, *I speak to them thusly* when my life—not my words—brings the world to light in its irreducible, unexpected, perplexing, mysterious diversity.

And thus we are not concerned here—in this affirmation of the world, the kind of affirmation to which Zarathustra exhorts us—with "true knowledge" of the world, with access to the real structure of things (their "irreducible diversity"). The point is not certain knowledge as to how things really are. Zarathustra seeks another kind of wisdom. Zarathustra does indeed say, "this blessed certainty I found in all things," but this does not mean that he has found some universal structure within them, some common denominator, and thus a solid ground.[33] On the contrary, Zarathustra is certain only that there is no such structure, no such common denominator—in other words, that such a structure, such a common denominator, is nonsense. For every step in my life, each successive experience of the world around me, is *accidental*, not completely determined. In other words, in my every experience the world begins anew.

The *blessed certainty* that Zarathustra has found in all things is a certainty that all things "*dance* on the feet of Chance."[34] They dance—they do not lie prostrate, ordered, in expectation of discovery. They "*dance* on the feet of Chance" and thus not according to a pre-established order, a ready-made pattern, a script. It is in this dance, in each individual step, that the world—"all things"—comes to light.

Only this kind of wisdom is possible for Zarathustra, a wisdom that "is mixed in with all things," through chance.[35] It is not necessity that binds all things together, not the chain of causes and effects, not a logical connection, not a structural relation. This is a wisdom that teaches me that every experience opens new, unlimited fields of possibility, and only there does the meaning of the things I encounter—and my own identity as well—arise. Wisdom that makes me ready for the incurable inconsistency and discontinuity of the world, for the encounter with the otherness hidden in it. Wisdom that gives me courage and makes me *brave*. The wisdom of life, not of words or concepts. Wisdom that binds all things, *dancing*—that binds all things with a *brave* life, one that is open to the new and the other.

A wise person is someone who is sensitive to the unexpected, the alien, the incomprehensible—to *chance*. A wise person is someone whose life is not solely an adaptation to the things he finds, even if they are merely ideals attainable only later, not today or even tomorrow (happiness, social justice, general prosperity, etc.). A wise person is someone who, with his own life, reaches beyond the given, the found, the dreamt-of, the planned—"to the stars." "I say unto you," Zarathustra says unto us, "one must still have chaos in oneself to be able to give birth to a dancing star."[36] Only then, when my life will not surrender to the rules I encounter—actually, to any rules at all (because, constantly overcoming itself, it must go on creating them anew)—only then will I manage to create something that surpasses me, only then will I become a place where a new form of the world can come to light.

The affirmation of the world's diversity, the *blessing unto things* to which Zarathustra exhorts us—this is not therefore merely our agreement that things are various. It is I who, with my life—which cannot be crammed into any frame but is unhindered, chaotic, *wild*—permits things to come to light in their as yet unencountered diversity: I reveal the fragility and vulnerability of their momentary meaning, I unveil to them the unbounded novelty, the otherness, of their future. My unhindered, chaotic, *wild*—creative—life opens the pure, deep, abyssal heaven above every thing: "But this is my blessing: to stand over every single thing as its own heaven, as its round roof, as its azure bell, and eternal security; and blessed is he who blesses thus."[37]

A wise person is one who knows life as it is. But this does not mean, in my understanding of Zarathustra, that the relationship between *wisdom* and *life* is the same as that between "true knowledge" and "reality." An unwise person, a stupid person, is not one who thinks that two and two make five rather than four, is not one who thinks that life is otherwise (eternal, pleasurable, easy) than it is in reality (too short, full of suffering, dangerous). *Life* is not one way or another irrespective of *wisdom*, irrespective of my knowledge of it, of the kind of knowledge I accumulate not only with my consciousness, not only by looking, touching, listening, understanding, and then packing what I have seen, heard, and understood into conceptual bags, but also—or, rather, primarily—with each movement of my body, with each successive step in my life. Life is, to a certain extent, always already "understood," assimilated by my knowledge of it, covered by a web of meanings, which refer to what I do or am able to do: here is a house, here a mountain, here a hammer, and here a triangle. But not completely. For life, after all, is always something more than what I know about it or am able to know, for it is always slipping out from the web of meanings in which I try to catch it. For life, after all, always has this other side, this other, alien face. It is different from what I can call my own, a deep, vast, insurmountable difference.

Accordingly, *wisdom* will never—however successfully it has assimilated life, however far or deep it has cast its web of meanings—be identical to life, will always be too short, too shallow, and thus momentary and correctable. Not because life is too difficult to understand. No, but rather because my knowledge, accumulated in life experience, is itself life, because it forms and creates life, because it is creative (and the more creative it is, the wiser it is). For this very reason life slips away from it, and for this very reason *wisdom* differs from life in its ever-insurmountable difference.

Life and *wisdom* are indeed, to a certain degree, identical. "Deeply I love only life," Zarathustra says. "But that I am well disposed toward wisdom, and often too well, that is because she reminds me so much of life. [. . .] [I]s it my fault that the two look so similar?"[38] Similar, but not identical; identical to a certain degree, but different. Life will never be like wisdom, though it wants to be wisdom. Life, after all, is an attempt to inhabit, to settle in, to establish the world as my own, to tame it; it is (also) an aspiration to (some kind of) order. "And that I like you, often too well, that you know," Life says to Zarathustra, "and the reason is that I am jealous of your wisdom."[39] And wisdom will never capture the life that is constantly slipping out of its grasp—for the very reason that wisdom itself co-creates life. Isn't death the best witness to this? Doesn't the inevitability that I will die testify to the fact that life will always slip out of my hands, no matter how wise I may have been? "O Zarathustra," Life says to Zarathustra, who is full of wisdom, of that wisdom that Life envies him, "you are not faithful enough to me. You do not love me nearly as much as you say; I know you are thinking of leaving me soon."[40]

Is it strange, then, that in the face of their inevitable mutual defeat—the irreparable and ultimate defeat of understanding, which life will never allow to tame it, and for which life will always remain insurmountably alien; and the inevitable defeat of action, which will never succeed in ordering the world, which would pacify the longing for order, for structure, for the stability inscribed in every action—is it strange that, tasting the bitterness of this defeat on their lips, "we looked at each other and gazed on the green meadow over which the cool evening was running just then, and we wept together"? "But then life was dearer to me than all my wisdom ever was."[41]

7

Human life is therefore—this is the sense, I believe, of Zarathustra's message—irreducibly diverse and thoroughly dangerous. We are constantly trying to rebuild our home within it, constantly trying to glue all the pieces of the world we live in into a whole, to order it, to turn it into "our world." But we will never be able to remove from this world the threat of catastrophe, of destruction, of the end; we will never achieve certainty that the next step in our lives won't march us into the abyss, into which everything that has been familiar till now, everything nice and warm and orderly, vanishes. ("I am ever over an abyss," Nietzsche notes.)[42] In other words, an essential feature of life as we live it is *chance*: the new, unexpected, alien side of my life. In its every moment, life is torn open, discontinuous, fractured: diversified. But let us remember that this difference is not like that which obtains between left and right, or between the glass shards of a vase that has just been shattered: it does not leave us alone. At every moment of my life, that which is other, new, alien, and unexpected places a question mark above everything I am, and thus it concerns me, and this is no accident: it co-creates the meaning of my (fragile, endangered) identity. It hurts.

If this is so, then Zarathustra was right when he said that there is no *chance*, in the sense of something that has nothing to do with me. In fact, such a notion makes no sense. Otherness, *chance* eternally escaping rationality—this is me, too, that other, mysterious side of my continuously self-overcoming life.

Zarathustra does not, therefore, teach us relativism and indifferent tolerance, just as he did not teach us nihilism. The diversification of our world, as he understands it, does not provide a suitable premise for a gentle gaze that discovers many different paths toward truth and good and no reason to choose one of these paths over another. No—Zarathustra teaches us that such a gaze would be self-deception, evidence of hidden weakness. The diversification of the world is always seen from the perspective of who I am, from the point of view of my own life. In other words, my life is always a challenge to the world, just as the world I encounter over the course of my life is a challenge to me, to every brick in the house I have built myself, to every cell in my body, to every corner of my soul.

How difficult, how impossible it is to live like this! And so we are always coming up with new means of negating life's incurable diversity and horror. Nietzsche maintains that the culture we live in is also a collection of such means: the culture of *Gleichschaltung*, nihilistic and relativistic culture. The ideal of man in this culture—Zarathustra calls him *the last man*—is man equal to others. The ideal of social life in this culture is the equality—identity, in a certain respect—of all its participants. Of course, differences are acceptable, but they have to be differences within pre-established limits, differences that presuppose some common denominator—"civilization," "humanity," "rationality"—and thus differences that can be understood "rationally." One who crosses out beyond these limits and, in this sense, "thinks differently" is a nutcase: "Everybody wants the same, everybody is the same: whoever feels differently goes voluntarily into a madhouse."[43] Or else is a criminal: Nietzsche maintains that in this culture, morality, too, is a means of taming differences, a method of pacifying them. Just like the concept of universal rationality, our morality is also an order that is universal in design, a spider web that our nihilistic culture tries to impose on our lives so that the differences that divide us, and thus our world as well, will become solvable, so that they will no longer be dangerous. The establishment of a universal reason and a universal morality is precisely our culture's strategy for eliminating danger and difference.

It was not always so, Nietzsche believes. "Formerly," he writes in *Daybreak*, "thinkers prowled around angrily like captive animals, watching the bars of their cages and leaping against them in order to smash them down: and *happy* seemed he who through a gap in them believed he saw something of what was outside, of what was distant and beyond."[44] Forget about whether Nietzsche is right regarding the past; perhaps today, too, somewhere deep within each of us, under the surface of an allegedly universal rationality and morality, such an animal is still running. If so—and I think that this is exactly what Nietzsche wants to tell us—our nihilistic and relativistic culture is only one aspect of our lives.

V

The Time Is at Hand

As we have seen, Nietzsche maintained that all knowledge is inherently moral. This is especially true of science. Regardless of the content of scientific assertions, scientific activity is an endeavor undertaken for one reason or another and, as such, expresses the conscious or unconscious preferences of those who engage in it; it testifies to what they believe is good, what evil. Science carries this moral sense, too, which is hardly to suggest that this is all it amounts to.

Let's examine this argument more closely.

We should note that science and its functions are not Nietzsche's primary concern here. His principal concern is different: he addresses the moral sense of science, I believe, to discover something about the human condition expressed therein.

The term "discover" carries a specific meaning in this context. To discover the morality behind science does not mean to uncover some true figure behind an appearance, the prince in the pauper's clothing. Tearing off the mask, we not uncover the naked truth; we do not exchange what is only apparently true for what is actually true. Tearing off such a mask, we merely increase the freedom of our own action. "That the destruction of an illusion does not produce truth," Nietzsche notes in 1885, "but only one more piece of ignorance, an extension of our 'empty space,' an increase of our 'desert'—."[1] What is meant here, therefore, is "practical" (in other words, "moral") knowledge: the opening of a new, predominantly hidden perspective on life.

But does science—scientific activity, science as a particular way of organizing life—have an essential significance in matters that determine the human condition, in matters that we habitually think of as crucial or essential? Here I do not have in mind the otherwise interesting question of whether scientific results are a blessing or a curse on humanity. Rather, I would like to consider whether, in an everyday life that is today permeated by science, there might not also be some hidden answer to ultimate questions, to questions of the meaning of life and of death.

For Nietzsche this is indeed the case. Science, he believed, is in this sense heir to a very ancient tradition. In *The Gay Science*, he writes:

[I]t is still a *metaphysical faith* upon which our faith in science rests. [. . .] [We] godless anti-metaphysicians still take our fire from the flame lit by a faith that is thousands of years old, that Christian faith which was also the faith of Plato, that God is the truth, that truth is divine.—But what if this should become more and more incredible, if nothing should prove to be divine anymore unless it were error, blindness, the lie—if God himself should prove to be our most enduring lie?—[2]

But if we are to better understand this "faith that is thousands of years old" and Nietzsche's interpretation of it, I think that we must first reach for the Book of Revelation and the ongoing discussion of what it really means.

2

The Apocalypse (Revelation) of John of Patmos is, in the King James Version, "The Revelation of Jesus Christ, which God gave unto him, to show unto his servants things which must shortly come to pass; and he sent and signified it by his angel unto his servant John" (Rev. 1:1). That "which must shortly come to pass" is the (horrible) end of the world as we know it and the beginning of a new life whose magnificence exceeds our ability to imagine it.

The question that troubles anyone who ponders the meaning of Revelation's message is: How shortly is "shortly"?

"The time is at hand," John admonishes us (Rev. 1:3). Another, noncanonical text of the same genre (*The [Syriac] Apocalypse of Baruch*) announces that "the pitcher is near the well, and the ship to the harbor, and the journey to the city, and life to its end" (2 Baruch 85:10).[3] How are we to understand this?

Perhaps as a cosmic or historical event, like a flood or a meteor smashing the Earth to pieces, an event that will happen sometime, though no one really knows when. Next Friday? Next month? In (God willing) another hundred years? If so, then we know more or less what will happen. Actually, not more or less—we know precisely what will happen. According to this interpretation, the apocalyptic vision of John offers a rather precise scenario, without any room for anything really new. A scenario that foresees a bigger or smaller role for me as well, with a happy ending or none; what has to happen does not involve me directly, but for me and others it designates a place in an event that is independent from me, in an event that involves everyone—a flood, a cosmic catastrophe, the end of the world as I know it—insofar as I have to ready myself for all of this and somehow organize my time while I'm waiting for things to get going.

Understood in this way, the Apocalypse shifts the most important event in the life of a Christian—the beginning of the new life—from the world around me in the here-and-now to the "hereafter," from my life to the Afterlife.

"The time is at hand." When I define this time as an extraordinary event with familiar parameters (a flood), for which I can prepare appropriately in advance (say, by filling sandbags), I draw it away from the moment I am living in toward some future, toward a later time. As a result, I can sleep well—assuming, of course, that I have prepared well.

It may be, however, that something else is meant here—not an event, a singular moment in time, but each individual moment of time. Each moment—according to this interpretation—each instant (not just that one, as yet unknown, next Friday or one hundred years from now) conceals within itself a potential end, a limit, an edge, a closing of the world as it is—and of a new beginning, of a departure beyond the borders of what is and can be known, the potential for a world that is radically new. If so, if this is what has to happen, what the Lord revealed to Christ, and Christ to the angel, and the angel in turn to John, so that he would tell us—if so, then what has to happen has already happened, or better yet, it is happening, in every moment of my life, as much now as next Friday. The Apocalypse is happening all the time; Christ arrives at every moment of our lives and, by this token, tears each of us out of the world as we find it, out of the world as we know it, and calls us into the new one. This Apocalypse is no longer a blueprint in which I have an appointed place beside others. This Apocalypse touches me directly, just as it does us all, so that in my every movement, in every act of my life, the world ends and begins anew. Each of these moments is different for each of us; we therefore cannot know in advance how it will happen. It is therefore nonsense—so the argument would go for anyone understanding the Revelation of John in this way—to take John's metaphors literally as a scenario that applies to everyone: first the breaking of the seal, then the horsemen, then the sounding of horns, and so forth. And therefore I cannot prepare for the Second Coming—the end of the world as I know it and the beginning of the new—as I might prepare for a flood or a meteor smashing into Earth. I must live differently, right away, at every moment, and forget about stacking sandbags on the embankments. Nor do I have any time to spare: the Horns of Jericho are already blaring, right now, and there is no time to put my affairs in order and play cards, self-satisfied that I have met my responsibility in waiting for the return of the Judge. "Jesus will be in agony until the end of the world," Pascal would write. "We must not sleep during that time."[4]

According to this formulation, the time of the Apocalypse cannot be deferred into the future, whether it is defined or not, for the time of the Apocalypse is the very same time in which we are now living. Consequently, I have no hope of peace, of security, of untroubled dreams, no chance to be quite certain that I will be well prepared when I am awakened.

As we can see, the narrative that John of Patmos provides about the end of the world as we know it and the birth of a new world hides a tension between two potential interpretations. In the first, this may be a story about a future catastrophic event, whether historic or cosmic, whose subject is humanity as such, a story that furnishes its listeners with enough information about what will transpire for them to be prepared when it happens. This story, in deferring the catastrophe into the future, opens the possibility for peace and security, at least for the time being. Gerhard von Rad writes that, in this formulation, the eschatological scriptures "want to comfort us and, through the perspective of the impending crisis, press us to hold on."[5] On the other hand, John's narrative may be understood as a symbolic tale about the human condition, not as a narrative of future events: a tale about human life, in every moment of which (and not only in the one, singular, catastrophic moment) Christ dies and is reborn, and through which the world ends and begins anew. Such a tale would no longer be an objective report on what is going on (with humanity or the cosmos) but rather an appeal, addressed to each of us individually, that tears us from our sleep and tells us to live in the face of the world's end—right away, not later, here and now, not eventually—to stay awake.

3

What does science—science as we understand it today, modern science—have to do with all this? How does the scientific organization of life—with its attendant claim, explicit or hidden, to an exclusive rationality—relate to an apocalyptic view of the human condition? Pascal has a great deal to say on the matter.

Every attempt at understanding oneself and one's own place in the world through new scientific concepts, Pascal assures us, inevitably leads to desolation and despair:

> When I consider the brief duration of my life absorbed in the eternity that lies before and after [. . .], the small space I occupy and can even see, engulfed in the infinite immensity of spaces I do not know and that do not know me, I am frightened and astonished to

see myself here rather than there; for there is no reason why I am here rather than there, why now rather than then. [. . .] The eternal silence of these infinite spaces frightens me.[6]

What can one do under such circumstances? How can one live a life that is, in the face of time's infinitude, which we have only just recognized, irrevocably short? Telling the story of a cosmic catastrophe that will end the world as we know it so as to make room for a happy new world now ceases to be a potential source of comfort: there is no room for such a story in Pascal's world of infinite time and infinite, undifferentiated space. And yet one must find some way out, make some decision, since desolation and despair don't help us orient ourselves. A decision that is irreversible, because every moment of one's life is irrevocable, beyond return, because there are no second chances. A decision we have to make for ourselves—no one else is capable of making it for me—because the life about which I am deciding is so very much my own that I cannot exchange it for anyone else's. Our confrontation with death makes this clear: "We will die alone. We must therefore act as if we were alone."[7]

This irreversible and lonely decision, a decision that cannot be deferred to later or simply forgotten, is actually, Pascal tells us, always the same decision; everything I do ultimately boils down to one and the same question: Is the soul immortal, or not? Naturally, this doesn't mean that every person is supposed to be capable of articulating such a question, nor a well-grounded answer to it. Not without good reason, Pascal does not see the skill of formulating concepts as more important than the skill of chopping wood or harvesting potatoes. We answer these most important questions by living one way or another, whether by living in the world as though we were foreign to it, as if we were merely passing through for a while, or else by living as though the world as we know it were our only home:

> We must live differently in the world, depending on these different assumptions:
> Whether we could always exist in it.
> Whether it is certain we will not exist in it for long and uncertain if we will exist in it for one hour.
> This last assumption is ours.[8]

This is a decision with far-reaching consequences, a decision that, despite the fact that each of us must choose for ourselves, depends on more than us alone: whether we will find our home somewhere else, beyond the world we know (if we are saved), depends, according to Pascal, on God's mercy. The drawbridge we may cross toward that other side, to our home, must (as Jacob Taubes once wrote) be let down from the other side, not from ours.[9] To put it differently, the kind of knowledge we can attain on our own, knowledge of the world as we see it, is insufficient. We must succeed in crossing out beyond the world as we know it, to reach out toward what is unknown and radically new. And in order to do this, Pascal tells us, we need a divine intervention. If it does not come, we are forever lost in the world and, as a result, are condemned forever, with no second chance.

For Pascal, just as for Nietzsche, human life is a constant journey along the edge of an abyss. Every moment, every step, is a choice—a choice beyond our control—between salvation and damnation, and thus a choice between openness to the unknown and that which is yet to pass—which cannot be assimilated into known, familiar, "worldly" categories—and damnation in what is, in the apparently familiar and known, which actually leads us to desolation and despair: "Between us and heaven or hell, there is only life in the interval, the most fragile thing in the world."[10]

Naturally, no one enjoys living at the edge of an abyss. Accordingly, we seek out various diversions for ourselves: tasks, games, worries, money and linguistics, dancing and politics, sex and mathematics. If only to distract us from the fact that each subsequent step may be our entry into Paradise, to eternal salvation, or else may end with a fall into the chasm, without bottom, without return. If only to forget this infinite gamble, that each step—this one, the next—wagers everything on a single card. That there is no railing protecting us from the abyss, nothing to hold onto when we stumble: "We burn with desire to find firm ground and an ultimate secure base on which to build a tower reaching up to the infinite. But our whole foundation cracks, and the earth opens up into abysses."[11]

The second, most common answer to the basic question of human life is forgetting, flight into what is, hunkering down into preexisting matters, mechanisms, into what one finds, an attempt to fill my time so that its emptiness won't confront me with its apocalyptic dimensions, with my very self. Pascal calls this response "diversion," having in mind not only hunting for wild boars or rabbits, playing soccer or dancing (his own most frequent examples), but everything we do that draws us away from the most important decision in our lives, that draws us away from the eternity hidden within time. Among other things: science, that new kind of pastime, which is all the more dangerous because it draws in intelligent people more than others. (If you really have to play, Pascal says, then choose mathematics.) Scientific activity is, just like any other pastime, a waste of time—but none of us has any time to waste. *The time is at hand*, now, right now: the Last Judgment is happening at this very moment; the sentence that determines whether I will be damned or saved is being passed right now.

As we can see, Pascal is deeply convinced that the Apocalypse occurs at every moment, and not just once, at some time, that it is not an objective event, like a storm, but that it touches each of us individually, that it is a challenge to the individual life of each and every one of us. Instead of the terrifying account (also full of solace and comfort) of the coming end of the world, which in the world of modern science is relegated to a fairy tale, there emerges a new form of "diversion" that provides us with more effective, though just as deceptive, activity, meaning, and support than previous forms had: science itself.

4

Nietzsche similarly believes that science is a form of *diversion* but that it is not like any other form of it: science (in the sense of the set of a scientist's activities) is for Nietzsche a deception. Not just any deception but the most important, central, primary deception, the self-deception of modern man.

Let us consider, then, what this means.

First of all, science is an apparatus, an institution—and by no means accidentally so but of its own internal necessity. "Science is an institution," Heidegger will later note, "not because it is practiced in scientific institutions; the institutions are necessary, for science in and of itself has an institutional character."[12] This institution of science designates a particular researcher's place in line, offers him the role of a cog in the machine—a machine that works slowly, maybe even endlessly, but surely, because it moves to achieve goals that it designates for itself. In this way, each particular researcher enjoys a sense of the meaning of what he is doing, regardless of what he himself has achieved; he gains a solid ground beneath his feet, regardless of the meanderings of his own individual destiny. A scientist becomes a functionary of the institution that defines him, at the cost of his own personhood beyond the institution. "The presupposition of scientific work," notes Nietzsche in 1886, is "belief in the unity and perpetuity of scientific work, so the individual may work at any part, however small, confident that his work will not be in vain."[13]

Thus the scientist toils on, like an ant (in Nietzsche's eyes), for the future, gathering the little leaves, sticks, and needles that may prove useful to future ants. He labors on with the feeling that the more leaves and needles he can collect, the more likely it is that in the future there will still be some ants doing similar work, that there will still be a future at all.

A scientist par excellence is, from this point of view, a mediocre scientist. Science as an institution depends on mediocrity; this is what it works for and is served by. Mediocre people are, according to Nietzsche, "who matter most, [. . .] the procrastinators *par excellence*, slow to adopt, reluctant to let go, and relatively enduring in the midst of this tremendous change and mixture of elements. [. . .] [M]ediocrity consolidates itself as the guarantee and bearer of the future."[14] Attaching ourselves to a slowly laboring scientific apparatus—slow because it is unending, because it does not labor toward the achievement of any ultimate goal (and is there some goal whose achievement would allow science to quit working further, meeting its own criteria for rationality just as well as before?)—we attain a feeling of stability and security. In other words, we become increasingly certain of the future. To accomplish this goal, the machine of science irons out differences, removes potential conflicts, introduces continuity where we have seen none before, constancy amid flux. It changes the world into a garden where manicured paths always lead to a place determined in advance. The more efficient this machine is, the easier it is for us to fall asleep—we, the judicious, the virtuous, the fortunate—certain that the following morning we will awake to find the world exactly where we've left it.

Nietzsche's Zarathustra wants to disturb this peace, to wake us from this dream: "It is time! It is high time!" he announces.[15] Zarathustra informs us that the dream of scientific rationality is a veil that conceals the unknown side of human life. Without it, life would not be life, and man would not be man. Sleeping on means to miss what is most important.

Nietzsche maintains that, succumbing to the temptation of science, dreaming our dream of the garden, of order and security, all we are doing is providing evidence of our own weakness. Any unity is a manifestation of inertia, and you, modern people, by inserting yourselves into the cogs of the Moloch of science and thereby lying down comfortably in the world it governs, are merely demonstrating your indolence, your feeblemindedness, your lack of courage.

For one needs courage in order to accept the fact that the future can be in no way certain, neither in the sense of knowing what will happen nor—what is more—in the sense that we know that anything will happen at all. The future means an infinite openness to the change of every moment as we live through it, which means that in every moment I live the future as such is questioned. In every moment I live, the world dies and is born anew—from which it naturally does not follow that I, Krzysztof Michalski, am a god, able to destroy the world or create it, but that the future does not occur beyond me, independently of me, in the same way as it rains even in May.

Which means that the future, though uncertain, necessarily concerns what is going on with me, and only if I wish—out of weakness, indolence, lack of courage—to make it as dead-certain as thunder after lightning may I rid it of this relation. Only weakness or drowsiness, therefore, can extricate me and my responsibility, however we wish to describe it, from the world—and thus you and your responsibility, him and his responsibility, and thus, finally, the very differences between us. And where is there any guarantee that these differences will always lend themselves to a smooth and peaceful resolution?

If, Nietzsche tells us, toiling for a certain and infinite future in the gears of the machine of modern science, we dream of the world as of the garden, we lose sight of that other side of the world, the world that troubles because the future is constantly called into question—the threatening world, because conflict can never be removed from it. The world where there is no time to sleep, because at every moment, for each of us, the meaning of our lives is constantly being decided anew.

Nietzsche warns us, "Not to desire to deprive the world of its disturbing and enigmatic character!"[16]

Naturally, such a world is menacing and terrifying. But it is not menacing or terrifying in the same sense as the sight of an enraged, quickly approaching bear might be. Nietzsche does not paint us a portrait of the world that he takes to be true (terrifying) so as to supplant a false (reassuring) image of the world as portrayed through modern science. The world is menacing and terrifying, Nietzsche seems to say, because we ourselves are the ones who make it out of the scattered fragments of sense left over from the preceding generation, because we do not find any pre-established harmony there. The world is menacing and terrifying because we, each one of us, carry a responsibility for what happens to it. We—this does not mean all of us together, in solidarity and joy (if such a unity were still to be achieved), but also against one another, divided by irreconcilable differences, in conflict. Furthermore, we know in advance that we cannot put this world in order once and for all (and rest, like God, after six days of toil) because each lived moment opens a new perspective of limitless change: the uncertain future.

It is unsurprising that in the face of all this we feel a need for stability and order, a hunger for a future we might depend on, for a peace and security that do not require a constant struggle for self-affirmation. The desire to ground responsibility in some lasting basis. The longing for a world like a garden, orderly, stable, and secure, whose fruits and shade one might enjoy at least for a little while.

Science as a certain way of living, Nietzsche argues, is the modern recipe for satisfying this need.

The metaphors and concepts that Nietzsche employs to express the side of life that is otherwise hidden from scientific rationality often allude to the apocalyptic themes of the Bible. Zarathustra: "The figs are falling from the trees; they are good and sweet; and, as they fall, their red skin bursts. I am a north wind to ripe figs. Thus, like figs, these teachings fall to you, my friends; now consume their juice and their sweet meat. It is autumn about us, and pure sky and afternoon."[17] This image only appears to be idyllic: "autumn" and "afternoon" and the cold "north wind" herald the coming winter and twilight: the end—and this is precisely what Zarathustra's "teachings" are about, mature, falling, and therefore foretelling the end, the conclusion of everything that we call the world. The end, which is also the beginning: "And what you have called world, that shall be created only by you," Zarathustra says later.[18] The figs falling from the trees: the end, the death of the world as we have known it, is at the same time a call to create, to start all over again: "Indeed, there must be much bitter dying in your life, you creators."[19]

Zarathustra's apocalyptic exhortation—"It is time! It is high time!"—is therefore not addressed to me as I am, to all those features and characteristics I have gathered over the course of my life. All of that is marked by the coming winter, by the inevitable end: it is tipping toward the end. Rather, Zarathustra's exhortation arouses in me—in each of us—the potential for total renovation, and therefore for a child now being born. The creator, Zarathustra declares, has to "be the child who is newly born."[20]

In this we distinctly hear echoes of the New Testament. "Children, this is your final hour!" John announces (1 John 2:18). And Mark responds: "And from the fig tree you shall learn resemblance: as soon as its branch is young and opens its leaves, you know that summer is near. So, too, is it with you: as soon as you see that all this is happening, you will know it is near, at the door" (Mark 13:28–29).

So do not sleep: "Remain alert, for you know not when the time will come" (Mark 13:33).

Nietzsche is fully aware of the ambiguity of the apocalyptic motifs I mentioned earlier. "What are the 'glad tidings'?" he asks in *The Antichrist*. "True life, eternal life [and thus the end of life as we know it, a new beginning], has been found—it is not promised, it is here, it is *in you*. [. . .] Everyone is the child of God—Jesus definitely presumes nothing for himself alone."[21] In this way, Jesus underscores the fact that the Apocalypse is inscribed within the time of our own lives. It is Paul, Nietzsche says, who "transposed" the end of the known world and the beginning of the new one, and therefore "life's center of gravity not in life but in the 'beyond.'"[22] No longer is the Apocalypse a dimension of life as we live it but a future event prophesied in detail by John, though also by Mark: "in those days [. . .] the sun shall be darkened, and the moon shall not give her light. And the stars of heaven shall fall [. . .]. And then shall they see the Son of Man coming in the clouds with great power and glory" (Mark 13:24–26).

5

I started this essay with the Revelation of John and two completely different possibilities for interpreting it. According to one, the Apocalypse is a narrative about what will happen, about a catastrophe that will occur at some point, about a certain distinct moment of time—and therefore not about the moment that I am living through now, not about the moment in which I now find myself. If this is the case, then this version of the Apocalypse may also be an instrument of delay, a deferral of all those terrible things that allegedly await us then: even if all this will happen, at least it's not happening now, but later, maybe even in an hour or a day from now (God forbid!), but in any case not at this moment. Furthermore, if the Apocalypse is a narrative about some future event, some cosmic catastrophe, then it concerns me the same way it does all others who will be affected by it—and therefore I am not all alone with this terrifying vision: I can confer with others, share my fear and my responsibility, and prepare.

Therefore, while the narrative about a catastrophe that ends the world as we know it presents the reader with a portrait that provokes fear and trembling, at its core it is a means of consolation, a tool that helps us feel settled in the world as it is, at least for the time being.

But not entirely. The kernel of disquiet, which this interpretation cannot dislodge, is bound to the announcement that all of this—the end of the old world, the birth of the new—will happen "shortly." For maybe the Apocalypse isn't a narrative about a distinct moment in time at all but rather about every moment, about each individual instant. Maybe it will not happen eventually but is already happening, now, in the moment we are now living through. If so, then it isn't a means of deferring that which is supposed to happen in the future: the Apocalypse cannot be deferred—the future is happening now. Nor is there time to prepare for it. There is neither means nor opportunity to share our responsibility or the horror we experience in facing it: since the Apocalypse occurs in every moment of time I live through, I am irrevocably alone with it.

Apocalypse in this sense offers no consolation; it does not allow us to settle into the world as we know it. On the contrary, it lays bare the fragility and ephemerality of every habit, every truth, every moment of happiness and calm.

Under the growing influence of science, the modern European, as we have seen with Pascal, situated his narrative interpretation of the Apocalypse among fairy tales: terrified by the everlasting silence of time and space, seventeenth-century man is no longer capable of believing that after a certain time some horsemen will come and put everything in order. Despite this, Pascal's vision of the world and of the human condition is, in one of the senses I have noted, apocalyptic—because for him, too, eternity is present in every moment of time: each instant of our lives is a choice between eternal salvation and eternal damnation. And yet in Pascal's world, too, man cannot live without some consolation. But where can one find it, if the motley Horsemen of the Apocalypse no longer terrify or reassure us? Science—life shaped by science—assumes the place vacated by these horsemen; science, that new kind of *diversion*, which binds us to the world as it is and, by the same token, allows us to forget that the world as it is is not our proper place; a *diversion* more engrossing than all those games, hunts, amusements—and therefore more effective.

Nietzsche will later call this function—the function of consolation and support—*intoxication*. The institution of science performs this function better than its mythological predecessor had, for it promises world domination. The institution of science also promises our mastery over the future, its subordination (so that we can be sure of it)—and thereby postpones the end of the world as we know it (and the beginning of the new world), *ad calendas Graecas*, and ensures that for now we can live without apocalyptic dread. But just as tales of golden horses, harlots, and cities made of diamonds, frightening and consoling, could not entirely suppress that anxiety with which my life here and now undermines all the sense gathered therein, so too does modern science fail in its attempt to give life a solid foundation. If we listen closely to the noise of its slowly turning wheels, we may also hear—in the distance, not too clearly—the trembling of the ground beneath our feet, and perhaps even the stomping of hooves.

6

This, according to Nietzsche, is therefore what the moral character of modern science consists of—its *lie*, its *deception* (in other words, its *nihilism*): that it tries to turn our attention away from the Apocalypse, from the end of everything and the new beginning hidden in every moment of our lives. From the fact that *the time is at hand*, as close as it could possibly be—already here. This function is older than modernity, for the truth that God revealed to Christ, and Christ to the angel, and the angel finally to John, who revealed it to us—this truth can perform this function as well. In this sense, "we godless anti-metaphysicians still take our fire [. . .] from the flame lit by a faith that is thousands of years old [. . .] that God is the truth."[23]

This does not mean, however, that we can extinguish this fire, unmask the deception. No—without this deception, Nietzsche tells us, we would be unable to live: it is as much a part of our lives as the Apocalypse inscribed in every moment. To "reveal" this deception, Nietzsche assures us, is to reveal potential, the hidden possibility of life—life as possibility. "That lies are necessary in order to live," Nietzsche notes, "is itself part of the terrifying and questionable character of existence."[24]

The two visions of the Apocalypse we have discussed are not therefore merely two conceptual interpretations, one true, the other false. They are rather two sides of the human condition that cannot be distinguished the same way we can tell red from green, a square from a triangle, or a true statement from a false one. And if this is so, then every version of the Apocalypse, including that of John, must be an enigmatic tale, irremediably unclear, a tale about human nature, in which terror cannot be separated from consolation, and our search for solid truth from the mostly hidden belief, deep down, in its fragility.

VI

The Death of God

Do you remember how, in *Phaedo*, Plato recorded the last moments of Socrates' life? Phaedo, a friend of Socrates, shares with his acquaintance, Echecrates, his final discussion with Socrates. The subject of their discussion is death. But this discussion is unlike others. It is during this discussion that Socrates drinks the poison and dies, carrying out the sentence of the rulers of Athens.

His circle of friends, Phaedo among them, have come to bid him farewell. They are troubled, distressed, and look to the future, a future without Socrates, with sorrow and worry. But Socrates is cheerful and full of confidence; he is preparing for death the way one would prepare for a fascinating, albeit lengthy, journey. He assures his friends that their sadness is unfounded; rather, they should, like him, rejoice in his approaching death. For death is not nothingness, dying is not the same thing as the withering of a flower or the rotting of cheese. Nor need it be a step into the unknown; it is possible to have knowledge of what awaits us after death, though this knowledge may not be easy to attain. A person's death, Socrates tells his friends, is his liberation, the beginning of his true life.

Only one who does not know all of this, Socrates argues, anticipates his own death with anxiety, or even with terror, and mourns his departing friends. Fear of death arises from ignorance: it is stupidity. When prepared appropriately for death, we have nothing to be afraid of. On the contrary: we have something to look forward to. Just as we need not be afraid when we are well prepared for a journey to familiar places, it would be childish to fear death after a life well lived. Let's just pack warm things, a raincoat, a change of shoes, and hit the road!

Socrates says to his friends, who are already mourning him: "And now, O my judges, I desire to prove to you that the real philosopher has reason to be of good cheer when he is about to die, and that after death he may hope to obtain the greatest good in the other world. [Other men] do not perceive that he is always pursuing death and dying."[1]

Of what, then, does this true life, this complete goodness we are to reach only after death, consist? Where do we go after we die, and what are we supposed to bring with us?

Socrates' argument is as follows: life cannot be understood on the basis of everyday experience, in reference to what we see, hear, and feel. Each attempt at understanding life necessarily leads us beyond that experience, beyond the world of the senses. How could we have seen anything, if we hadn't known geometric figures, which themselves cannot be seen (since we can see only the things they organize)? How could we hear something without knowing the laws of harmony, which cannot be heard? How could we know what is beautiful, what is true, what is good, if we haven't known beauty, truth, and good, when we cannot encounter them in the world of our daily experience, not even when (for the wise and happy among us) this world is full of beautiful women, true theories, and good deeds?

This necessary surplus of meaning over that which we experience through the senses every day—necessary if our daily, sensory experience is to be organized into some kind of comprehensible whole—Socrates calls *ideas*. What distinguishes ideas from things that we can see or hear, from the objects of our daily lives? Above all else, the fact that things that are visible or audible have their own beginning and end, whereas ideas do not: in the garden beyond the window an apple will fall, will probably get smashed against the hard ground, and will rot in time, but the law of gravity is eternal and always the same; time has no effect on it, just as geometric figures, the laws of harmony, and beauty and truth are themselves eternal. Setting out beyond the world of everyday experience, Socrates argues, is also therefore a departure from time. To understand everything that arises and passes away, gets old, disintegrates, decays, everything that changes—to understand the world of our everyday experience—we must refer to that which does not arise and pass away, that which does not change: *ideas*.

"Life" without ideas, Socrates maintains, is therefore merely an empty word: it's nonsense. It is the eternal, indestructible ideas that impart any meaning to life, that make it what it is, its truth.

Thus, if we are to understand the life around us as it is, doesn't this also mean that we, people, are also thereby participating in the world of ideas? This is the very core of Socrates' argument: our very capacity for understanding demonstrates, he asserts, that we are more than mere things that one can touch or hear. More than just a clump of earth or a stone. More than just a bundle of muscles and nerves. More than the body, this "wind going on its way and not returning," as Saint Augustine would later say.[2] Our ability to comprehend life testifies to the fact that each of us contains within him- or herself something that does not disintegrate, that does not decay, something unaffected by time: *the soul*. It is because of this that we live.

These three things—life, ideas, the soul—are therefore inextricably bound together: and if so, the soul, that part of me that allows me to move out beyond the sensual world that surrounds me every day and thus to comprehend it, is immortal.

The immortal soul—and not the body, which putrefies over time—is our access to the truth about life:

> And thought is best when the mind is gathered into herself and none of these things trouble her—neither sounds nor sights nor pain nor any pleasure [. . .]. [. . .] It has been proved to us by experience that if we would have pure knowledge of anything we must be quit of the body—the soul in herself must behold things in themselves.[3]

It is alleged that Democritus, following this same advice, gouged out his own eyes so that the visible world would not draw his attention from thought. "This is, of course, untrue," Jorge Luis Borges comments, "but beautiful."[4]

Thus if we wish to attain true knowledge, we should die. Death, the complete separation of the soul from the body, is the necessary precondition for knowing truth: "and then we shall attain the wisdom which we desire, and of which we say that we are lovers, not while we live, but after death."[5]

By now we can plainly see (or, at least, this is what Socrates wants of us) that philosophers have no reason to fear death, that they should look forward to it: "The void holds no terrors for a philosopher," we hear later from Homais, the pharmacist in *Madame Bovary*.[6] And they should prepare for it in their own lifetimes, striving as best they can to break the soul away from the body, that it might live on, now without the body, after death (just as we ready ourselves for difficult travels in cold countries, doing our calisthenics and packing our long underwear). "And the true philosophers, Simmias, are always occupied in the practice of dying, wherefore also to them least of all men is death terrible."[7]

"To philosophize," Michel de Montaigne will write, "is to learn how to die."[8]

So too goes the argument of which Socrates, in the story told by Phaedo, wishes to convince the friends gathered around him in the last moments of his life.

But is the argument convincing? Does Socrates really convince the friends who have come to bid him farewell? Are they now unafraid of death, and do they join Socrates in looking forward to his departure? What do you have to say about it, Phaedo, Simmias, and Cebes?

> Cebes answered with a smile: Then, Socrates, you must argue us out of our fears—and yet, strictly speaking, they are not our fears,

but there is a child within us to whom death is a sort of hobgoblin: him too we must persuade not to be afraid when he is alone in the dark.[9]

What does Cebes have in mind when he says that there is a child within each of us? To what does this metaphor refer? Perhaps it means something like this: I am still a child, despite my age and experience, insofar as I am something more than just a "person," a "rational subject," or a "philosopher." As a philosopher, as a rational subject, I am convinced (let's assume, for the sake of argument); I know now that a thinking person shouldn't be afraid of death. But this does not yet mean that I, Krzysztof Michalski (or perhaps the little kid, Krzyś, within me?), no longer fear death. For it is I, Krzyś, who is supposed to die, and that's what I'm really afraid of—I am not afraid of a "person" dying, or a "rational subject," a "philosopher" (sad as it may be that butterflies live for but one day, it's still almost time for dinner). I, Krzyś, am the one who desires consolation, I'm the one who wants somebody to take me by the hand and let me know that there's nothing to be afraid of, that it—death—will not be so horrible after all.

By referring to the child within each of us, Cebes is therefore really asking whether the insight into the essence of life that you, Socrates, are offering us, your friends (and, through Plato's mediation, to us as well, your later audience), affords any solace to the soul, alone in its fear of death.

What can Socrates say? Can his argument—about life and the body's inseparable connection with ideas, and consequently about the immortality of the human soul—also persuade the child within us all?

Socrates' response might look like this: No, of course I can't convince the child you say is within each of us; at best, I can tell him a fairy tale about the beautiful and happy country we go to after we die, just as we tell children about knights and faraway lands at bedtime. I can only convince someone who is rational, someone who can already think, who is grown up. Fear of death is irrational: to understand this, one must stop being a child. I can't help it if Krzysztof Michalski continues to behave like Krzyś Michalski, just like I can't do anything about someone not believing that two and two is four. Knowledge of life and death, like knowledge of the rules of mathematics, rests on lucid, unshakeable, eternal foundations (*ideas*).

Of course, Socrates could add, the child's irrational fear of death (or that of the child in us) is not entirely irrational. Nobody, not even children and immature or unwise adults, fits within the world of everyday experience: everyone, whether he likes it or not, whether he intends it or not, in thinking necessarily moves beyond what he sees and hears, what he can touch: beyond what is known and familiar. This is the source of his anxiety. Up to a point—when he matures and grows wise, when he understands the essence of life and the immortality of the soul from which it arises—this anxiety will go away.

From Socrates' point of view, then, there is no room for the fear of death in the rational world of adults. Insight into the immutable, eternal essence of life allows us not to fear time; it allows us to see in the ongoing mortification of the body—in the new effort it takes to get up from the chair, in the unpleasant surprise of failing to catch the bus—joyful signs of our approaching liberation, harbingers of the coming spring.

This also allows us, for the time being (so long as we're not dead), to make decent, respectable lives for ourselves, to restrain and control the body and its needs, and to render the soul, insofar as it is possible, independent from the body. Life has its own internal, essential order, its own truth; he who is driven by chance passions, by sudden needs, momentary desire, or fear (of death, for instance), distorts this order and lives poorly. Discovering the immutable essence of life will allow the soul to break free from the caprices and anxieties of the body, thereby introducing peace and order into our lives. Then we will be able to live justly and in moderation— just as we are told to, it happens, by custom and tradition. (It would seem that Socrates lived in different, happier times than our own.) This will bring us our reward after death:

> Some are happier than others; and the happiest both in themselves and in the place to which they go are those who have practiced the civil and social virtues which are called temperance and justice, and are acquired by habit and attention without philosophy of mind.
>
> Why are they the happiest?
>
> Because they may be expected to pass into some gentle and social kind which is like their own, such as bees or wasps or ants, or back into the form of man, and just and moderate men may be supposed to spring from them.[10]

Death, correctly understood, does not corrupt the order of life, does not disturb the peace. On the contrary, it is just this kind of understanding of death that reveals the usually invisible order in life, thereby giving us a chance at true peace. This is Socrates' message, as Phaedo relates it to Echecrates. When we become wise, we will be able to live like ants (finally!)—no disorder, no anxiety. Socrates ratifies this message with his death; in Phaedo's account, he dies the death of a decent citizen, concerned with the everyday affairs he wishes to put in order and leave that way, like a prudent traveler checking whether everything is in order, whether the windows are locked, for the last time before leaving the house. And then death—a sense of anticipation, but nothing to be afraid of (I'll finally get to see Majorca!).

He was beginning to grow cold about the groin, when he uncovered his face, for he had covered himself up, and said—they were his last words—he said: Crito, I owe a cock to Asclepius; will you remember to pay the debt?[11]

Later, in different times, Epicurus had found other, equally apt words in which he embraces this same vision of the world: "Don't fear god, don't worry about death; what's good is easy to get, and what's terrible is easy to endure."[12]

Did Plato, who recorded Phaedo's telling of Socrates' last moments for us, find himself convinced by Socrates, as his friends had been? We do not know: he wasn't there. "Plato," Plato—the dialogue's author—has Phaedo, the narrator, say, "Plato, if I am not mistaken, was ill."[13]

2

How dramatically different are the last words of Jesus Christ in Matthew! Crucified, Christ calls out "with a loud voice, saying, *Eli, Eli, lama sabachtani?* that is to say, My God, my God, why hast thou forsaken me?" (Matt. 27:46). And a moment later: "Jesus, when he had cried again with a loud voice, yielded up the ghost" (Matt. 27:50).

This is not the death of someone who knows what awaits him after death. Christ is not setting out, well prepared, on a long and interesting journey. He does not issue last wishes from the cross ("Mary Magdalene, before I forget..."). He dies in great terror, in the mounting anxiety of his uncertainty, in a feeling of solitude and of having been abandoned by everyone, his God and Father included. He is unprepared: everything he has experienced till now, everything he has done, now seems to have become useless—it does not illuminate the now impenetrable darkness of the future, nor does it give peace.

But what is it supposed to mean that Christ dies in fear and uncertainty? How is it possible that God is terrified? What could "God's anxiety" possibly mean? What could be its source? Do we not expect that God knows rather than that He does not, and thus don't we expect His certainty rather than anxiety? Don't we expect Him to behave in the face of death like Socrates, whose knowledge of the essence of life and death allows him to die as if he were taking the (summer) train from Warsaw to Krakow?

What is Christ afraid of? Is he afraid of nothingness, like the child within each of us, like the little Krzyś afraid of being left alone in the dark, where he can no longer see what he knows, what he's used to, what he loves?

Let's take a moment to consider this fear, the fear of nothingness. It is not the fear of one thing or another, of being robbed, of the flu, or of bears; nothingness is nothing of the sort, so it cannot be an object of dread. When I say that, fearing death, I am afraid of nothingness, I mean the end, disintegration, the annihilation of everything I know and can imagine, of all the flies, feelings, equations, concepts, obligations, and everything else that one can call "something." The prospect of death places this "nothing"—the edge of all possible knowledge and, by the same token, of the person in me, the person I know, the person who sees, feels, runs, and knows—before our very eyes. It is the end of my world. As D. H. Lawrence suggested, "To know is human, and in death we do not know, we are not human."[14]

Death is not a "something" that one can understand. Death is the annihilation of all conditions for understanding, of all the conditions by which we think something, ourselves included. In the same way, the prospect of death pulls the ground out from under us, it subverts all possible support, it takes away our chance for a place to sit, for certainty, for peace. Death exposes the limit of all concepts, and so death itself is incomprehensible. "From that plenitude of our being," William Hazlitt notes in reference to Shakespeare, "we cannot change all at once to dust and ashes, we cannot imagine 'this sensible, warm motion, to become a kneaded clod'—we are too much dazzled by the waking dream around us to look into the darkness of the tomb."[15]

This is why death arouses our fear, our dread.

If God's outcry on the cross is therefore an expression of such anxiety, of such fear, then the Gospel of Matthew contradicts the words of Socrates as Phaedo relates them. As I understand Matthew, our confrontation with death places us face-to-face with something unimaginable and unthinkable—and not, as Socrates wished, the one true object of knowledge: the *idea*. There is no possible object of knowledge to be found here, so that the words "we" and "I" also lose any meaning they have held till now. To the question of death—of its meaning, which differs from that of life, of its reality, also different from that of life: the question of what comes next—there is not, nor can there ever be, an answer. As Gadamer writes, "Does any one of us know what he knows when he knows that he must die? Aren't our questions regarding death always and necessarily a cover [. . .] for the unthinkable, for non-being?"[16]

If this is the case, then death is incomprehensible not only to ignoramuses, not only to those who, for one reason or another, are mentally undeveloped, and not only to those (as Phaedo's Socrates wished) who are locked in the prison of the decaying body. It's just as incomprehensible to God. Death does not resemble a mathematical problem so complex that only God could solve it. There is nothing here to know. God the Father cannot console the Son dying on the cross by revealing a solution to the mystery that torments Him. Gadamer again: "When Jesus, in the moment of his dying, calls out to God, it can do no good. For [. . .] a knowledge that would render death comprehensible and bearable can never be assumed."[17]

And yet we know about death: we know that we are going to die. God knows it, too, the God who is dying on the cross, the God who became man. What kind of knowledge is this?

If death cannot be understood, then I must know of it differently from the way I know that Aunt Edna's birthday is on Friday. Levinas says that "[death's] own acuteness [. . .] is its scandal (each death is the first death)."[18] Not so, of course, with Aunt Edna's birthday. Regardless of how much we know about the process of the body's decay, about clinical death, about the extinguishing of consciousness, regardless of our knowledge of funerary rituals and of how our own culture or others' relates to death—regardless of all of this, my death, like yours, is unrepeatable, one of a kind, outrageous. It cannot be generalized. Death touches me differently, more radically and imperceptibly, than any other relation or relationship: it touches me not as a specimen of my species, nor as a member of my society, nor as a representative of some profession, but me as me alone, the me who this time cannot be replaced by anyone else, for no one else can die in my place. Death is closer to me than any character trait or any momentary characterization, it is more mine than the person I love most or my most important task. Without it—without death—there is no me. Death defines me: me, an unrepeatable individual, and not merely a particular case of something. It is only this prospect of death that makes the life I am living my own.

Death is therefore the most intimate feature of my life. I live; this means that I am going to die. But what it means that I will die—this is not something I can explain to someone else, since there are no concepts for it. My "knowledge" of death is my life. My life is suffused with an anxiety that can never be relieved completely; it is mined with a horror that is constantly threatening to explode. My life, which inevitably escapes all concepts. Thus it is not ignorance that makes me afraid of nothingness, just as it is not ignorance or a momentary incomprehensible weakness that is expressed in the cry of the dying God. In this anxiety, in this fear, in this chronic weakness, the specific quality of my life comes to light. My—human—condition.

If the confrontation with death characterizes my life every day and not just on occasion, then every moment of that life—and not just the very last one—contains some trace of it. Death is not merely one of many—the most important—moments in my life, merely one of many events. No moment, no instant of my life, is comprehensible without the relation to death concealed within it, without the relation to the nothingness of the world, without the negation of everything that is familiar, of everything comprehensible. The possibility of the end of the world, the Apocalypse, is inscribed in every moment, in each individual instant of my life. This possibility severs the continuity of my time; time is no longer just the diligent accumulation of meaning, the gradual construction of identity, morning to night, Sunday to Saturday. Between morning and night, today and tomorrow, between "now" and "in a minute," the bottomless abyss of nothingness opens wide, the end of everything I know, of everything I can know, of everything I can rely on. Kafka writes:

> Wonderful, entirely self-contradictory idea that someone who died at 3 a.m., for instance, immediately thereafter, about dawn, enters into a higher life. What incompatibility there is between the visibly human and everything else! [. . .] In the first moment the breath leaves the human calculator. Really one should be afraid to step out of one's house.[19]

Permeated by "knowledge" of death, human life turns out to be similar to a volcano: an unquenchable fire is roaring somewhere in the depths, ready to consume everything in this life that seems lasting, accomplished, all set, all meaning, every object of knowledge. A fire that spares nothing that we know or can know. A fire that burns not only what Saint Augustine calls "this body of death"—no part of me, no "soul," is a diamond left unaffected by this fire. Nothing can be saved for the other side. What does "the other side" mean, anyway? What do we mean by "after death"? Since death destroys all conditions by which something can be understood, if it destroys the possibility of knowledge, then these are empty, meaningless words.

The fire of nothingness. Or perhaps the fire of God? "God," Saint Augustine once prayed, "[you] who are a devouring fire."[20] And the Prophet Micah warns the Samaritans: "For behold, the Lord cometh forth out of his place, and will come down, and tread upon the high places of the earth. And the mountains shall be molten under him, and the valleys shall be cleft, as wax before the fire" (Mic. 1:3–4).

From the perspective of our concepts, of experiences we have had, from the perspective of all that we know, death is nothingness: it is utterly incomprehensible and transcendent. It has no meaning. Death and life—insofar as life is something I know, familiar, comprehensible—are completely alien to one another, they have nothing in common, they don't fit. Thinking about death, we therefore should not refer to metaphors that draw on the world as we know it for their content. Death is not like the breakdown of a mechanism, the smashing of a delicate object, the decomposition of something complicated. When I say that death is nothingness, that it is the end of the world, I mean exactly this foreignness, this transcendence, this incompatibility—and not the destruction of some object, the end of some time, the limit of some space. Thus we are also not dealing here with two realms, two independent countries, the country of life and the country of death, with the known and with that which is, for the time being, unknown. Socrates' tale of the land the soul is supposed to go to after death may be beautiful, but it is certainly a fiction, or perhaps it would be better to say: it does not mean anything.

> But there the whole earth is made up of [colors], and they are brighter far and clearer than ours; there is a purple of wonderful luster, also the radiance of gold, and the white which is in the earth is whiter than any chalk or snow. [. . .] And in this fair region everything that grows—trees and flowers and fruits—are in like degree fairer than any here; and there are hills, having stones in them in a like degree smoother, and more transparent, and fairer in colour. [. . .] They are the jewels of the upper earth, which also shines with gold and silver and the like, [. . .] making the earth a sight to gladden the beholder's eye.[21]

In reality there is no place where life ends and death's country begins. Death—its absurdity, its incomprehensibility, its mystery—permeates my life, is hidden in everything I know in living. The meaning of my life—and thus I myself, my personal identity—cannot be understood without this other, dark side, without this nonsense, this incommensurability, this transcendence. In this way, the prospect of death brings something into my life that cannot be assimilated, that cannot be incorporated into what I already know: a radical otherness, a difference that cannot be removed, a crack that cannot be sealed over, a fissure across which no bridge or overpass can be cast.

This is why Nietzsche writes, in *The Antichrist*, "The whole concept of natural death is lacking in the evangel: death is no bridge, no transition [to another world]. The 'hour of death' is *no* Christian concept."[22]

I understand better now the anxiety in Jesus' cry on the cross. It is not just one's anxiety before an important, perhaps the most important, event in one's life but rather the eruption of the kind of inconsolable anxiety the prospect of death hides in every moment of our lives. Death is the *spur in the body* of life, a spur that cannot be pulled out. Hidden most of the time, though always there, every so often the prospect of death blasts through our knowledge of the world, as well as our identity. Or perhaps it's better to say that it is only when we sense this explosion, this earthquake, which can happen at any moment, which is right around the corner, which might begin at any second, this fire burning inside me, ready to destroy everything—it is only then that we will understand the essence of human knowledge of the world, knowledge that can never be enclosed in concepts, the essence of human life, the *conditio humana*.

Rending every moment of my life with the possibility of nothingness, thereby introducing a radical, irreparable discontinuity, the prospect of death, by the same token, opens my life to something entirely new, to the possibility of an entirely new form of life: Paul can take the place of Saul, the "overman" can take the place of man, the "resurrected body" can replace Krzysztof Michalski. I don't have in mind a new form of something I already know, a mutation, transformation, development, or evolution. I am talking about leaving behind everything I know now and can anticipate. The "resurrected body" is not the same me, just a more beautiful, stronger, healthier, and wiser me. On the other side of the fissure my identity up to now is just ashes, and the "I" that I know becomes a dead letter.

Thus the prayer of Simone Weil: "Father, tear this body and this soul away from me, to make of them your things, and let nothing remain of me eternally but that tearing-away itself."[23]

The prospect of death, the prospect of nothingness, is therefore also the anticipation of something that has been entirely unknown until now, of something that has no place in familiar concepts: of a new beginning. Thus understood, the prospect of death does not force us to obey any rules, it cannot be the ground for any ethics, for any virtue in waiting. It is utterly different from the prospect of travel, which requires us to prepare rationally and thoughtfully. Unlike a trip to Krakow, there is no way to prepare for death. Departure schedules, tickets, maps, guides, dictionaries, manuals—everything that enables us to plan for the future—facing the prospect of death, these lose all meaning; they are no longer important. Here life shows us its uncomfortable side: it turns out that we cannot settle into it completely, we cannot nestle into it, we find no solid ground there. No ethics, no institution, can provide such a ground; the prospect of death reveals their temporary, relative nature.

In this way, the prospect of death, inscribed in my life, undermines all ethics, all human institutions.

If death is therefore not only the event that ends life, if it is not (and what could this mean?) a footbridge linking life in time (and doesn't "life beyond time" make as little sense as a "four-cornered triangle"?) with eternal life (isn't that an oxymoron?)—if death, the possibility of death, is first of all the rupture of every moment of my life, which in this way becomes open to the New, then in our confrontation with death the world shows itself to us from a side we have not yet known. No longer just as a place that we leave in death (all these flies, feelings, and tasks), no longer just as a web of meanings determined (at least in principle) by what I can touch, see, or understand.

The prospect of death imparts new meaning to the world in which I live, a meaning that is, as such, unfinished, open, and temporary. In other words, the prospect of death demonstrates that the world and thus I myself as well contain more than we can hold.

"Knowledge" of death, which permeates every pore in my skin and every second of my life, is thus not only a natural source of fear. By confronting me with nothingness, with the end of everything known and familiar to me, it also opens me to the possibility of something radically new and entirely unknown. It shows the world breaking apart, a world that is always something more—though to the question "What more?" there is no answer. We can therefore say that the prospect of death arouses not only fear but also longing—a longing that cannot be satisfied, because unlike hunger or lust, here I don't know what I am longing for or what could serve to satisfy this longing. Saint Augustine again, praying: "What is the light which shines right through me and strikes my heart without hurting? It fills me with terror and burning love."[24]

The fabric of my life is therefore suffused with longing, a longing that we might call metaphysical, since it does not refer to anything that comes from the world I know and in which I am home. An infinite longing, since it cannot be fulfilled, and because of this it leads out beyond all things. Unlike a concrete need (say, for money) or lust (I won't say for whom) or curiosity (who's winning?), it is a desire that cannot be satisfied. A fire impossible to extinguish with any satisfaction.

Isn't this the place, in this eternal fire, in this infinite longing for something other, new, and unexpected, that God can reveal Himself to man? "[A]nd, behold, the bush burned with fire, and the bush was not consumed" (Exod. 3:2). I believe that this is precisely what Matthew wishes to tell us: Christ's cry on the cross reveals the world as the place where we are waiting for God.

If this is all true, then human life is radically, infinitely free. If every moment of our lives is marked for possible destruction, for annihilation—if in every moment of our lives there burns a hidden fire that can transform it unexpectedly and radically—then this would also mean that nothing binds me completely, no knowledge already attained, no conditions already defined: the fact that I live frees me from every situation I might find myself in and gives me the possibility of distance from everything I do, the possibility of freedom. "To practice death is to practice freedom," Montaigne would write. "Knowing how to die gives us freedom from subjection and constraint."[25]

So there is nothing strange in the fact that death—this trace, this brush with the unknown, visible to neither mind nor eye, that exposes the fragility of each moment, its openness to the unforeseen future, and by the same token my own unlimited freedom—cannot be understood.

Just as Phaedo's account of the death of Socrates was supposed to provide the Athenian youth with an example of proper conduct in the face of death and thus also an example of a good life, so too is the death of Christ on the cross in the Gospel of Matthew supposed to be, as I understand it, testimony regarding the human condition: what's important in life, what it's all about. God became man in order to confront us with the truth about ourselves. Matthew tells us about Christ's death so that the cry of the crucified Jesus could ring forever in our ears, that we might then know who we are.

"Jesus will be in agony until the end of the world," Pascal would write. "We must not sleep during that time."[26] Jesus' anxiety is supposed to infect us as well; to live, to live truly, is to wait continuously for the unknown, to be on alert. To fight against the sleep toward which everyday life entices us with appearances of order and the peace it fosters. Saint Augustine: "The burden of the world weighed me down with a sweet drowsiness such as commonly occurs during sleep. The thoughts with which I meditated about you were like the efforts of those who would like to get up but are overcome by deep sleep and sink back again."[27]

The fear and longing that pierce my heart in the face of death do not allow me to lose myself in everyday concerns, in that which is today, in what I know. They do not let me fall asleep. The cry of the dying Christ can be heard everywhere I go. Levinas: "I am, myself, torn from my beginning in me, from my equality with myself."[28]

But life has its necessities: we need to sleep. This is why we create tools that make things easier on us—institutions, patterns of behavior, moral rules—so as not to hear, to forget, to fall asleep. The tools of *diversion* (Pascal), the *means of intoxication* (Nietzsche). Do you recall Socrates challenging us to live like ants, without disorder, without anxiety? "Now I understand clearly what was once sought above all when teachers of virtue were sought," Zarathustra says after meeting one such teacher. "Good sleep was sought, and opiate virtues for it."[29]

In the Gospel of Matthew, Jesus' cry is supposed to awaken us, to tear us out of our sleep. Which means: to make us aware that we have been sleeping until now, that the reality in which we have been living is not the ultimate, absolute form of reality. Awakened, we see the fragility of everything around us, of everything that we have regarded as hard, solid, and unshakeable. Awake, we see ruins where in sleep there had been houses; we wake up, and the earth shakes, the ground slips out from under our feet. The order of the world, the institutions that ensure the stability of our lives, the concepts that allow us to understand this world, and finally I, me myself, my identity, what I am—they all reveal their temporary nature, their irremediable vulnerability, their exposure.

The suspicion that we are asleep when we think ourselves awake also tormented, as is well-known, Descartes. We will never be completely successful in eliminating this suspicion from everyday life, though a healthy mind constantly pushes it off to the side. The only real defense against it, Descartes concludes, is mathematics: two and two is four, regardless of whether I am asleep or awake. From the mathematical point of view, the difference between waking life and sleep, between life and dream, loses all meaning. But doesn't this also mean that mathematics and science, like the knowledge of *ideas* in Phaedo's tale about Socrates, stop having any significance at all when we are asking about the meaning of human life, about the *conditio humana*?

Either way, the Cartesian argument about the indistinguishability of waking life and sleep undermines the conviction that the form of the world as I know it from everyday experience is already the world as it truly is. Of course, this does not mean that it is merely an illusion, just a dream, that there really isn't such a world at all. Descartes didn't think this either. But there is a possible point of view—so Descartes would say, so too will I—from which this reality looks limited, one-sided, and therefore relative. Just as dreams are.

Matthew's Christ crying out on the cross is supposed to shake us from this dream. It's supposed to prevent us from falling asleep. His cry is supposed to force us to struggle further with the heaviness of our limbs and thoughts, with resignation, with the temptation of peace and order, with the comfort of our identification with the institutions, virtues, and concepts we have found—with the temptation of sleep.

Let's sum up. Plato's *Phaedo*, the Gospel of Matthew: two narratives about death, two visions of human nature. Christ's cry on the cross, as told by Matthew, gives voice to an understanding of human life that is radically different from that of Socrates (if Phaedo understood him correctly). For Phaedo's Socrates, the truly important things in life are *ideas*: the eternal order of the world, the understanding of which leads to unperturbed peace and serenity in the face of death. The dying Socrates wanted to give us concepts that would provide peace, concepts that will soothe our anxiety in the face of death. The Gospel of Matthew, as I understand it, is the complete opposite: it testifies to the incurable presence of the Unknown in every moment of my life, a presence that rips apart every human certainty built on what is known, that disturbs all peace, all serenity—that severs the continuity of time, opening every moment of our lives to nothingness, thereby inscribing within them the possibility of an abrupt end and the chance at a new beginning.

Two visions of death, two visions of the human condition. Perhaps the unrelievable tension between them is something more than just the opposition between truth and falsehood. Perhaps it is precisely this tension that constitutes the only possible meaning of human life.

VII

The Flame of Eternity

From when I started speaking until this moment, you realize you have grown older: you cannot see your hair growing; and yet, while you stand around, while you are here, while you do something, while you talk, your hair keeps on growing on you—but never so suddenly that you need a barber straight away: so your existence fades away—you are passing. [. . .] Let a few years go by: let the great river slip forward, as it always does, passing through many places, washing, always, through some new tombs of the dead.

THIS IS AURELIUS AUGUSTUS—SAINT Augustine, Bishop of Hippo—in the fifth century, preaching.[1] How long since that city has passed! Only these words strike me, after all these centuries, as they surely must have struck the faithful gathered in that church.

What is the source of their strength?

It is not easy to understand what he's talking about. Unlike then, today the eye, when properly equipped, has no real difficulty seeing how hair grows. And yet we cannot see passing now, either. The eye, whether so equipped or naked, cannot see the change of what is into what has already been, the change of "now" into "then." Sure, it's easy enough for me to make out the changes in my face when I compare my reflection in the mirror to an old photograph. But where, in the mirror or in the photograph, is that feature that tells me that the face in the photograph used to be, whereas the one in the mirror is?

I can't find it.

Which means that the experience of passing, my knowledge that the world as I know it—and I with it—will pass away, cannot be freed from the suspicion of unreality that usually accompanies it, from the suspicion that this experience is merely the result of (our) limited point of view, while in reality nothing is really passing. Since we are incapable of seeing how something passes, does this not mean that nothing is passing? Since, looking at my face in the mirror, I can see wrinkles, fatigue, and gray hair that are absent from the old photograph—while I can't make out any "today" or "yesterday" in one or the other—does this not mean that in reality there is no "today" or "tomorrow," that maybe in reality things do not differ in this way? That perhaps it is only things that are real, not their succession? Of course, we see things one after the other—this yesterday, that today, something else the day after tomorrow—but might this be just because we are incapable of seeing them all together, whereas this might be possible from some other, better point of view? Perhaps there is a perspective—that of God? of Truth?—in which everything is simultaneous, the "I" in the photograph and the "I" reflected in the mirror. The objects of the soul succeed one another, a suspicion once formulated by Plotinus: "—now Socrates; now a horse; [. . .] but the Intellectual-Principle is all and therefore its entire content is simultaneously present in that identity [. . .]; nowhere is there any future, for every then is a now; nor is there a past, for nothing there has ever ceased to be."[2]

The presence of things seems to contradict the assumption of the world's transience: the world as I see it—just is.

The assumption that I, too, will someday pass away seems even more scandalous. Doesn't the very notion—that I'll be gone someday, the thought of a world without my presence—contradict every tiny little fragment of my experience? Isn't it completely absurd? Despite what I know—from other sources, abstractly—about the world (that everything comes to an end), about others (that they die)?

What seems to be the irrefutable self-evidence with which the world is present to me, as well as the absurdity of thinking about my own eventual absence from this world, incline us toward a spontaneous distrust of the suggestion of transience.

We might also formulate this idea as follows: the kinds of tools at my disposal for understanding and expressing what I see—my concepts, my words—seem to be geared toward grasping that which is; the world as I see it, the world as I know it, just is, and does not pass away. This passing—of the world, and me with it—seems to guard against all categorization, to escape words and concepts, to slip out from knowledge.

And yet, and yet: "What nonsense!" one wishes to say to the thesis that time is an illusion. Doesn't the person who asserts something along these lines also contradict the evidence of our experience? After all, I remember well how I was standing at my friend's funeral, and time split apart into "now," without him, and "then," when he was still here. In such moments as these, the past breaks off from the present, becomes resistant and foreign, it turns into a stone, a burden. And it hurts. Or rather: in such moments the world's presence splits into present and past, leaving a wound, a painful wound.

Borges writes that "succession is an intolerable misery."[3]

And so it is: we do not see passing. True, in the clear presence of the world, and of myself in it, passing seems to be just an illusion, a bad dream, stupidity. And yet our assumption of the transitory nature of things is deeply ingrained in our experience. Though I do not see it, I feel it. Nietzsche writes:

> You feel that you will bid farewell, and perhaps soon—and the evening blush of this feeling shines within your happiness. Pay heed to this testimony: it means that you love life, and yourself with it, indeed, that you love the life that you have lived until now, and that has shaped you. [. . .] But know this!—that transience is always singing you its brief song, and that, hearing its first lines, one can die of longing, at the thought that all of this can pass away forever.[4]

The evidence provided by experience thus seems internally contradictory: what we intuit from it seems to be difficult to reconcile, since our experience simultaneously proves the reality of passing—the reality of time—and denies it.

Following Nietzsche, let us reflect on this contradiction.

2

"Space," Nietzsche notes in the summer of 1882, "is, like matter, a subjective form. Time *is not*."[5]

What does he mean?

Time is not a *subjective form*—that is, it is objective, real. That is, the world is of necessity constantly changing, the world is becoming, the world is passing, and this change, this becoming, this time, is not merely a subjective illusion.

Nietzsche tells us: forget about eternity, which renders time a dream. Set aside theories that persuade you to wake up, to tear off the veil of time, in order to face the world as it (ostensibly) is. These are just ruses, futile tricks. Oh, I know full well why you are so easily persuaded, I know where your ingenuity in finding escape routes comes from: time hurts. Death is horrifying. The shadow of mystery, the shadow of an incomprehension that cannot be removed from the constantly changing world, irritates, inclines us to ignore what changes and to seek out something that simply is. And yet this is the only reality you have: this pain, this fear, this incomprehension. Time.

There is no escape from time: this, too, is the message of Christianity, revolutionary in the Greek and Roman worlds where it appeared. The questions of who you are, your fate, the meaning of your life—Christians preach to the Greeks and Romans—are to be answered here and now, in the always too-brief span of your life, and nowhere else—in a span you can live through only once, irreversibly, with no second chance, just as "Christ also hath once suffered for sins, the just for the unjust, that he might bring us to God" (1 Pet. 3:18). Time, and with it the pain of passing, the fear of death, the incomprehension of the changing world, is also real for Christians; for Christians, too, it is no illusion.

What does this irremediable change consist of? What does it mean that the world passes away?

Nietzsche answers this question with the help of a couple of metaphors. This is not merely a heuristic operation, nor is it an attempt to illustrate a meaning that is otherwise available to us. The metaphors cannot be removed from his answer; the meaning of what is happening to the world, to us, cannot be told without them. "And the best metaphors," Nietzsche notes, "speak of time and becoming: they should be praise for and a justification of passing!"[6]

Let's have a look at some of these metaphors.

3

One of the metaphors that praise and justify passing is Heraclitus's metaphor of the world as a river. It is true, Zarathustra says, "Everything is in flux."[7] We are unable to see it, though. The river of time eludes our instruments of perception and understanding. Nietzsche notes that "we are not refined enough to peer into the ostensible, absolute river of happening."[8] But beyond our perception, under the surface of phenomena, "seethes and seethes, a river of darkness" (D. H. Lawrence)—the dark river of passing. Continuously, without end, without beginning.[9]

"'How now?'" Zarathustra anticipates an objection. "'Everything should be in flux? After all, planks and railings are *over* the river. Whatever is *over* the river is firm; all the values of things, the bridges, the concepts, all 'good' and 'evil'—all that is *firm*.'"[10] Yes, of course, some things break apart, decay, perish—but not everything! For example, concepts that are universal in their validity, like the concepts of good and evil: even if everything around us has changed, they at least are immutable, time has no effect on them!

Nietzsche had obviously been reading Hölderlin. "Your tutelary spirit, splendid friend, illuminates the earth!" Pausanias says to Empedocles in *The Death of Empedocles*, "And all of this should pass away?"[11]

Only "blockheads" ask these kinds of questions, Nietzsche responds (as Empedocles does to Pauzanias: "Silly boy! does not the holy spirit of life / Nod off to sleep and hold its purity transfixed / At any place where you might hope to bind it?").[12] Nietzsche is not interested in compromises: no, the river of time cannot be resisted, nothing can ever hold it back, "the holy spirit of life" never sleeps, never rests. Things cannot be divided into mutable and immutable, these things embraced by the river, those other things eternal, atemporal. There can be no liberation from the river of time, and morality does not liberate us from it either. Only fools believe in the possibility of such liberation, and only madmen seek it out. "Alas, where is redemption from the flux of things?'" Zarathustra says. "Thus preached madness."[13]

A compromise would be impossible anyway; in this case, Nietzsche claims, *tertium non datur*: anyone who believes that at least some things, though not all, are unaffected by time (for example, triangles, which do not age, versus Mrs. Smith, who does), anyone who believes in "bridges" and "railings" leading over the river of time—such a person is challenging its very existence. If we believe that something, whatever it may be, exists beyond time, then we have also stopped believing in the reality of change in general. These two positions cannot be reconciled. A belief in an atemporal "something" casts a shadow of doubt on the reality of time: this is "there," not "here" (we then believe), the world is as it is.

If there does exist something that does not change, it is difficult to believe that anything changes, that time is real.

Nietzsche often presents this idea in the form of the following argument:

> If the world could stand still, shrivel, die out, and become nothing, or if it could attain a state of equilibrium, or if it had any goal at all, durable, immutable, attained once-and-for-all (briefly and metaphysically: if becoming could be encapsulated in being or nothingness)—then such a state would have to have been achieved already. But it is not.[14]

The belief that there exists something that is not subject to change often appears, Nietzsche argues, in the form of the thesis that becoming, the change we recognize on a daily basis, has some purpose, some goal, no matter how remote. In other words, that becoming is the becoming "of something" (of freedom, for example, or of human destiny, which will be fulfilled at the end of days, or of the essence of humanity, which, with a bit of luck and great effort on the part of the working class, will finally be realized in communism, etc.). To this Nietzsche says that if the world's becoming had some purpose (and thus if a state of things no longer subject to change were possible, a state of things beyond time), then such a state would already have been achieved within the infinitude of time that has flowed up till now. If the world is to become "something," then why is that something, that ultimate goal, yet to arrive, despite the infinitude of time past?

To really understand this argument well, let's dwell for a moment on what it might mean that "time is infinite," what this "infinitude of time that has flowed up till now" is.

What is meant here is certainly not an objective, infinite process stretched out between "way back when" and "the present moment." Such a notion would be utterly incomprehensible, for it would assume that time has no direction and that it therefore doesn't matter whether I am going backward (from the present to the past) or forward (from the past to the present). Time without direction is time with no difference between past and future, and what kind of time doesn't differentiate past from future? "If I were to regard the direction of *time* (whether forward or backward) as immaterial, then its head would become its tail."[15] That is, the concepts of the "past" and the "future" (and therefore also the concepts of "infinite past" and "endless future") would lose their meaning. Time, like a snake biting its own tail, would become a circle, a negation of itself.

The only way to understand time as infinite, Nietzsche writes, is by "withdrawing from the moment in which I find myself, to confirm that 'I will never reach the end'; the account accumulating from the moment forward is similarly infinite."[16] It is only from the perspective of the moment in which I find myself that time's infinity acquires meaning, since it is only from the perspective of such a moment that time has a direction and that, consequently, the concepts "past" and "future" mean anything.

To say that "time is infinite" is therefore tantamount to saying that from the point of view of the moment I'm living through right now the notion of "the end of time" is impossible.

Therefore, when Nietzsche writes that "If the world [. . .] had any goal at all, [. . .] then such a state would have to have been achieved already," he means something like the following: when I speak of the "end of time" from the perspective of a person having some past behind him and some future in front of him, I'm talking nonsense—such a concept is meaningless in this regard. It has meaning only at the expense of negating change, of denying the difference between past and future, of negating the perspective of today.

If the world is moving toward some ultimate state, toward the end, toward the edge of time, then the fact that the world is now changing is entirely incomprehensible.

The situation is similar with the concept of the beginning: if it were possible to have an (atemporal) state of things from which time flows, if it were possible for there to be an (immutable) beginning from which the changing world arises, then it would be entirely incomprehensible how the world was able to leave that state and start changing.

If it were possible to have a state of things that does not become, a state of things without past ("the beginning") or future ("the end"), then there would be no way of understanding the difference between past and future, no way of understanding this becoming. Time is not something that happened (like spilled milk), time did not become, nor will time become anything. Time is simply becoming, without beginning or end. Nietzsche writes:

> The world exists; the world is not something that becomes, it is not something that passes. Or, rather: it becomes, it passes—but it never started to become, and it never stopped passing.... The world lives on itself: its excrement is its nourishment.[17]

If the world that I am looking at, the world where I live, is really changing—if my presence in this moment is not full, whole, if this moment is ruptured, if it has a fissure through which the nothingness of what was and what will be seeps, if the difference between the future before me and the past behind me is real—in short, if the world is really passing away and does not simply exist (as Nietzsche, it so happens, believed)—then that passing, that change, that becoming, never began and will never end.

> If the world were capable of standing still and lasting, of "being," if it had such a capacity, if only for a single moment, to "be"—then by the same token all becoming would become impossible.... The fact is [. . .] that becoming proves that the world has no goal, that it has no end, that it is incapable of simply being.[18]

There was no beginning, and there will be no end: no moment of time can be either. From the perspective of the beginning or the end, change would be utterly incomprehensible.

Tertium non datur.

This is why the "blockheads" not only indicate to Zarathustra places where the "river of time" cannot reach but also ask him, "Does not everything stand still?"[19] Isn't the river of time a mirage (they suggest), and isn't the real world—the world as it is, the whole world—unchanging, like those bridges and railings, like such universal concepts as good and evil?

No, Zarathustra argues, and Nietzsche, too, through his lips—the river of time has no borders, it is the world as it is, the ephemeral world, without beginning, without end. There is no other.

If the river of time has neither beginning nor end, if it is not something's becoming, the transformation of one thing into another, then time cannot be destruction, decay, or the corruption of something that had been at the beginning, that was there before time, and that would still be whole, intact, undisturbed, innocent, if only time had not begun to flow. It is for this very same reason that time is not, and cannot be, merely some "not-yet," anticipation, hope for something that will arrive and stop it. For, after all, the "beginning" and the "end" of time are concepts just as nonsensical as a "square circle" (or Mrs. Smith never aging).

But doesn't this mean that time is entirely beyond our understanding? Is there another way to understand time than from the perspective of something becoming in time, something changing (or not), the way a disease can be understood only as the pathology of a given organism that is otherwise normal and fine without it? Can time be understood other than as just "the dark river of dissolution," as D. H. Lawrence calls it, the "black river of corruption," as the "silver river of life, rolling on and quickening all the world to a brightness, on and on to heaven, flowing into a bright eternal sea"?[20] As the degeneration of what once had been a healthy human nature, the gradual corrosion of the divine gift under the influence of sin, "the great river [flowing] forward, as it always does, passing through many places, washing, always, through some new tombs of the dead," as Saint Augustine would have it, or as the path toward a luminous future, Paradise, redemption, socialism, democracy, an end amid angels and trumpets?[21] In short, isn't it true that change is comprehensible only from the point of view of something that does not change? Isn't the disruption of identity comprehensible only from the perspective of something that is identical?

This is precisely the position of Edmund Husserl, for example. Husserl sought to unravel the mystery of time ("Why does it flow?") in the deep structure of consciousness that is inaccessible in everyday experience, ultimately to find the source of time in the cleft driven into consciousness by our relation (*intention*) to objects, in the disruption of our primal conscious unity by the signifying intention of objects. Husserl therefore saw temporal difference (the difference between past and future), he saw discontinuity, the becoming that is time, from the perspective of unity and continuity, from the perspective of a being that is *not* becoming (yet? any longer?): "the consciousness of otherness, of difference, presupposes a unity."[22]

It is a position shared by Leszek Kołakowski. In "Historical Understanding and the Intelligibility of History," he writes about the seemingly constant change of life around us, noting that history can in no way be understood as a meaningful structure if we do not assume an ahistorical essence incarnate in its course. Without assuming such a structure, "history is forever obscure."[23]

Nietzsche would say that Husserl and Kołakowski were trying to reach "land somewhere in the sea of becoming," believing that becoming could not be understood without this dry ground.[24] From their point of view, becoming can be understood insofar as it is no longer becoming, time insofar as it is "standing still," no longer flowing. It is therefore unsurprising that in this regard time is always merely something "lesser," destruction or progress, a path toward something (or away from it) that is not time, an anticipation, a shadow, a lack. Time, as a mirage, is comprehensible—as Kołakowski believed, and Husserl before him, and others besides—only insofar as the true (atemporal) reality within it shines through.

Nietzsche, meanwhile, believed that a "true" reality "standing" beyond time is, as we have seen, nonsense: there is no such thing. Only "block-heads" insist on it. "True" reality does not "stand" but "flows": "being [. . .] is [. . .] changeable, non-identical with itself. What 'stands still,' what lasts, exists exclusively because of our rough-hewn organs."[25]

Maintaining that the world "stands still" rather than "flows," we err, according to Nietzsche, but this is not simple ignorance. It is *our organs* that lead us astray, it is *our organs* that are mistaken. In Nietzsche's argument, this hardly means that we have some other access to reality that is independent of our organs and through which we might see how the world truly is (that it "flows" and does not "stand still"). The point here is not the fallibility of the senses (which can be corrected, if only through mathematics) nor the finitude of our consciousness (which scientific advances are surpassing bit by bit). We are not dealing with the kind of error that one might correct but with the kind of *error* "toward which our vital organs are disposed"—and thus the organs about which Nietzsche writes are the "vital organs," those one needs in order to live.[26]

The assumption—the postulate—of a self-identical world (the kind of "error" that "blockheads" make)—to reformulate Nietzsche's idea—is therefore the precondition for the possibility of life. In other words, in order to live, we must think, we must know, and knowledge demands a self-identical object. In order to live, we must know (and move around) all those tables that stand in our way, we must smell all the smells (and seek after their source), hear all those thunderclaps (and hide for a while). In short, in order to live, we must know the world as it "is." The precondition of such knowledge is a world identical with itself, a world that lasts, that stays as it is. Without such knowledge, life would be impossible.

Consequently, the constantly changing world—*the river of time*—cannot be an object of knowledge: "Our intellect is not formed to comprehend becoming."[27]

The absolute river of becoming "cannot be perceived."[28]

Or, to put it another way, "the ultimate truth about the river of all things cannot be assimilated."[29] It cannot be "assimilated" because it is not the "truth" in the same sense that it is true that the table stands in my path to the door, or that it is true that I smell an enticing aroma, that I hear thunder. Because it is not a "truth" that I can—that I *must*—incorporate into my life, assimilate, as I have those other truths, in order to live. I cannot know the *river of time* in this sense: it has no place in my life, it is fundamentally impossible to fit it in.

The *foolishness* of those who seek the borders of the *river of time* thus cannot be compared to the ignorance of someone who does not know how things really are. It is a foolishness that I cannot escape, so long as I am alive. It is the necessary foolishness of life.

Let's try to formulate this argument yet another way. Since our ability to live is dependent, as Nietzsche would have it, on the premise that the world is essentially immutable, lasting, and atemporal, then this means that our ability to live requires that our lives also have an inert, passive, uncreative aspect. This (our inertia) is evidenced by the very fact that we know something, by our knowledge, for it is this very fact that posits the existence of an independent object that can be known, of something that, as a thinking subject, I should adapt to. Adapt, discover—but not create.

The concept of the immutable world, of the world that "stands still"— this, Nietzsche writes, "is truly a winter doctrine, a good thing for sterile times, a fine comfort for hibernators and hearth-squatters."[30] That which is barren in us, fruitless, uncreative, that which is passive in us, our laziness, which demands that we remain by the fire and accept the world as it is: this is the other aspect of our ability to know something. The point here is not, I should say just in case, that scientists are stupid, lazy, and have too few children but that there is an indispensable aspect of our lives, its incorrigible foolishness, an inertia that cannot be eliminated, and a laziness that stems from it and is therefore necessary—as is the image of the world as eternally, immutably the same, which corresponds with it. "'At bottom everything stands still'—*against* this the thawing wind preaches" (while Empedocles says to Pausanias in Hölderlin's *The Death of Empedocles*, "Pass away? / But it's enduring, like the stream the frost / has fettered")—and this is so, that as long as I live, my life is passive, uncreative, barren.[31]

Life, which is a condition for the possibility of all knowledge.

Knowledge of the world as foolishness, as an expression of inertia, laziness, and barrenness—isn't this also an ancient Christian theme?

Thus the point is me, how I live, and not the order of a world that is independent of me (or of its absence). The thesis that everything flows needs to be understood in this context. Its point of reference, its necessary background, is the thesis that *everything stands still*. This happens (everything seems to be standing still) only insofar as we accept the world passively, adapting ourselves to what we take for granted, only insofar as we do not create reality but merely strive to learn what it is. If the thesis that everything is in flux is to come true, our lives must be something more.

That *everything flows*: from Nietzsche's mouth, this is not simply a description of the world, the theses that it is this way and no other, that the world "flows," that it passes away and does not "stand still," that we cannot say that it simply "is." When Nietzsche speaks of the "ultimate truth" of this assertion and of the "error" of its opposite (that *everything stands still*), he does not have in mind the opposition of two views of reality, one true, the other false, of a reality that is as it is ("fluid" or not) independently of those assertions. He does not presuppose any meaning for these terms— "world," "knowledge," their mutual "relation," "error," "ultimate truth." Rather, the metaphor of the river of time places them in the only context where, Nietzsche maintains, they can mean anything at all: in the context of life as we are living it.

Accordingly, this concept of time, of *the river of time*, is not a description of the world independent of what I do. Nietzsche is not talking about such a world, that everything in it "flows" (and does not "stand still"): this is not a physical, cosmic thesis. The "world"—the found, given reality to which one must adapt in order to live—is the projection of a passive, inert, exhausted life. "Time is endless," "change never ceases," "becoming is absolute, aimless": "everything is in flux"—these are not theses about the order of the world, about the cosmos. They are an expression of the belief that the ice that enchains the river of time might thaw at any moment, that at any second the river of time may flow on, shattering the next series of dams, washing away the next set of bridges: undermining the allegedly unshakeable foundations of the forms it will take next, which to us seem durable, stable, and immutable. That life contains within itself an explosive charge that will blast through that ice, that it passes by, in spite of our best efforts to hold it back, ever anew.

Please note that the "life" we are talking about here—the life that makes the river of time flow—is not a descriptive category either. Nietzsche does not describe life the way one might the weather or a headache; "life" is not that kind of object—it isn't an object at all. Placing some concept in the "context of life" does not mean simply assigning it a particular category; it is not a methodological tip for us not to confuse triangles with potatoes. It means, rather, that these concepts—like all concepts, like everything we know—cannot be divorced from what we do, that they are unthinkable without their expressive function, and that they also express our effort (greater or lesser), which we call "life." When I say (when Nietzsche says) that "everything is in flux," I have in mind the fact that this effort is irresistible, that it will meet no obstacle that cannot be overcome, that, in other words, nothing will satisfy it, nothing will pacify it—that this is not an effort to achieve anything.

What we mean here are the conditions for the sensible use of concepts. This is not a description of some object ("life").

Can we then say that the "river" is a good metaphor for time? A river is a movement of water, water's transfer from one place to another, from its source to its mouth, an "A" changing into a "B." If, however, time, change, and becoming have neither beginning nor end, then we have neither "source" nor "mouth," and there is no state "A" that could change into a state "B." "Today" does not differ from "tomorrow" the same way as "the Mississippi at St. Louis" differs from "the Mississippi at Memphis" (or as young Mrs. Smith from old Mrs. Smith); it is a completely different kind of difference. Passing is not a process by which one thing transforms into another. Moments do not pass like things, Levinas once remarked against Husserl.

Time, unlike a river, is not a process in which "something" changes, whatever it may have been; time is not the transformation of something into something else. The difference between the past and future—time—cannot be reduced to the difference between two states of a thing.

The *river of time* is not, therefore, a river like the Mississippi. The Mississippi starts somewhere and ends somewhere else, it widens and narrows again, it flows faster or slower, for we can find something that, relative to it, does not change, that can serve as a measure. We can look at the Mississippi from its banks. At the bank-less, unlimited river of time—no. It has no such measure.

Thus it may be that the metaphor of the river, the image of flowing water, of the constant motion of something from one place to another, is not a good point of departure for understanding time. It may be that, wanting to understand reality as becoming, the world as time, wanting to understand how it is that this very moment, this "today," this "now," gives birth of necessity to a "tomorrow," a "later"—if we want to grasp the difference between past and future—we must refer to other concepts than "motion" or "change."

And yet we have nevertheless learned something from discussing the metaphor of the river of time: that everything flows, and thus that the world is constantly changing, becoming, and that this statement makes sense only from the perspective of the moment I am now in, the moment I am living, and thus that it cannot be understood independently of what I do and how I live; that this endless becoming is not the becoming of something, that it is, therefore, neither disintegration and degeneration, nor an approach toward some goal, a stairway to heaven—that, accordingly, this constant change, the river of time, cannot be an object of knowledge like the tree out the window or mathematics, that it is not information about the world that can be added to other such information—information, knowledge, without which our lives would be impossible.

We have learned that *time is flowing*, that the *world is changing*, in the effort that is my life. When this effort slackens, the *spirit of life* lies down to sleep, and the river of time starts to *freeze over*.

A warm wind contradicts this wintry perspective, says Nietzsche. Summer is coming, "a destroyer who breaks the ice with wrathful horns."[32] This wind, the hot breath of approaching summer, thaws everything that has been frozen till now: "Have not all railings and bridges fallen into the water?"[33]

"O my brothers," Zarathustra announces, "is not everything in flux now?"[34]

As we can see, besides the metaphor of the river of time we encounter here yet another metaphor, that of wind. Let's consider that next.

4

"This book," Nietzsche writes in the preface to the second edition of *The Gay Science*, "seems to be written in the language of wind that thaws ice and snow: high spirits, unrest, contradiction, and April weather are present in it, and one is instantly reminded no less of the proximity of winter than of the triumph over the winter that is coming, must come, and perhaps has already come."[35]

Wind: this is, in Nietzsche's writings, a metaphoric name for "spirit" ("the storm that is called 'spirit,'" he writes in *Zarathustra*, the spirit that "says No"), which destroys everything solid and permanent and in this way removes all limits, borders, obstacles—that liberates.[36] It is "the wind of the great freedom," Nietzsche says in *Ecce Homo*.[37]

To this extent wind is also a metaphor for becoming, a metaphor for passing.

Not even death is an obstacle for this wind; the wind-spirit "tears open the gates of the castles of death."[38] In the perspective opened here, death, too, is no longer final. It ceases to be the ultimate—immovable, immutable—border, dam, or rock face that the *river of life* merely runs up against, unable to overcome it.

What could it mean that not even death can impede the spirit, that not even death can delimit passing? I'll come back to this question. In this thought of Nietzsche one can also hear an echo of the Bible; for God, too, Saint Paul wrote to the Romans, death is not an insurmountable boundary, since God "quickeneth the dead" (Rom. 4:17).

What is this wind, this spirit? Whence does it come? "I am this wind myself," Nietzsche notes in 1882.[39] The hot "wind," because of which the frozen river starts to flow again, is the *blast*, the *breath* of my soul, the blast and breath that my soul itself is.

The soul is a "warm exhalation," Heraclitus is said (by Aristotle) to have believed.[40]

But what is the soul, who am I in this context? Certainly not Krzysztof Michalski, a professor of philosophy of a certain age! "I want to be the power [. . .] where the wind blows, and I want to blow within it," Nietzsche writes.[41] I am therefore "wind," insofar as I am "power," insofar as I am strong. Zarathustra is exactly this: "Verily, a strong wind is Zarathustra."[42]

I am, therefore, *wind, spirit, freedom*, insofar as I am like Zarathustra, insofar as I am as *powerful* as Zarathustra.

Who is, what is, this Zarathustra?

Zarathustra—the strong wind, the wind-spirit that knows no impediment in its course—I as Zarathustra, the Zarathustra in me—is everything within me that resists my passivity, my laziness, my barrenness, everything that runs counter to my ability to adapt, to my being hindered by what is. Zarathustra is me, insofar as I am creative, active, free, insofar as I do not adapt to the world I encounter but rather create one anew. It is *power*, my life-strength, a power that assures that the world is becoming other (more or less) by the mere fact that I am. That it changes, it *flows*.

Zarathustra is that element within me that makes it impossible for any aspect, any quality, any ability or characteristic to be entirely me; it is that wind Jarosław Iwaszkiewicz calls "heavy, terrible, inhuman breathing, the kind not meant for our lungs." In other words, "Zarathustra" is our name for the fact that my existence, my life, cannot be reduced to anything that is.

Thus there is no simple answer to the question "Who is Zarathustra?"—we cannot say that Zarathustra is X, Y, or Z. "Zarathustra" is the name we give to the fact that "a hot wind is blowing," that "the ice is melting," that "the railings and footbridges are tumbling into the water," that the world is becoming, that time is flowing. Nietzsche has a name for this fact: "life." "Zarathustra" is that *strong wind*, it is the basis of life, the world insofar as it is becoming, changing, and flowing: the world that lives. In order to answer the question of who Zarathustra is, we must therefore tell a story, the story of some life, bearing in mind that this story, like life, never began and will never end, that, in other words, there was no Zarathustra before this story began (for it did not begin), and there will be no Zarathustra once it ends (for it will not end).

What has happened in this story can therefore never be settled completely: there is no one, ultimate answer to the question of the "meaning of life." And if "to understand" means "to find the ultimate answer," then life cannot be understood.

Hence it is no accident that the book *Thus Spoke Zarathustra* takes the form of a narrative. This is not merely a means to provide a colorful illustration of a doctrine that might just as well have been presented otherwise. It cannot be. There is no doctrine—a kind of "Teachings of Zarathustra"—independent of the narrative.

We can encounter the metaphors that organize this narrative elsewhere as well. First of all, in the Old and New Testaments. After all, we are already familiar with the metaphor of the "winds of freedom," with the metaphor of a breath or spirit that enlivens what is otherwise dead, whether from Genesis, which tells us how "God formed man of the dust of the ground, and breathed into his nostrils the breath of life; and man became a living soul" (Gen. 2:7); from the psalmist who sings of God and creation, "thou takest away their breath, they die, and return to their dust" (Ps. 104:29); or finally from the Prophet Ezekiel, who speaks of his vision of his dry bones restored to life:

> And when I beheld, lo, the sinews and the flesh came up upon
> them, and the skin covered them above: but there was no
> breath in them.
> Then said he unto me, Prophesy unto the wind, prophesy, and
> say unto the wind, Thus saith the Lord God; Come from
> the four winds, O breath, and breathe upon these slain, that
> they may live. (Ezek. 37:8–9)

In each of these instances the same term, *ruah*, appears in the sense of "breath" and "wind."

This *wind-spirit*, this *wind-Zarathustra*, clears away sleep, it drives us away from the warm hearth. "Rush, O wind, drive!" Nietzsche remarks. "Drive away my every satisfaction!"[43] It is this *wind* that does not allow us to be reconciled to the world as it is, to the world that invites us to adapt to it. It is the wind that proves that the world around me, the world that wants to enclose me within it, is incomplete, inconsistent, pitted. Kafka writes:

> Among the young women up in the park. No envy. Enough imag-
> ination to share their happiness, enough judgment to know I am
> too weak to have such happiness, foolish enough to see to the bot-
> tom of my own and their situation. Not foolish enough; there is a
> tiny crack there, and wind whistles through it and spoils the full
> effect.[44]

It is a wind that stirs unrest.

We should not confuse this unrest—the unrest stirred by the *wind-spirit*—with our terror before some external danger, with my unrest before an event I am anticipating. No, the kind of unrest symbolized by the wind (Zarathustra) does not come from outside but is in me, in each of us. It is an indispensable component of my existence, the unrest that arises from the fact that I am simply never completely myself, that I am not just some "A" or "B," that I am never completely at home, at rest, by the hearth, in my own identity. None of us is.

Consequently, no knowledge—about the eternal order of things, about the cosmos, about a frame of reference, purpose, or mission by which my life might find its ultimate meaning—can assuage me, none can soothe this unrest within me. Every attempt to obtain such knowledge is merely a projection of my weakness, an attempt to escape from life, a pointless effort to take shelter from the "strong wind." In the last years of his sane life, Nietzsche would write that he felt "[p]rofound aversion to reposing once and for all in any one total view of the world."[45]

From this it naturally follows that the "hot wind" threatens all identity, all sense, any institution that we take for our own, our very home. Be aware, therefore, that "the ice that still supports us has become thin: all of us feel the warm, uncanny breath of the thawing wind; where we still walk, soon, no one will be able to walk."[46]

The "warm wind" blows—and "everything is in flux." The "railings and bridges" have "fallen into the water." There is no escape from the *river of time* once it is released. Destroying what remains, the *wind of the spirit* simultaneously liberates us and opens us to new forms of life: it provides *unlimited freedom.*

And thus Zarathustra announces, "'Woe to us [as we are]! Hail to us [as we might be]! The thawing wind blows!'—thus preach in every street, my brothers."[47]

Here we can hear an echo of God to Jeremiah: "Proclaim all these words in the cities of Judah, and in the streets of Jerusalem" (Jer. 11:6).

We already know that the point here is not really to propagate any discovered truth (*"Eureka!* A body suspended in water...! etc."). News of the "hot wind" is a call to cast off everything we already are. In every house I build for myself, "The wind blew through my keyhole and said, 'Come!'"[48] "And the Spirit [. . .] say[s], Come!" (Rev. 22:17). In every house: and thus this "Come!" is not a call to cross from one place (some Sodom or Gomorrah) to another (where it is decent and pure). It is a call to abandon all houses. It is a call to nowhere.

In other words, the news that "the warm wind is blowing" is news of the end of all the things we know, about an end brought about by *wind, storm, spirit, hot breath*: by Zarathustra. Not eventually, in the future, someday, but any second, now, already, because everything that seems lasting to us, immutable, eternal, is just an ice sculpture melting under the breath of the "warm wind," in "the hot breath." This is news about the end of the world as it is—the frozen river—when the "warm wind" blows, when Zarathustra comes into being, when my life exhibits the strength to tear itself away from everything that is.

Come—this is the call for the Horsemen of the Apocalypse to ride (Rev. 6).

It is also possible to interpret this call, "Come," in a completely different way, as a summons to the eternal peace that awaits us, who have been exhausted by everyday cares. Saint Ignatius may have had something like this in mind when he says, according to the Catechism, "there is living water in me, water that murmurs and says within me: Come to the Father." The unrest from which I think Saint Ignatius wished to be liberated is the kind of unrest that we find in life: worry for our loved ones, fear of disease, the unrest brought on by curiosity, ambition, or desire. It is the kind of unrest that now we feel (usually), now we don't, so to have, in those rare moments free from it, a taste of eternal rest, beside the Father, and to long for it.

Whereas the unrest that Nietzsche describes is the *spirit*, the essence of life, an unrest that cannot be relieved, that has no end. It is because of this unrest that the world lives: it passes away. Jose Ortega y Gasset writes:

> It is not by accident that the wind has always been, for the human imagination, a symbol [. . .] of pure spirit [. . .]. The essence of wind is disquiet. So, too, is the essence of spirit, in one way or another, to be disquietude, a vibration beneath the dead mass of the universe.[49]

What, then, does Nietzsche's metaphor of the wind teach us?

First of all, that seeking out the source of time is also necessarily a narrative about the human condition. That the answer to the question "What is time?" requires a simultaneous response to the question "Who am I?" And at the same time that the necessary connection between these two questions, the impossibility of understanding the difference between past and future in isolation from my life or yours—from the life that is itself the *wind*, the *spirit*, the *breath* that destroys every given form, that overcomes every obstacle, subverts all foundations, in short, the life that time is—that the mutual dependency of these two questions renders an ultimate answer to each impossible. No concept can provide an answer to these questions: only life can answer them. With every step, gesture, or action I undertake, it answers them anew, and thus it can never do so completely. For, as D. H. Lawrence writes, "Only ideas are final, finite, static and single."[50] Not life.

Life is the effort to change, an effort capable of overcoming all resistance, and in this sense without end. Nietzsche also calls this by another name: "the will to power."

As we can see, the "I" in this context is not a known quantity. How could it be? It's not just that I don't know but that I *cannot* know completely who I am: this is, necessarily and irremediably, an open question. Life, this effort to overcome the world I have been born into, is always my own—or, to put it another way, the world is comprehensible only in the context of my effort to overcome it, of my effort to overcome what is—but this "I," too, can be defined only through this effort, and thus it can never be derived exclusively from previous achievements, never just as this or that. It can never be ultimately defined.

This strength hidden within me, this strong wind, is Zarathustra. Not somebody, not something, no institution. An ungraspable, indefinable, invisible force—like the wind.

Thus the metaphor of the wind leads us, I believe, a bit further than the metaphor of the flowing river. Or rather: it allows us a better understanding of that earlier metaphor, since unlike the metaphor of the river it no longer refers to the movement of certain objects, and it no longer suggests that the change of something into something else and the change of past into future are the same thing.

The wind, a symbol of the spirit—the hot wind, the warm breath, the power of my life, the "Zarathustra" within me—cracks and melts the ice that covers the river of time. It undermines all identity, any claim to a "being" beyond time, eternal, unchanging. *The hot wind:* the metaphor of the wind leads in this way to the subsequent metaphor, that of fire.

5

"With regard to fire or the soul being the animating principle for Heraclitus," Hegel writes, "we find an expression that may seem bizarre, namely: 'The driest souls are the best.'" He goes on to note that "'dry' here means 'fiery.' So [. . .] the driest soul is pure fire, [. . .] vitality itself."[51]

Dry breath, hot wind, fire: vitality itself.

"[The] world, the same for all," Heraclitus writes, "no god or man made but it always was, is, and will be, an everliving fire, being kindled in measures and being put out in measures."[52]

What Heraclitus meant is difficult to say. With regard to our problem, what is important as a point of departure is the interpretation of the Stoics, which was also popular later, in modified form, among the Church Fathers. According to the Stoics, "fire" is an element that suffuses the entire universe and is planted within it like a sponge in the depths of the sea (the simile belongs to Saint Augustine). Or, to put it another way, for the Stoics the world is like a volcano that is forever active, now and then erupting and destroying the mountain that has arisen out of the lava that has solidified around it.

In one of these Stoics, Seneca the Younger writing to Marcia, we read:

> For if the fate that all share can bring comfort to your sense of loss, realize that nothing will remain where now it stands, that time will

bring all things to ruin and take all things with it. And not only humankind will be its plaything (for how trifling a part of Fortune's realm is man?) but places, countries, and areas of the universe. Whole mountains it will level and, elsewhere, it will force up new rocks into soaring crags; it will drink up seas, divert rivers, and, destroying communication between nations, it will overthrow the association and commerce of the human race; elsewhere it will swallow cities in enormous chasms, shake them with earthquakes, and from the depths below send up pestilential vapors; it will overwhelm with floods the inhabited world and, deluging the earth, will kill all creatures, and in mighty conflagration will scorch and burn everything mortal. And when the time comes for the world to be destroyed so that it may assume new life, these things by their own strength will bring destruction on themselves, and stars will clash with stars, and all that now shines in orderly arrangement will burn in a single fire, as all matter is consumed in flames.

We, too, we happy souls that have gained the lot of eternal life, when God shall decide to build the universe anew, shall constitute a tiny addition to this destruction, as all things collapse in ruin, and shall be transformed once more into our previous elements.[53]

The world, like your pain, your fears, your sadness, your memories, Marcia—the world will one day perish in a universal, ultimate blaze. Nothing that is mortal will remain there—"What stands high, must fall," Seneca writes—all that will be left is that which is good enough to be eternal.[54] In this manner, the apocalyptic fires will purify the world and restore it to its primal innocence that it might then arise again from the ashes.

There is therefore no reason to grieve excessively for what is lost (as you have, Marcia, for your beloved son). For despair and sorrow, too, will pass away. This is the common fate of all people, of all things. When you understand this—and turn your mind and your life toward that which is lasting and eternal—you will find solace, you will discover joy.

In this "conflagration of the world" the Church Fathers (regardless of whether they shared the Stoics' views on its periodic return) later recognized the *conflagration of the Last Judgment*, the fire that awaits sinners in order to destroy the stain of sin within them and purify their souls, preparing them to meet God. Here they might have invoked Paul's letter to the Corinthians:

Now if any man build [with his life] upon this foundation
   gold, silver, precious stones, wood, hay, stubble;

> Every man's work shall be made manifest: for the day shall
>   declare it, because it shall be revealed by fire; and the fire
>   shall try every man's work of what sort it is.
> If any man's work abide which he hath built thereupon, he
>   shall receive a reward.
> If any man's work shall be burned, he shall suffer the loss: but
>   he himself shall be saved; yet so as by fire. (1 Cor. 3:12–15)

Origen then comments:

> For when from our evils we cause vices and passions to come upon
> God's creation, which is good from the beginning, then we are
> mixing brass, tin, and lead with silver and gold. Fire then be-
> comes necessary to purify it. And that is the reason one must take
> great care that, when we come to that fire, we may pass through it
> unscathed. Like gold, silver, and precious stone that are without a
> trace of adulteration, may we not so much burn in the conflagra-
> tion as be tested.[55]

And the Prophet Isaiah warns that "under his [the sinner's] glory he
shall kindle a burning like the burning of a fire. And the light of Israel
shall be for a fire, and his Holy One for a flame: and it shall devour his
thorns and his briers in one day" (Isa. 10:16–17).

The fire they are talking about is the test, the measure of our lives. It
separates that which ingratiates us to God—and which is accordingly lasting and eternal within us, that which the fire will not destroy (gold, silver,
precious stones)—from all the rest, of baser provenance (wood, thatch,
straw, copper, tin and lead, thorns and briers), which is cast to the flames.
The part of us that is truly important, the trace of God, is safe, even in the
fire; this is the part of us that, as Origen says, clings to God's Word like a
hot iron to the whiteness of fire.[56] Insofar as we are made in God's image,
we need not fear being consumed by the flames.

Knowing this brings us security, peace, and consolation.

In this way, the fire cleanses us, it heals us of being sick with the world.
It destroys the evil within us, for it is only this evil that is subject to being
consumed:

> And the devil that deceived them was cast into the lake of fire
>   and brimstone, where the beast and the false prophet are.
>   [...]
> And death and hell were cast into the lake of fire. This is the
>   second death.

> And whosoever was not found written in the book of life was
> cast into the lake of fire. (Rev. 20:10, 14–15)

The fire destroys evil. Or: what passes away is unworthy of lasting, is evil. Time as such is evil. Death is evil. After we are showered in flames, all that remains of us will be that which is good and eternal, that which does not know time.

Driving upward, dancing between heaven and earth, the fire's flames are (according to this interpretation) like human hands reaching up, begging to be plucked out of time, dread, fear, death, into the heaven of the eternal and the peaceful.

But might Heraclitus have had something else in mind? Might we not also interpret the Old and New Testaments in some other way?

Hegel writes: "But it is also spoken that Heraclitus spoke of a world conflagration or, as we picture it, of the world perishing in flames. But we can see at once that this burning-up is not the end of the world as a whole but only expresses the general life of the universe as a whole."[57]

The fire, Hegel tells us, is a metaphor for life, life and nothing more. Hegel writes that "fire is physical; it is restlessness. Although fire is, it is the consuming of itself as well as of its others. [. . .] [I]t is not lasting, [it is] physical restlessness or process."[58] It is precisely on this that life depends, that it is constantly changing, that it is constantly becoming. Life is not change from one thing into another; the point here is not that life is one thing at one moment and something else later, like an actor or a swindler. Each form of life necessarily contains some relation to something else (which is to say, to itself as other, past or future), and no identity that we can discover in life can be understood without the diversity contained within the very notion of identity—that it passes away.

Becoming, passing—Hegel argues that this does not happen to us, though it might just as well not happen. It is not a river that one can step into and not step out of later. Becoming, passing—this is inscribed in the concept of every form of life individually. No life can be understood otherwise, divorced from the fact that it is becoming.

So, Hegel continues, is it not some changing, becoming, passing subject that allows us to understand change, becoming, and passing. It merely seems to us that we understand change when we relate it to two states of any given subject: a "before" and an "after," fat Mrs. Smith and the post-weight-treatment-yet-still-the-same Mrs. Smith. No, Hegel asserts: diversity, reference to another form of itself, and thus change, becoming, process, constitute the meaning of each particular form.

This is why, according to Hegel, this fire, this "restlessness," works as a metaphor for the very process of life, for life as a process.

In this interpretation, "fire" is no longer our name for some event (occasional or otherwise), for the end of the world (whether onetime or endlessly repeating); it is not an intervention from outside (in relation to life) that separates the wheat from the chaff, the gold from the straw, what passes from what is eternal, from what truly is. "Fire" is now the name just for what truly is, for life itself.

Furthermore, this "fire" is also not a process external to me, its subject; it is not something that happens to me, a trial I am necessarily put through in order to prove my worth. No, Hegel asserts: I myself am the life-fire, this is my identity. Or, rather, "I" is actually non-identity, it is change, becoming, passing—the passing of everything around me, and my passing as well. One thing cannot be understood without the other.

"Fire": becoming, and thus "being" and "non-being" at the same time, not "something" that is but existence itself, being itself. Comparing life, comparing existence to the fire, we expose the fact that it cannot be understood in relation to "something," whatever it may be, that it cannot be comprehended with regard to some identity, as identical with itself. Because it actually isn't. Because each moment of life is torn, non-identical, incurably diverse within: it is becoming. Which is precisely what it means that it "is."

Hegel had a good grasp of this tearing, this diversity, this wound within existence. At the same time, he tried to mend it, to make it whole, to heal it, for he believed this to be the only way of rendering it comprehensible. As a result, according to Hegel, becoming—mine and the world's—turns out to be a process that somehow begins somewhere and ends somewhere else, a process whose particular elements, from start to finish, are bound together by an internal logic (the "dialectic"), thus forming a comprehensible whole. What is other is thereby absorbed, assimilated. Difference, the tear in existence, its becoming—these are placed in a system of reference within which they can be grasped and understood. Instances of becoming are indeed, for Hegel, no longer differentiated the same way as things are; indeed, he does not identify the difference between one moment of life and another with the difference between two objects (like the fat Mrs. Smith and the Mrs. Smith who has dropped the extra pounds); indeed, he does not regard the "other," that to which every moment of existence refers, as "another object," "another content," yet he nonetheless binds this otherness, to which each moment of my existence necessarily relates, this other side of that existence, through (dialectical) logic, to what is given, making them a single whole. He captures otherness, difference, in the net of rationality. He domesticates it.

In this way, he heals the tear in life. Or, to put it another way, the tear, the diversity within existence, because of which "to be" means "to become," is, for Hegel too, a wound that demands to be healed, a pathology awaiting treatment: time is an infection within being.

When we peer deep into the flame's dance, Hegel seems to be saying, we discover a certain pattern within it, a certain regularity, a certain logic. The fire, too—and thus becoming as well—obeys a certain logic, it burns according to a certain order. Which is the very thing that allows us to understand it.

Hegel therefore also ultimately understands the fire—becoming, change, time—from the point of view of identity, order, unity; in his eyes, too, the fire symbolizes a (necessary and thus also comprehensible) lack, disruption, disintegration (of identity, order, unity). And Hegel, too, believes that we can grasp life through knowledge and in this way find the plenitude threatened by time, find totality, find peace—find solace. For Hegel, too, knowledge can heal the wounds inflicted by time.

Heidegger made the next attempt to understand our metaphor, to understand the word "fire" as Heraclitus uses it. We should consider, Heidegger writes, "that fire illuminates, glows, rages, and opens a sort of space—but also that it consumes, dies down, fades, smolders, and goes out. Fire burns, and in so doing it separates light from dark; bursting into flames binds and separates light and dark."[59] In this way, the bursting into flames, the ignition of fire, suddenly—for can something burst "gradually" into flames? Can this be a "slow" process?—creates a "space" in which something can manifest itself. In the blink of an eye, a single moment—like lightning—bursting into flames distinguishes the darkness from the light; it allows the words "darkness" and "light" to assume their meaning, just now, in mutual distinction. It is this moment of ignition, this lightning, that, according to Heidegger, defines the essence of fire. And Heidegger says that Heraclitus was already aware of this: "The thunder-bolt [lightning] steers the universe."[60] "By 'lightning,'" Heidegger adds, "Heraclitus means eternal fire."[61]

In Heidegger's interpretation, the fire, the flame's play, symbolizes life as play, in which all difference is constantly disappearing and reemerging, and which by the same token creates and destroys the conditions for the possibility of everything that is. This play, irreducible to anything else, cannot be explained by any external factors. It is play that unfolds according to no plan, in which there is no internal logic; it is diversification, which never stands still, which never reaches its end. Life as "fire"—this is the unity that does not remove differences, that does not posit a common denominator between them: the flame's play symbolizes a diversification whose particular elements, that which is different within it, are not joined by any logic, any dialectic, any rules.

In such life-fire, there can be no remainder, nothing can survive, not even the fire itself; such fire is not an immutable structure that we somehow know, it is not a system of reference (and, in this sense, a "bridge," a "railing") that allows us to understand what is going on within it.

"Fire" is now—if we are following Hegel and Heidegger, and not the Stoics—a metaphorical expression for how the world exists, a metaphorical response to the question of what it means that something "is." It is life, which cannot be encompassed by any logic, by any knowledge (now we are following Heidegger beyond Hegel)—the life that is raging behind the ostensibly immutable forms of things. Nietzsche writes that "had you keener eyesight, you would see that everything is in motion: just as burning paper curls, so too does everything change and curl thereby."[62]

It is just this kind of fire that the Nietzschean Zarathustra brings into the world.

At the beginning of Nietzsche's narrative, Zarathustra descends from the mountains into a valley. "[W]ould you now carry your fire into the valleys?" Zarathustra is asked by the hermit he meets on the road.[63] Indeed, this is precisely Zarathustra's intention, to bring people fire, his own fire, the fire that he himself is. To ignite the souls of the people. "What I teach I have drawn out of my fire."[64] The doctrine "comes out of your own fire."[65] From the fire that wants to flow "to spirit."[66]

Fire poured into the spirit: here is the birth of the hot wind: "The wise man," Nietzsche-Zarathustra says about himself in an unpublished note, "is like a great, blazing inferno that summons its own wind, a wind that feeds it and carries it farther."[67]

Such a wise man feels the heat of the flames beneath the cool surface of phenomena, who, as Nietzsche writes in *The Gay Science*, feels "the heat in things that feel cold to everybody else."[68]

Zarathustra wants to be a "fire [. . .] for all dry souls."[69] For "dry" souls and thus for those that submit to the fire, for kindling. (Let us recall Hegel's reference to Heraclitus.) "To me you are dry grass and prairie," Nietzsche-Zarathustra notes, "but I wish to make of you a raging wildfire."[70] You are "like dry grass and prairie—and verily, [. . .] languishing even more than for water—for *fire*."[71] Much like the "bones" of the dead, "dry" and cast into the valley and waiting for God to restore them to life in the vision of the Prophet Ezekiel (Ezek. 37:1–14).

"My book," Nietzsche wrote to a friend regarding *Thus Spoke Zarathustra*, "is like a volcano."[72] It is supposed to issue hot lava that will scorch the soul of everyone who reads and understands it. (The metaphor of the volcano is the same one the Stoics used, but how different the interpretation is! For the Stoics, the volcano was a metaphor for the order of the world, which arises periodically from the flames that consume all that is mortal. For Nietzsche, the volcano is Zarathustra, who awakens the force of being within me, who ignites my soul and thereby ignites the world, causing everything I touch, and not just this thing or another, to become, not just to be.)

In this way, by setting our souls on fire, Zarathustra wants to give us life, to liberate the life within us. "Life," Nietzsche writes in *The Gay Science*, "means for us constantly transforming all that we are into light and flame."[73]

Zarathustra sets our souls on fire, summoning the life within us. In other words, Zarathustra is the fire that rages in us when we are alive. It is a dangerous fire: no form of humanity achieved thus far, no shape of life until now, no fashion of this world, no institution can resist it. Everything that has heretofore determined us as people begins to shake and crumble, comes into question. So, too, with what we hold most dear, with what we love most, with what is most our own—and these things especially, for it is precisely that which is most dear, most loved, most our own that binds us most powerfully to what is, to the here and now. "Shatter your heart, full of admiration and honor, at precisely the moment when it is most bound to something": this is what Zarathustra calls on us to do.[74] He calls on us but on himself as well: he "shatters his own heart, full of love for his friends, for his animals, for everything he has held dear."[75]

"May the divine Word [. . .] burn out our souls," Origen writes, "so that as we listen we might say: 'Did not our hearts burn within us?' (Luke 24:32)."[76]

You must therefore "cast off not just the chains that weigh you down," Nietzsche warns, but "the time must come for you to flee from what you hold most dear. [. . .] You must be ready to abandon your woman, your country, everything you find beneficial, your closest-held belief."[77]

As though seconding Nietzsche, D. H. Lawrence writes of this moment when hearts burst:

> So they go down to the sea, the sea-born people. The Vikings are wandering again. Homes are broken up. Cross the seas, cross the seas, urges the heart. Leave love and home. Leave love and home. Love and home are a deadly illusion. Woman, what have I to do with thee? It is finished. *Consummatum est.* The crucifixion into humanity is over. Let us go back to the fierce, uncanny elements: the corrosive vast sea. Or fire.[78]

Only this fire will give you freedom.

Lawrence writes of sailors setting sail; sailors are Zarathustra's favorite audience as well. Not by coincidence: a seaman, like a tightrope walker or an artist, lives dangerously. These professions require a willingness to cast aside what is given and to risk the unknown, whatever that unknown might bring with it. It is for just this reason that the life of the sailor, tightrope walker, or artist is for Nietzsche a testament to life as it is. It is a testament to the unrest inscribed in life, the fire raging within it, a fire that cannot be extinguished—so long as I am alive.

And thus, Nietzsche writes in *The Gay Science*, "Build your cities on the slopes of Vesuvius! Send your ships into uncharted seas! Live at war with your peers and yourselves!"[79] This is a call to no one in particular but to everyone, an appeal to the life in each of us, a life that cannot be enclosed in any form, in any characteristic, in any identity.

This is Zarathustra's task: to kindle the fire that is smoldering inside us, to liberate the life within us that is caked in some given form. His words are supposed to be like embers, like burning lava, like the hot wind that melts whatever ice has encased the river of time, like a blaze on the arid step, like the fire that consumes the dry bones of the dead, like the hammer that smashes petrified, long-since-dead forms of life.

When I, following Nietzsche, speak of "freedom" and "liberation" in this context—of the kind of freedom or liberation that Zarathustra's fire brings us—I naturally do not have my own freedom in mind: the point here is not Krzysztof Michalski's liberation from what have been the oppressive conditions of his life. Nor do I mean the liberation of the true, perhaps hidden, humanity within me, the essence of the human species, the potential I could develop in order to come closer to an ideal of humanity, were it not for all these awful circumstances (for example, man's oppression of man). No, the freedom I have in mind is absolute, and thus it has no measure. It is the freedom of life, overcoming, burning away all obstacles, the freedom of life that blasts away, that burns all identity.

Man (man as we know him, man as we can imagine him, any form of mankind) is therefore, as Zarathustra tells us, "something that must be overcome."[80] Not in order to achieve some ideal, not to replace man with some other, better species (the "overman"). No, for there is no measure for this overcoming; it occurs for the sake of no one and nothing but is an expression of the absolute freedom of life that, as fire, burns every form of humanity, all measures of man, every ideal, all identity. This overcoming is a step into the unknown, into nothingness. "I hold the hammer in my hand," Nietzsche commands the mature, happy Zarathustra to say, "that will overcome man."[81] And he wants to teach us "How One Philosophizes with a Hammer"—the subtitle of *Twilight of the Idols*.

(A bit later Kafka would write to a friend, "A book must be the axe for the frozen sea inside us.")[82]

Is this not similar to what God tells us through the lips of Jeremiah? "Is not my Word like as a fire? saith the Lord; and like a hammer that breaketh the rock in pieces?" (Jer. 23:29).

Of course, not everyone wants to follow such a call. It is hard to expect that words that burn through the soul, words that engulf the heart in flames—and thus words that threaten everything we hold dear, everything we love—to be greeted by general enthusiasm. Zarathustra wants to be a blaze and thus a danger "for all dry souls"—and this is why the hermit asks Zarathustra, carrying fire into the city, "Do you not fear to be punished as an arsonist?"[83]

And, in fact, Zarathustra's very first speech to the townspeople crowded in the marketplace is met with a lack of enthusiasm and open hostility: "When Zarathustra had spoken thus, one of the people cried: 'Now we have heard enough [. . .]!' [. . .] And all the people laughed at Zarathustra."[84]

Is it even possible for Zarathustra to find a receptive audience? Indeed, Nietzsche believes that there are specific historical reasons for modern culture's resistance to Zarathustra's call, but Nietzsche's Zarathustra is supposed to be a danger not only for this culture, not only for us. Every culture, Nietzsche notes, "is like the thin skin of an apple covering the *chaos* glowing within."[85] We have all been, we are all, we will all be like the "dry grass" waiting for the fire. Every culture thus constructs defensive mechanisms; every person, every parched soul, desires water, protection, consolation.

"And it came to pass, when Jesus had ended these sayings," Matthew tells us, "the people were astonished"—Luther translates this as "shocked"—"at his doctrine" (Matt. 7:28).

The crowd mocks Zarathustra, is shocked and scandalized by his words, because Zarathustra (Zarathustra the "hot wind," Zarathustra the "arsonist," Zarathustra the "hammer") wants to ignite hearts, to ignite souls, to smash everything one holds most dear. For Zarathustra brings unrest and risk with him—freedom—while the people he meets want to be left alone. It is on precisely this need, the need to "make society secure against thieves and fireproof," that, according to Nietzsche, modern society is built.[86] For modern man, Nietzsche writes in *Daybreak*, "security is now worshipped as the supreme divinity."[87]

"Our steps sound too lonely through the streets," Zarathustra tells the hermit he meets in the forest about his contemporaries. "And what if at night, in their beds, they hear a Man walk by long before the sun has risen—they probably ask themselves, Where is the thief going?"[88]

Was it not this same worry, this same terror, this same need to shut the door, to guard one's sleep, that Saint Paul had in mind when he wrote, "the day of the Lord so cometh as a thief in the night" (1 Thess. 5:2)?

This is why Nietzsche states that today's false prophets are those who deceive us with the illusion of eternal peace and convince us to base our social order on this illusion. Because eternal peace is a mirage inimical to life, to life that is in fact necessarily unrest, risk, openness to the unknown and the new. The Prophet Ezekiel may have had similar false prophets in mind, those who lead people astray, saying "Peace; and there was no peace" (Ezek. 13:10). But—"Thus saith the Lord God; Woe to the women that sew pillows to all armholes, and make kerchiefs on the heads of every stature to hunt souls!" (Ezek. 13:18). And so (God says, according to Ezekiel, to us all): "Your kerchiefs also will I tear" (Ezek. 13:21).

Nietzsche faults his contemporaries for lacking the courage needed to understand Zarathustra's words: "You lack the courage to immolate yourselves, you fear your own destruction; thus you will never become something new. What lifts us up, what gives us color, dress, Power—let it all be ash tomorrow."[89] But could anyone, at any time, have an easier time understanding this? Can this kind of courage—the courage of self-immolation, the courage to engage in endless war with oneself—ever be the natural behavior of any kind of human being?

Everything I am, everything we are—Nietzsche tells us through Zarathustra's lips—every form of the world is a future sacrifice to the fire, future ashes ("our whole world is ash," he notes).[90] "Had you keener eyesight," you would see the tongues of this fire among the people laughing in the marketplace, in the background of our daily rat race, and then it would seem so much more important, so much more absorbing. Thus Zarathustra says, "Woe unto this great city! And I wish I already saw the pillar of fire in which it will be burned."[91] The critique of modern culture (of the society secure against fire and thieves) is here intertwined with a message about human nature (that a person lives only insofar as he overcomes himself). In this way these words of Christ are so close to those of Zarathustra: "Woe unto you that laugh now!" (Luke 6:25). And these: "I am come to send fire on the earth; and what will I, if it be already kindled?" (Luke 12:49).

Zarathustra: the "hot wind" that is invisible to our eyes, the wind that kindles the fire of life and ignites the world as it is with this fire: the spirit. A flame that exterminates everything but also a liberation, the liberation of life that is constantly changing and thus always new. It is the "pillar of fire" that heralds the end—to those who have the courage to know, to those who are ready to go to sea—but also a beginning. "And though I am usually invisible," Zarathustra says of himself, "I wish to show myself on the masts of solitary sailors and explorers—as a flame."[92]

And once again in the Bible, this time from the Old Testament: "And the Lord went before them [. . .] to lead them the way; and by night in a pillar of fire" (Exod. 13:21).

So, then, what has our analysis of the fire given us?

It joins together all three metaphors we have discussed: the *fire* poured into the spirit gives rise to a hot *wind* that melts the ice, thereby freeing the *river of time*.

Above all else, the fire turns out to be a metaphor for the radical discontinuity of human existence. Insofar as I am dry grass waiting for the fire that will burn me away, insofar as the essence of my life is the fire raging somewhere in the ground beneath it, which might engulf me, all of me, in its flames at any moment, a fire that does not allow me to stand still for long, to be resigned, to fall asleep, that orders me to leave my love and my home—insofar as I am such a fire, each moment of my life is a chance at a new beginning, a chance to begin all over again, from zero. This is an absolutely new beginning, birth from the ashes, or better yet, from the nothingness of everything else. Strictly speaking, the word "new" is out of place here, since the term "new" establishes a distinction from that which is "old," "ancient," "till now," whereas the life-fire begins in this very moment, completely anew, and thus has nothing "old" or "ancient" in the background, nothing from which such a distinction could be made.

When I speak of "two different moments" in my life (the walk I took yesterday, today's visit to the doctor), I have in mind moments of another kind (units of time placed one after the other: instants) and differences of another kind (two states of things). Then I am assuming a kind of continuity (instants that follow one another), and I am also assuming something that succumbs to change (my biography) within that continuity. Whereas the metaphor of the fire demonstrates the disruption of this continuity, it exposes my life as an absolute non-continuity, absolute diversification, absolute beginning, in every moment.

If we want to find an answer to the question of time, of the source and nature of passing, then we should seek it—so, I believe, the metaphor of fire instructs us—precisely in the unrepeatable, singular moment of life and not by comparing two (or more) instants, two states of affairs. For such a comparison will at best show us the difference between a wrinkled face and a smooth one, between a pimple and none, but it will not allow us to find in that face any trace of the fact that this face is no more, that it has already passed away. In order to recognize that the young face in the photograph "was," that it no longer "is," we must somehow know what "was" means. The difference between two moments—the walk, the visit to the doctor—will not explain to us why that walk "was," why that visit to the doctor "is" right now. Passing, becoming, and time are a different kind of difference than any objective diversity, any diversification of moments. Passing, becoming, and time are the internal diversification of this single—though not one of many—moment, a diversification that precedes all identity (and thus both the walk and the visit to the doctor), the moment in flames, burning all the way down, "laps[ing]," as Borges writes, "into nothingness as if blasted by a lightless fire."[93]

And it is only in this sense that it "is."

Two moments can differ from one another, like the "past" from the "present" or the "future," insofar as this difference (time) has already been established. Insofar as every moment—discrete, singular, "a" moment outside of the context of other moments—"becomes," "passes." Insofar as life is torn, radically discontinuous. Without this radical discontinuity of life, without this unique kind of diversity uncovered by the metaphor of fire, time would be incomprehensible.

This moment of existence—unique, singular, though not one among many—is the moment in which I find myself, it is my presence in the world. By "moment," I do not mean "this moment" (today) as distinct from "that one" (yesterday, tomorrow). Rather, I mean *how I am*. And it is precisely because of the fact that I am this way and not another—that, existing, *I burn*—that all of these yesterdays, todays, and tomorrows become possible.

Time is thus not independent of what I do or what people do. Time erupts in my every gesture, in my every movement, my every step: my life, in each of its moments, undermines the world I have encountered and challenges everything that "is," that "lasts." Time flows, the world passes, thanks to the flames of my life.

In other words, insofar as "being" means "becoming," the only sense that "being" and "existence" can have for me is that which my life imparts to them. "Being" and "life" cannot be separated from one another. My life, a human life, is the only path toward understanding becoming, toward understanding the constant becoming of existence.

Let us remember, however, that when I say "life," whether "my" or "human life," I am not referring to historical, sociological, or biological concepts. I am not speaking of the "human species," of "human history," or of what we already know about the specifics of human social behavior. Or rather, not just about those things. When I say "human life," I am not trying to differentiate it from the life of an ant or a camel; I do not presume to know what a human being is. Because I don't. I cannot. When I say "human life," I am not presupposing any "subject" of that life who would make that process, "life," comprehensible (this is a "life" different from, for example, that of an ant or camel). The "life" I mean here has no subject, or perhaps it has no one subject. In each moment of life its subject, some subject, is re-created anew. It is a life that, at every moment, challenges every form of humanity, as well as every biological, social, or historical form. In fact, life questions humanity itself, everything that we take for its indispensable essence, no matter when, where, or who. *Man is something that must be overcome.*

Why, then, do we call life "mine," "ours," or "human" at all? Because the "life" we are discussing goes on in our actions, in our gestures, in what we do. Only here. So much so that the meaning of that little word, "we," is open, never completely definable.

It is not I who am the subject of life, but the Zarathustra in me. Zarathustra, who is not a tailor, a carpenter, a clergyman, a philosopher, or a

customs officer—who is not a someone, one way or the other. But Zarathustra is also potentially each of us, insofar as there is in each of us the
power to overcome everything that is. Insofar as the life we live is "fire."

As we can see, the attempt to understand the time that flows necessarily
leads us to the question of man, and on the other hand the story of human
nature is inextricably intertwined with the story of the world that becomes.
"Time is the substance of which I am made," Borges writes. "Time is a
river that sweeps me along, but I am the river; [. . .] it is a fire that consumes me, but I am the fire."[94] I? Who is this "I"? "The fire [. . .] breaking
apart, falling to ashes," Stanisław Brzozowski writes in his *Memoirs*, "these
constant actions, never a bottom, never a harbor, [. . .] this is a human
being."[95] This is the only possible answer.

As we know, to this fundamental, essential characteristic of life as we
live it Nietzsche applies the term *will to power*. In *Zarathustra*, Nietzsche
says that the will to power is "the scalding scourge of the hardest among
the hardhearted," that it is "the dark flame of living pyres," that it is "the
earthquake that breaks and breaks open everything worm-eaten and hollow; [. . .] the lightning-like question mark beside premature answers."[96]
In short, that it characterizes life as an effort at change that knows no insurmountable opposition, at change that cannot be encompassed by any
rational schema, in any design (from here to there)—at change that dis-
rupts all continuity, any linkage between what has come before and what
might come after, that tears each moment of life from the context of other
moments, and thus also from the context of time as a succession of instants, as the difference between "yesterday" and "today."

Life as flame, the moment consumed by fire, disconnected from what
was or will be. In this sense: eternity.

Life, the will to power, which overcomes everything that the succession
of instants gradually accumulates around me, the continuity of time, making me this, and not that, Michalski, not Mrs. Smith—the effort that
places me on the plane of eternity.

"This infinitely small moment," Nietzsche writes, "is the higher reality
and truth, a glimmer on the eternal river."[97]

"A glimmer on the eternal river": eternity as a dimension of time, without which time is unthinkable—this is the only eternity. There is no other.
Eternity as infinite duration, eternity as the negation of time: this is an
illusion. "[A]nd all that is 'permanent,'" Zarathustra says, "is also a mere
parable."[98]

And one more note from Nietzsche, from the same period: "Against the
value of that which remains eternally the same [. . .], the values of the
briefest and most transient, the seductive flash of gold on the belly of
the serpent *vita*."[99] For Nietzsche, as for Heidegger, "fire" is an image
of discontinuity, of suddenness, the instantaneousness of lightning. This

lightning-fire, irrevocably inscribed in my life, rends its fabric and makes each moment therein a potential new beginning, and in this way places that moment beyond any connection with "yesterday" and "tomorrow," in the perspective of eternity. In this way, the lightning-fire makes life flow rather than stand still and makes the difference between past and future possible.

If, however, the "fire" of life tears apart the continuity of instants, making each of them a single moment of its own, an absolute beginning, is it any wonder that life—and therefore time and passing—hurts? After all, the continuity of instants constitutes my life as I know it, everything that I, Krzysztof Michalski, am, everything that I hold dear, my memories, my biography. Breaking this continuity, tearing me out of the context in which I have become who I am, causes pain. This pain is identical, then, with life; it is a pain without which life would be unimaginable. The "fire" that tears apart the continuity of instants that are slowly constructing my house, the meaning of my life, my identity, opens a deep "wound" within me, a wound that cannot be healed so long as I am alive. A wound that hurts.

How different these words, "wound" and "pain," seem to us now, as opposed to what they had meant to Hegel. True, then and now, time tears the continuity of my life apart: each moment of life is a fire that consumes everything that is given, a lightning bolt that hits everything that is. It hurts. But now—as opposed to in Hegel—it is not a pain for which there can be any treatment. It is not a trauma that must be soothed. This pain, this trauma, is life itself. Origen writes:

> But fire has a twofold power: to illuminate, and to burn.... [. . .] But this fire which Jesus came to cast upon the earth really does "enlighten every man coming into the world" (Cf. John 1:9), and yet it also has a burning quality to it, as they profess who say: "Did not our hearts burn within us while he opened to us the scriptures?" (Luke 24:32)[100]

The heart, when it burns, hurts. But what kind of heart doesn't burn?
Lou Andreas-Salomé once wrote of Nietzsche as follows:

> Nietzsche's genius derived from the vivacious fire behind his thoughts, which showered those thoughts in such glorious light, such that no logical insight could have done.[101]

And earlier in the same study:

> [The] greater clarity, the bright light of knowledge demand [of Nietzsche] a glowing soul—yet this glow gives off no pleasant

warmth, but rather must wound with its singing fire and burning flames: [. . .] suffering is necessary here.[102]

But is it possible to live with this "knowledge"? In fire? Can one live, ignoring the cool surface of things, "the thin skin of an apple" covering the embers, the burning fire? How can one deal with such an eruption of fire, a fire that consumes everything, in a life where the main thing is not to be late, to catch the falling wine glass, not to forget to pick up some butter on the way home? How can one live with the open, festering wound of torn, broken continuity, from birth till now, from yesterday to today, from the bend in the road to here, this door, through which I'm about to walk in order to buy that butter? The continuity of life that constitutes who I am and thanks to which I gain what is near and dear, dearest, to me?

Of course, it is not possible that such a life is not possible. "The ultimate truth [. . .] cannot be assimilated."[103]

"Who among us shall dwell with the everlasting fire? who among us shall dwell with everlasting burnings?" (Isa. 33:14).

Except: "Saints live *in* flames" (E. M. Cioran).[104] And indeed, "After the death of the holy Joseph of Copertino," Piero Camporesi quotes an eighteenth-century hagiography, "according to custom":

> death having been legally certified by public authority, the body was then opened and embalmed with sweet-smelling herbs and spices. The surgeon found in the process not only that the pericardium was dry but also that the ventricles were devoid of blood, indeed the heart itself was dry and desiccated, not through the natural burning of a fever, but through the supernatural flame of Divine Love; a phenomenon which the surgeon had encountered previously during his experience and therefore attributed in this case.[105]

But we mere mortals need continuity in order to live, we need knowledge (which assumes a world that is, not one that burns), passive assimilation, sleep. To live, we assume one or another form, we take on features, characters, institutions, and we become encysted in the world, facts, hard reality. We look on time with mistrust.

With the help of metaphors that are more powerful than any of their interpretations, Nietzsche wants to demonstrate that this is not the ultimate reality. Life, Nietzsche tells us, also conceals within itself an absolute unrest, thorns that cannot be removed from one's sides, nor assimilated: this unrest, this thorn, is its essence. Nietzsche wishes to show us the flames behind everything we see and know. He wants to show us the blaze that consumes everything, the embers beneath the cool surface of things. He wants to teach us how "[to transform] all that we are into light and flame."

But this does not mean that Nietzsche wants to show us some other world, the kind of world that is concealed behind the (alleged) illusion that surrounds us, behind all these walls we cannot hit our heads through, these sidewalks on which I bang my knees, the stones that might hit me in the head—another world, which would allow us to flee from our responsibility for the one we live in, to relativize it. No, of course not. There is no other world. The very notion of another world hidden behind the one about which we can have some knowledge is nonsense. There is only that which surrounds us. There is nothing to be seen "beneath it." The flames, the embers—these are not a glimpse into another world; the fire we are discussing here is invisible. When I say that Nietzsche wants to show us this fire, I am using the term metaphorically. This fire is burning here, and here alone: this fire is life, our lives, the life I am living here and now.

What is at stake here is not knowledge of another world. Nietzsche is not trying to expand our knowledge about the world, to add another bit of information to what we already know. The "fire" is not a structure, nor is it the order of the world, which can be known and described. The "fire" is not a potential object of knowledge. "Knowing the fire," which would supplant other knowledge we possess, is impossible. Rather, the metaphor of fire is supposed to teach us that everything I do, each moment of my life, conceals a lightning bolt that burns everything I know. In other words, that my life contains a potential for boundless freedom, that it is unconditionally creative. And as a creative power, Nietzsche notes, "all knowing must also be unknowing."[106]

Life is like fire, and thus each moment of my life refers not only to other moments but also to the nothingness of them all, to eternity—an eternity that cannot be known. This radical discontinuity challenges everything I know in every moment of my life.

Thus one cannot know the fire of life; knowledge of the eternity that penetrates all things is impossible. Only our unrest, only the pain of life— this indispensable horizon of all our knowledge, the necessary ground of all knowledge as our own—brings it to the fore. In this regard, knowledge is ashes. Words are ashes. As Kafka would write:

> And if from this ash a flame will rise, bright and hot, great and strong, and if you stare enraptured into this flame, then.… But these pure thoughts cannot be written by a clumsy hand and the rough strikes of instruments. One can only write these white, modest scraps.[107]

VIII

Eternal Love

"WHAT IS LOVE?" Plotinus asks in the *Enneads*. "A God, a Celestial Spirit, a state of mind?"[1]

Love: how numerous its forms, how various are all those aspects and moments of life to which we apply that word. Any attempt to reduce them to a common denominator would be foolish. Among this enormous diversity there is also the meaning I will now address: eternal love.

This love is a trace of eternity. It is the presence of eternity in time. It is the revelation of a certain kind of "now": here, under the apple tree, when I ask you to "set me as a seal upon thy heart, as a seal upon thine arm" (Song of Solomon 8:6)—this is the discovery of that "now" which signifies "always." The suspension of time. If "now" means as much as "always," the difference between "now" and "yesterday," "now" and "tomorrow"—and thus time itself—loses its meaning. Here, under the apple tree, past and future disappear, and thus death loses its sting: "for love is strong as death."

Such love sows immortality into the lives of any Dick or Jane, into your life and mine, into life between birth and death. It thrusts the seed of immortality into the ground of everyday life. Such love makes everything that binds you and me to time lose all meaning and vanish. Only you remain—and I. "Who is she that looketh forth as the morning, fair as the moon, clear as the sun, and terrible as any army with banners?" (Song of Solomon 6:10). It is you, my love—and it doesn't matter whether your name is Jane or Juliet. Or that my name is Krzysztof. In our love, we are at the ends of the earth. No, not Australia, but wherever the world ends, where there is no world anymore. After the end of the world. In love we are here, here in this place—but at the same time nowhere, neither in Verona, nor in Springfield, neither here, nor there. Time parts before us, it opens up—and we see the heavens. "Heaven is here, / Where Juliet lives" (*Romeo and Juliet* III.3).

Love: the place where earth touches the heavens.

So that Rilke writes:

> And now he has nothing on. And he is naked as a saint. Bright and slender [. . .]
> The tower room is dark.

But they light each other's faces with their smiles. They grope before them like blind people and find each other as they would a door. Almost like children that dread the night, they press close into each other. And yet they are not afraid. There is nothing that might be against them: no yesterday, no morrow; for time is shattered. And they flower from its ruins.

He does not ask: "Your husband?"

She does not ask: "Your name?"[2]

Perhaps it was this kind of love—eternal love—that Plotinus had in mind when he sought in love a deity or a celestial spirit. Perhaps this is the kind of love we read about in the Song of Solomon (8:6), translated in the New Jerusalem Bible as "a flame of Yahweh himself." If so, if it is about God and about a crack in time through which heaven seeps into my life, if in this way the human is connected to the divine, if it is here that we find that eruption of the absolute into my life and yours, into time—then it may be that in the kind of love I wish to describe here it is not just my affection for Jadwiga and hers for me that come to light. Maybe in this love, in this unrest that knocks you and me off the rhythm of everyday life, from what is familiar and our own, something more comes to the fore: a deep dimension of life as it is. Maybe this is where we find out who we are, beyond the fact that I am Krzysztof, and you are Jadwiga: the human condition.

Thus Mechtild of Magdeburg writes: "It is not our agility, our incorruptibility, or our eyebrows, that make us who we are; it is our love."[3]

2

Nietzsche writes: "What is *amor*, what *deus*, if there is not a drop of blood in them?"[4]

Nothing. It is a rhetorical question. There is no love without blood; it is not by accident that its organ is the heart. The pulsing of blood in one's temples: organs, full and quivering with blood, of lovers joined in an amorous convulsion. Open and joyful but also (at other times) the empty, broken heart, the heart in pain.

Because love hurts. It is a pain that cannot be separated from erotic ecstasy, the pain of merging and splitting, the pain of leaving this world, the pain of entering it anew.

It is also thanks to love that the world smells different. "As for the memory of Rodolphe," Flaubert writes of Emma Bovary, "she had lodged it down in the very depths of her heart; and there he lay, more majestic and more serene than the anointed corpse of a king deep-entombed. A vapour seeped out from this embalmed passion, permeating everything, scenting with tenderness the immaculate atmosphere in which she wished to dwell."[5]

Love also has a peculiar flavor: it is sweet. "O then, the burning of the fire!" Saint John of the Cross writes about the flame of love. "O how infinitely beyond all other fires dost thou burn me, and the more thou burnest the sweeter thou art to me."[6] This is a peculiar sweetness, undoubtedly quite different from the sweetness of sugar or the sweetness of a happy ending in some Hollywood film. How difficult it is—impossible, really—to compare it to anything else: this sweetness is as if "not of this world," something "celestial." This sweetness is the flavor of eternity. "It was [once] thought," Piero Camporesi writes, "that there rained down on earth like a heavenly sweat ('coeli sudor') or an undefinable saliva from the stars ('quaedam syderum saliva'), or a secretion/excrement of the air ('purgantis se aeris succus'), a honey in the form of gentle dew, the principal antidote to putrefaction, and thwarter of bodily decay, whether in life or death."[7]

Heavenly sweat, gentle dew, the saliva of the stars—and in the mouths of lovers a celestial sweetness, the sweetness of eternity: it is precisely here, in the sweat of lovers' bodies intertwined, in the saliva of mouths pressed together, that eternity enters human life.

Blood, the heart and pain, smell and sweetness: human love is then an embodied love: "only embodied souls can fully love," writes Mechtild of Magdeburg.[8] In precisely this manner: in love—in pain, in the bleeding of the heart, in the pulsation of blood, in the curious sweetness of the world, and in the new quality of the air—eternity enters my life. It *touches* me.

Consequently, eternity is a physiological concept, a dimension of our bodily presence in the world.

Or else, to put it another way, there is no other language for expressing eternity, beyond the language of time; eternity is inscribed within time, and love—eternal love—provides the evidence.

3

Isn't it the case, however, that our concepts and our imaginations rebel against such an approach? Doesn't it contradict arguments and metaphors, known for centuries and still with us today, which represent eternity—and therefore also love, which strives after it—as a *rejection* of the body, a *negation* of the senses, an *overcoming* of pain?

Let us return to Plotinus, who writes: "Eros is described as being either [Aphrodite's] son or in some association with her. [. . .] The Heavenly Aphrodite [. . .] must be the Soul at its divinest: [. . .] remaining ever Above, [. . .] so unreservedly an Authentic Being as to have no part with Matter—and therefore mythically 'the unmothered' justly called not Celestial Spirit but God, as knowing no admixture, gathered cleanly within itself."[9]

The attempt to reach this god—love—requires (as it would seem Plotinus claims) tearing oneself away from everything material and thus from everything that we call "body": from blood, pain, and the senses. In such an enterprise, the body is merely a hindrance deserving of disdain. Plotinus was not the first to think so, nor was he the last. A couple of centuries later Bernard of Clairvaux describes the human body as "nothing but stinking sperm, a sack of excrement and food for worms."[10] "Since we are nothing," he is seconded, now in the twentieth century and nihilistically, by one of the protagonists of Céline's *Journey to the End of the Night*, "but packages of tepid, half-rotted viscera."[11]

The body—and with it, Gregory of Nyssa writes, "sexuality, conception, birth, defilement, suckling, nourishment, excretion, growth from childhood to maturity, manhood, old age, sickness, death"—is nothing more than a "garment of skin" we must cast off as soon as possible.[12] The body is a "garment" because the essence of human life, the "soul," has nothing to do with the body, and thus the body is also a *dead* garment. "[W]ho set you, *soul*, about carrying a corpse?" another Gregory—Gregory of Nazianzus—asks.[13]

From this point of view, the body is a trap (set by the Devil?) for that part of man that determines his humanity, that lifts him upward, above worms, pigs, and wild animals. It follows that the body—blood, pain, the senses—poses a danger for my humanity, threatens to deprive my life of meaning. It must therefore be subjected to careful control. When the spark of eternity in man has nothing to do with flushed cheeks and hot blood, when it is "the Heavenly Aphrodite" having "no part with Matter," the body (these burning cheeks, this pulsing blood) becomes a "garment," a "corpse," a "grave," a "prison," a "chain," a "burden" (because it keeps the spark of life from becoming a flame). It also becomes a dangerous "enemy," the source of disorder, chaos, war, violence (because it disturbs the divine order). Finally a "veil," a "shadow," a "night" (because it obstructs our view of the Heavenly Aphrodite, our perspective on eternity).

Nothing more remains for us to do, then, but to *kill the body*, as John Climacus wants us to do. How else are we to reach the Heavenly Aphrodite, our chance at eternal love?

This is precisely what many have tried to do: hermits, monks, holy men, and those who wanted to become them. Climacus writes:

> With knees like wood, as a result of all the prostrations, with eyes dimmed and sunken, with hair gone and cheeks wasted and scalded by many hot tears, with faces pale and worn, they were no different from corpses. Their breasts were livid from all the

beatings, which had even made them spit blood. [. . .] They were
bedraggled, dirty, and verminous. [. . .] [T]heir bones stuck to
their flesh and they were dried up like grass (Ps. 101:4–12). [. . .]
You could see the tongues of some of them dry and hanging from
their mouths in the manner of dogs. Some [. . .] drank only
enough water as would keep them from dying of thirst. Some
munched on a bit of bread, flung away what was left of it and pro-
claimed themselves unworthy to be fed like human beings since
they had behaved like animals.[14]

The body, so many have thought, is in life already a hotbed of corruption
and decay; it was believed in the Middle Ages that lepers dramatize this
fact before our very eyes. Death will equalize all of us, lepers and those
who appear healthy alike, by exposing the true essence of the body, of this
decaying corpse. The inheritors of our bodily presence in the world are—so
it was believed—the worms generated by the body's disintegration. Pliny
maintained that the decay of a human spine could give rise to a snake.

Porphyry of Tyre writes that Plotinus so despised his own body that he
refused to bathe (until he died of diphtheria): "As he spoke [his last words]
a snake crept under the bed on which he lay and slipped away into a hole
in the wall: at the same moment Plotinus died."[15]

Let's take a closer look at the motifs of this terror, this disdain for one's
own body.

First of all, the body changes: "body" is a name for human mutability.
And change is often perceived as a threat, as degeneration, decay, passing.
Insofar as it yields to change so understood, the body is visual testimony of
how human existence has been corrupted, of the ephemerality of human
affairs, and—ultimately—of man's mortality. At the same time—so Plotinus maintained, and many after him—our humanity is determined precisely by what does not change: the soul, that spark buried in the body's
dust, which only awaits the moment when it will be called forth, to burst
into eternal flame. The trace of the Heavenly Aphrodite. Love, eternal
love, is, from this point of view, an attempt to brush the dust aside, to summon the flame, and therefore to discipline, to control, to kill that which is
mutable and ephemeral within us, what dies: the body.

This was precisely what the Egyptian monks of the third and fourth
centuries wanted to attain when they fled "from the world" into the desert.
But isn't this also the ideal goal (or perhaps the hidden dream) of the tor-
tures imposed on the body by scads of joggers and fitness addicts in the
twentieth and twenty-first centuries? At first glance it would seem that we
are dealing with contradictory ambitions: some (the monks) seem to de-
spise the body, while others (the fitness nuts) seem to deify it. In fact, both
want the same thing: to arrest change, to freeze the river my body is ("river

is not a bad name for the body," writes Origen).[16] To transform the body into an infinitely hard diamond, not subject to any kind of degeneration, something that never passes, that lasts forever. In short, they are both after the negation of corporeality—insofar as corporeality is an expression of change, and thus of degeneration, transition, and death.

Change must be arrested, for change is degeneration, disintegration, death. If the "body" signifies our susceptibility to degeneration, decay, and death, then it also must be subject to discipline, restriction and, if only it were possible, elimination. Can I do this myself, fleeing into the desert or enduring hours in a stuffy gym? Might it be that I rather have to wait for some external intervention, for the trumpets of Jericho summoning me to the Last Judgment (and from there perhaps to Heaven, where I will receive my "spiritual body," which is no longer subject to change)—or else for a revolutionary scientific discovery? Who knows. One way or another, from this point of view, life—real life—has nothing to do with passing, nothing to do with change. In this sense, it is not "corporeal." If I wish to live truly, I have to get rid of the "body."

The body does not merely change; it also differentiates. First of all, it differentiates men from women. This fact, too, makes the body a burden, a danger, an object of scorn—in the eyes of many.

Why? Why is the difference between women and men so important? What danger does it pose?

It is a threatening, and therefore important, difference because, as many authors have tried to convince us, it is particularly strong evidence of human degeneration, of human ephemerality, testimony to an inevitably approaching death. For gender difference bears witness to the necessity of procreation, to the need to have descendants—a necessity because children are our one chance at extending our own lives beyond death, the last hope of the mortal. Were we not fated to die, were we not sentenced to death, were it not for the fact that human life is a river flowing toward death through bodily decay, there would be no need to stop this flow, and it would therefore be unnecessary to produce children and engage in all those activities that reach that end.

The necessity we are talking about here comes to light, from this point of view, in lust, in an ostensibly irrepressible sexual desire; it is no accident that in early Christianity "necessity" was a Greek euphemism for the male member. It is this necessity, this lust, that binds us to bodily decay, to death.

It is also for this reason that the shadow of decay, passing, and death inevitably falls on the two lovers under the apple tree, as a good many believe.

And some tell us that maybe there was a time when no such difference existed: maybe woman and man were once one. Remember Plato's story about this unity and how it was split apart, so that we wander the earth looking for our missing half? Or it may have been that women and men once differed harmoniously (and were, in this sense, a unity): back then, the difference between them was not marked by lust and thus with death (in Paradise?). Today, however, as a great many have argued, our sexual organs are the still-stinging, barely healed wounds left by the dramatic and painful loss of this unity (of the first kind, or the second), by the loss of real life. Consequently, these organs testify to our degeneration, to our ephemerality: they herald our death.

Now and then, in an effort to overcome this fatal differentiation, an effort suffused with unconscious trepidation, we try joining our organs, thereby to return to the lost unity. In vain. This is a false path, or so says the argument I am tracing here. The only thing we can attain in this manner is the propagation of the species. Time, which degenerates every morsel of our lives, keeps flowing in the same direction as always: toward death.

Not surprisingly, this point of view regards the coupling of two bodies as "unclean rubbing that is from the fearful fire that came from their fleshly part" (Sophia of Jesus Christ).[17]

What makes this difference between men and women dangerous and threatening is, as we have seen, the lust that violates our freedom, this "fearful fire," a force that is stronger than our will, that attracts men and women to each other. (This affords a few authors a more benign approach to physical love. Saint Augustine, for example, argues that physical love is not simply evil but that it is lust that renders the communion of bodies an "unclean rubbing." The power of lust turns order into chaos and harmony into a potentially dangerous difference. Thus there is no reason why physical love should be excluded from Paradise—so long as it is without lust.)

Lust is inflamed primarily by women. (The monks, priests, and bearded theologians and philosophers who have written about this were all men.) "Because a woman's body is fire," we read in the sayings of the Desert Fathers—a fire that must be extinguished by every means possible.[18] In another saying, we find the following:

> A brother was tested by temptation in Scetis. The enemy brought into his mind the memory of a beautiful woman which troubled him deeply. By God's providence it chanced that a visitor came from Egypt and arrived in Scetis. When they met to talk, he told the brother that his wife was dead (she was the woman about whom the monk was tempted). When he heard the news, he put on his cloak at night and went to the place where he had heard she was buried. He dug in the place, and wiped blood from her corpse on his cloak and when he returned he kept it in his cell. When it

smelt too bad, he put it in front of him and said to his temptation, "Look, this is what you desire. You have it now, be content." So he punished himself with the smell until his passions died down.[19]

"For they say," we read in Clement of Alexandria, "the Saviour himself said, 'I am come to undo the works of the female,' by the female meaning lust, and by the works birth and decay."[20]

The Desert Fathers believed that in complete sexual abstinence they had found a radical antidote to the corruption of sexual differentiation. Many other men have followed their example (Origen allegedly castrated himself so as never to fall back into temptation), as well as many women. Virginity was to neutralize the awful differentiation of bodies, to heal the wound of sex—and thus to impart another meaning to our corporeality: to liberate it from lust and, at the same time, from its connection with death. In this context, virginity was an attempt to return to a "pure" life, "uncorrupted" by the degeneration of time, a return to Paradise. It is not by accident—from this point of view—that the first mention of sexual intercourse between Adam and Eve in the Bible appears after they have already been expelled from Paradise (Gen. 4:1).

The bodies of virgins became bodies in a new sense—new from the perspective of the frail, aching, aging, lust-ridden, mortal, stinking bodies of most other people. Carolyn Walker Bynum writes:

> Christina the Astonishing and Lutgard of Aywières exuded heal-
> ing oil and saliva; Dorothy of Montau swelled with mystical preg-
> nancy in the presence of the Eucharist; Alice of Schaerbeek and
> Lidwina of Schiedam shed bits of fragrant skin as they lay para-
> lyzed and dying. The bodies that experienced these emanations
> and breaches were those that were also wonderfully closed; they
> did not eat or waste away, excrete or menstruate, sicken or stink
> when death arrived.[21]

These virginal bodies were a foreign interjection in what would seem to be the inevitable and irremediable process of change and of the gradual degeneration that comes with it. Independent of potentially fatal sexual differentiation, inextricably bound to ephemerality and death, the bodies of these virgins became (for many) a reflection of eternity, a reminder—and at the same time a harbinger—of Paradise, witness to the fact that the corruption to which time subjects us is not insurmountable but can be reversed—that there is always time for a new beginning, for a return to Paradise. It is a reaching out toward heaven.

The women and men who succeeded in overcoming their lusts and, in this way, directed their corporeality toward eternity and heaven, and not toward death and earth—these are, in the eyes of many people of late antiquity, the Middle Ages, and even the Renaissance, the apex of humanity.

So the thesis that eternity is a physiological concept, that eternity is a dimension of our bodily presence in the world, which opens before lovers locked in an embrace, does indeed encounter a certain resistance in our concepts and metaphors, some of which, as we have seen, are quite ancient. The "body" is for many a word that calls to mind and imagination the dangerous, menacing mutability of human life, a word for degeneration and disintegration and sickness, which will sooner or later, in mounting pain, lead to death. A word that suggests the dangerous, menacing diversity among people, a diversity whose mark is our own sexual organs. Dangerous and menacing because it also binds us to death, through its symptom, lust, which disturbs the eternal order, threatens the eternal harmony.

Each of us, we are told by many saints and many philosophers, carries within us a perspective on the immutable, on the undisturbed unity, and in this sense on eternity: on "the Heavenly Aphrodite." This perspective is love, eternal love. The "body," all that binds us to destructive change and diversity: pain and the senses, "sexuality, conception, birth, defilement, suckling, nourishment, excretion, growth from childhood to maturity, manhood, old age, sickness, death"—the "body" so understood threatens this eternal perspective. One must therefore oppose it, negate it, overcome it, that is, one must pacify the change, tame the difference. One must relieve the body of its dangerous character, relieve it of lust—sever its connection to death.

Eternal love is, from this point of view, a longing for flight from the body, flight from earth, into heaven, into Paradise. Bernard of Clairvaux tells us:

> If we love this unstable and fragile life, which we maintain with a great struggle, [. . .] how much more must we love eternal life: there we endure no struggle, where there is always pleasure, complete happiness, blessed freedom and bliss, where men will be like the angels of God. There will be no sadness there, no distress, no fear, no suffering, no death, but enduring health will always abide there.[22]

Piero Camporesi adds the following:

> [The Garden of Eden] was a place immune to putrefaction, where neither human beings nor the fruits of the earth suffered degeneration. It was rather like a warm refrigerator or an enchanted

embalming laboratory, where matter that would normally perish, survived intact from year to year. Both body and fruit are as though "fixed" in eternity, time stands still for ever.[23]

Time stands still, and suffering, deprivation, and unrest disappear: there is no death, nothing but endless joy.

As witnesses to this resistance to corporeality I have called mostly saints, monks, and philosophers of early Christianity, for in their unusual words, often shocking to today's reader, the connections between concepts and metaphors sometimes emerge with greater force and immediacy than in the contemporary words and associations we might find more familiar. But these connections are still with us. Nietzsche formulated them anew in what the reader already knows as the vision of the *last man*, the ideal of a human being inscribed, in Nietzsche's opinion, in modern European culture as its ultimate goal. This *last man*, as Nietzsche presents him, feels no pain—and if he does, it is only a little, and for his own pleasure. He does not get sick. Consequently, he does not die—and if he does happen to be dying (so long as he has not yet managed to solve the problem of death), he dies happily. His connections with others are not dangerous, his conflicts are minor—"else it might spoil the digestion"—leading quickly to resolution.[24] In short, the *last man* knows neither change nor difference, insofar as they are painful, unrestrained, and therefore dangerous and fatal. Though he might work out, jog, and copulate, corporeality is alien to him, insofar as corporeality is also pain, suffering, sickness, and death.

Nietzsche assures us that we live in a culture that, despite its cult of the body, negates the corporeality of our bodily presence in the world, in a culture that is an agglomeration of techniques and tools for removing pain, suffering, disease, and death from our lives. It is also a box of anesthetics and sedatives, of narcotics, which allow us to keep on going pleasantly enough until such a time as these techniques and tools will be sufficiently perfected to fulfill their task. Our bodies will then stop decaying. We will be eternally healthy. For every pain we will have an appropriate anesthetic at our fingertips. We will all be thirty-three years old and will look like those people in magazine ads. As in Paradise.

Love in such a Paradise is merely pornography. "I can see what the future will be like," says another of Céline's nihilists. "An endless sex orgy.... With movies in between.... You can see how it is already."[25]

Hermits, medieval saints, *the last men*. Nietzsche writes:

> Looking at these figures [. . .], don't you have a sense of something profoundly enigmatic and uncanny? Don't you notice the spectacle before you, how they become ever paler—how desensualization is interpreted more and more ideally? Don't you

sense a long-concealed vampire in the background who begins with the senses and in the end is left with [. . .] leaves, mere bones, mere clatter? I mean categories, formulas, words.[26]

Categories, formulas, words that negate the corporeality of the human presence in the world and, by the same token, negate the reality of love: they negate the sole means by which eternity can be real for us.

4

Alright, then—"bones," their "clatter," empty words. But maybe there's something to this? Might it be the case that what is really eternal in man, his real life—and thus love, true love, which enables him to reach for this life—cannot be reconciled with "sexuality, conception, birth, defilement, suckling, nourishment, excretion, growth from childhood to maturity, manhood, old age, sickness, death"?

"To what extent can truth endure incorporation?" Nietzsche asks. "That is the question; that is the experiment."[27]

It is not an easy process. (The word "truth" assumes a new meaning in this context.) Our saints and monks did have a point: the presence of eternity in my body is sickness, it is strife, it is struggle. "We carry in our blood the poisonous dregs of the absolute," writes E. M. Cioran, "it prevents us from breathing yet we cannot live without it."[28]

The flame of love burns, it wounds, writes Saint John of the Cross: "For when this flame of divine life wounds the soul with the gentle languishing for the life of God, it wounds it with so much endearing tenderness, and softens it so that it melts away in love."[29]

True, love is sweet, but this sweetness stings. Its touch paralyzes, it kills, as Saint John of the Cross says: "That sweetness is such that if God had not had pity on its natural frailty and covered it with His right hand [. . .] it would have died at each vibration of the flame."[30]

What is the basis of this disease?

> *Juliet*: I will not fail: 'tis twenty years till then.
> I have forgot why I did call thee back.
> *Romeo*: Let me stand here till thou remember it.
> *Juliet*: I shall forget, to have thee still stand there,
> Remembering how I love thy company.
> *Romeo*: And I'll still stay, to have thee still forget,
> Forgetting any other home but this.
>
> —*Romeo and Juliet*, act 2, scene 2

When I am with you, Juliet—when I am with you, Romeo—I forget everything that was: what is it to me now? I forget your connections and my own, our relatives, responsibilities ("He does not ask: 'Your husband?'"): what could all that mean now? I forget the future, too. I pay no heed to consequences. Whether you'll get pregnant. Whether someone will find us out and make a scandal. Whether we'll get married. Whether we will then live happily ever after. None of that matters. There's no room for hope here, just as there is no room for obligations. Nor for the future, nor for the past. There is only "now"; what has been, what will be, vanish.

Thus it does not matter who you are. It doesn't matter who I am. ("She does not ask: 'Your name?'"). When I am with you, the world as it is no longer exists; there is no name by which to answer the question: Who are you, my love?

Now, when I'm with you, now, while I love you, there is neither past nor future. Love leads out beyond time. Beyond the world.

This "now"—this moment torn out of time by love—Octavio Paz calls "our share of paradise."[31] It is this that is our *heaven*.

> *Romeo*: 'Tis torture, and not mercy: heaven is here,
>   Where Juliet lives; and every cat and dog
>   And little mouse, every unworthy thing,
>   Live here in heaven and may look on her;
>   But Romeo may not. More validity,
>   More honourable state, more courtship lives
>   In carrion-flies than Romeo: they may seize
>   On the white wonder of dear Juliet's hand
>   And steal immortal blessings from her lips.
>
> *Romeo and Juliet*, act 3, scene 3

And Kafka, on Felice:

> Sometimes I thought she understood me without realizing it; for instance, the time she waited for me at the U-Bahn station—I had been longing for her unbearably, and in my passion to reach her as quickly as possible almost ran past her, thinking she would be at the top of the stairs, and she took me quietly by the hand.[32]

A moment torn out of time, a light touch: "the least, the softest, lightest, a lizard's rustling, a breath, a breeze, a moment's glance," Zarathustra says, but it is not an instant in the sense of a piece of time, Monday, six in the morning.[33] In this passing touch, "time breaks down"; nothing of it, no date, remains. "What happened to me?" Zarathustra asks. "Listen! Did time perhaps fly away? Do I not fall? Did I not fall—listen!—into the well of eternity?"[34]

Love, and especially this eternal love, is therefore not an attempt to extend the moment—this Sunday afternoon, in the garden, by the river—into eternity. Nietzsche notes, "All love things of the moment and of eternity, but *never* about the 'long term.'"[35]

The erotic act is a leap in the dark, into the unknown.

Consequently, love is uncompromising. It is ruthless. Selfless. "I have [. . .] kept nothing for myself," Heloise writes to Abelard of her love.[36] I have nothing left for myself because I have given all of it to you. This gesture of sacrificing everything one is to someone else, all in one flash, this gesture of utter self-evacuation, the smashing of all my toys, even those that are most important, like mathematics, like my country: this is the gesture in which love renders lovers utterly foreign within the world around them.

Of course, this is not the outcome of a conscious decision. Saint Augustine was right: the lover's sacrifice, the lover's destruction of time, is necessarily physical, material, and corporeal (lust)—not conscious, not rational. Thus its tendency to be expressed in the joining of two bodies—"Set me as a seal upon thine heart, as a seal upon thine arm"—in the short circuit of bodies, in the absurdly intense effort, oblivious to reason, decency, or moderation, to leave oneself in order to become, completely, that other person, to become utterly united with her; in the uncontrollable joining of bodies, too close for consciousness, too strong for the will; in the joining of bodies impossibly tensed, bursting with the blood in their veins, mindless, thoughtless, eyeless: past me, as I am, toward you, toward unity with you.

In order to offer ourselves to someone, we must sever the ties that join us to everything we hold dear. To sacrifice one's own heart, one must tear it out. Love is a movement beyond oneself, an abandonment of oneself, laying oneself upon the altar; it is violence and brutality against everything that I am and that you are. "Take now thy son, thy only son Isaac, whom thou lovest, and [. . .] offer him there" (Gen. 22:2).

Can such an operation ever be painless?

The touch of love commands me to move out beyond myself, to cast aside the person I was and lay it down as a sacrifice. By the same token, it rends the fabric of reality, yours and mine. Thus it hurts. This wound allows us to see heaven, to get there, but too fleetingly to make room for anything but you and me. To reach eternity.

Eternity, so conceived, is therefore also a burden, a curse. It is a volcano that threatens all commitments, institutions, and associations. Love, eternal love, is essentially subversive. It undermines what is already there.

"Love," writes Octavio Paz, "commingles heaven and earth: that is the great subversion."[37]

As such, the heaven that opens before the lovers—the eternity that erupts in their mutual caresses, our "share of paradise"—is hardly a promise of peace, quiet, and relaxation. This is not the place where "eternal rest" awaits us. "I am bent over under the weight of a curse called eternity," Cioran writes, "a poison of youth, a balm only for corrupt hearts."[38] Real eternity, the eternity that opens when the lovers' embrace demolishes time, is a painful illness, a sickness that undercuts all continuity, all stability, all peace.

Nor can eternity therefore be a "place" we can move to once we have abandoned time. We cannot abandon time; there's no getting out of it, certainly not the way one leaves the kitchen to get to the living room. Nor can they manage it, those who are under the apple tree—Romeo and Juliet, Abelard and Heloise. They're not somewhere else. Though so tightly intertwined, so indifferent to everything else, so alien—they are also here, under the apple tree, in the dark room of the tower. In a moment everything will start again: the rain will fall, I'll slip in the mud, a bird will shit on my head, her husband will come home. The very beat of the heart, its rhythm—boom, and again, boom, and once more, boom—reminds them they are in time, that he is her teacher, that she is his pupil, that she is a Capulet, he a Montague. Lucretius, as quoted by Jorge Luis Borges, writes:

> Like the thirsty man who in sleep wishes to drink and consumes forms of water that do not satiate him and dies burning up with thirst in the middle of a river; so Venus deceives lovers with simulacra, and the sight of a body does not satisfy them, and they cannot detach or keep anything, though their indecisive and mutual hands run over the whole body. At the end, when there is a foretaste of delight in the bodies and Venus is about to sow the woman's fields, the lovers grasp each other anxiously, amorous tooth against tooth; entirely in vain, for they do not succeed in losing themselves in each other or becoming a single being.[39]

Each scrap of time, each minute that binds lovers to the past or future, with time, is like a knife that cuts them apart.

Hegel writes that plants contain salts and soil—that is, foreign substances—within themselves. This is why they can decay. It is similar, he says, with lovers. What there is of the world within them—of past and future, of time—is like the grain of sand that jams the works, their striving after eternity. They cannot get rid of it; they are still mortal. They will not destroy all difference between themselves, they will not become a complete unity. Love will not enable them to break free of time. They are still dying.

Two lovers in time: Romeo and Juliet, Abelard and Heloise. In their love, they are no longer who they were, no longer anyone or anything: they give themselves to one another completely, and thus they lose their time and place, they lose the burden that draws them to some "here" and "now." They take flight, to soar in the empty sky, where one cannot tell up from down, left from right. And yet at the same time they are still here, they remain in the here and now. They do not abandon time. She is still Juliet, he is still Romeo, here she is, and here am I.

There's the flight, and there's the tethering to one place. There's "now" (Monday), and there's "now" (always and never). There's time, and there's eternity—but these are not two different states. They are a unity. The heart whose rhythm measures time and the one that is simultaneously pressing out toward Juliet are the same heart. So that Emily Dickinson writes:

> Might He [Romeo? Perhaps Juliet knew?] know
> How Conscious Consciousness—could grow—
> Till Love that was—and Love too blest to be—
> Meet—and the Junction be Eternity?[40]

Love, being sick with eternity, is therefore a different disease from all others. We do not fall ill with love only now and then, so as to return to normal life later (or else die). Unlike the flu or syphilis, this is a disease that questions and undermines the meaning of "healthy" and "normal." If we were capable of ridding our blood of the virus of eternity, we would not then turn back into "healthy," "normal" people. We would no longer be people at all.

This attempt to move out beyond oneself, beyond the "here" and "now," this effort to break free of time—in vain, for it merely leads us to the next moment, from Monday into Tuesday—this relentless questioning of everything that has ever been "human" till now, this constant transcending of "humanity," this sickness: this is the human condition. This is what we are. "[M]y soul [. . .] is the song of a lover," Zarathustra would say of himself.[41]

"All signs of the super-human," Nietzsche would note, "appear in man as sickness or madness."[42] We cannot live without the superhuman. Therefore this madness, this eternity-sickness, is our lives. Somewhere in the depths of our memories and expectations, of our obligations and hopes, which bind us to what has been and what will be—in the depths of time—there is a worm, a germ of eternity, which this time eats away, gnaws, digests. Sometimes, without warning, unexpectedly, this sickness flares up and becomes more acute: this is love.

By now we know a little more about sweetness, that taste of eternity that love leaves in the mouths of lovers. True, love is sweet—and its absence leaves bitterness. But this bitterness is not simply the taste of absence, a sense of missing something, as bitterness brought on by a lack of sugar in the organism. On the contrary, this bitterness is a symptom of being sick with eternity, of the stinging awareness of a wound that will never heal.

The nature of love: taking off into flight, into eternity, and the gravity that pulls us back to the nest, the fall into time—this is also the nature of man. "Love is the recognition, in the beloved person, of that gift of flight that characterizes all human creatures," Octavio Paz writes. "The mystery of the human condition lies in its freedom: it is both fall and flight. And therein lies the immense allure that love has for us."[43]

When the flame of love burns everything I otherwise am, when it burns time—when I give you all that I am—I am still me, the same me, but now in another, heretofore hidden sense, wrapped up in my names, functions, and interests. Love reveals an unnamed, as yet unknown identity within me, and within you. In this way, it also brings to light the common condition that we—people, these animals sick with eternity—all share.

5

This eternity-disease is a sickness unto death. "Loving and perishing," Nietzsche writes, "that has rhymed for eternities. The will to love, that is to be willing also to die."[44]

There have been a great many witnesses to the link between love and death. One is the poet Jarosław Iwaszkiewicz:

> Is there not death in the smile of loving?
> Is there not in every kiss
> A kernel of nothing?[45]

It is enough to look at the one and the other, at love and at death, to recognize the similarity. Or, rather, not to notice the difference. Hans-Georg Gadamer recalls a scene from Goethe in which someone (Pandora) asks, on seeing the act of love for the first time, "What is that?" and is told that it is death.[46] It's not a simple mistake: it could be both, one as well as the other, a state in which everything I have known till now, everything that has been my support, flies away into nothingness. Shuddering bodies struggling with something inhuman, alien, new, mysterious, desired. The convulsions, the scream. Ecstasy? Agony? Who can tell them apart?

Both love and death are brutal, a radical violence that breaks all resistance, violence done to what has been and what is now. As Tertullian said, "all death (even the gentlest) is violent."[47] All love as well.

In other words, death, just like love, is the experience of a radical limit, of radical difference, of utter alienation.

As we have seen, Saint Augustine tried to describe this alienation as breaking out of control, as a revolt against human will. In both cases—in death and in physical love—the human will reaches a limit that it cannot cross (at least, Augustine would add, not without some outside help). When we love, just as when we die, our bodies slip out of our control. Erection, orgasm, and agony—the example is Augustine's, not mine— place this fact before our very eyes.

Like death, love reveals the radical discontinuity of human life. In both cases I abandon what is known, familiar, my own, and enter what Levinas calls "a land not of our birth."[48]

Consequently, being "ready for love" is exactly the same as being "ready for death" in the sense that love allows us to accept death, to live with it; it allows me to integrate death into my own life. "Love is as strong as death." It is a different attitude from the (Stoic) acceptance of the inescapable fact that life ends. Love—that cataclysm of life as it is, that catastrophe in which everything I have built for myself so far comes crashing down—entails the acceptance of radical discontinuity, the acceptance of something alien that cannot possibly be assimilated, of separation with no hope of return. Acceptance of a life in which death is already inscribed.

The integration of life and death—the task of love, as well as its result— therefore does not signify assimilation; the point here is not to install the new part, fill in the hole, or heal the wound. No new, and this time really all-encompassing, whole will arise in this way, no undisturbed identity, that of the quiet life, with all its troubles behind it. No, this is not the point. Death is not a "something," it is not an object that we need to incorporate into a greater whole. The integration of life and death disturbs the identity of the former; it shows us that there is no "whole" to be made of it, that life cannot be "this" or "that." This integration exposes life's discontinuous, open (to the alien, to the unknown), and thus painful nature.

As Tadeusz Różewicz has written, love makes death "slide into life / like a knife into flesh."[49]

6

There, under the apple tree, when I am in love, death finds its place in my life. It is no longer the horsewhip, the sword of Damocles, an external threat: it "loses its sting." For there, under the apple tree, he and she, and thus life as well, discover their innocence.

In this sense, love is a return to Paradise. There, we are told in Genesis, Adam and Eve were still innocent; time was not yet a painful, irrevocable passing; it did not lead to death. There was no time as we know it. Accordingly, there was no room for guilt, nor for shame.

The expulsion from Paradise meant a fall into time, where the past differs from the present: time, whose horizon is death. The memory of what had been consequently became a greater and greater burden, innocence be damned.

The love I am writing about—eternal love—reconstructs the primary conditions about which we hear in myth. The time that consumes life disappears, and with it the difference between "was" and "will be." The past is no longer a burden—what do I care about this world?—and once again there is no room for guilt or shame.

Romeo and Juliet, Abelard and Heloise, my beloved and myself: we are innocent and without shame once more, like Adam and Eve in Paradise.

But not completely. Eternity and time, innocence and guilt—which Genesis describes, it would seem, as events that follow one after the other—are here, in us, in our love, inextricably bound, two sides of the same coin, even under that apple tree. "Sorrow and joy, guilt and innocence, like two hands indissolubly clasped together," Kafka writes. "[O]ne would have to cut through flesh, blood, and bones to part them."[50]

For us, innocence is possible only within the horizon of time, merely as an attempt to destroy it, to release oneself from it, to fly.

In vain, as we know. Thus pain—and shame, which arises anew. No longer is this the shame of love: What kind of lovers are they who are ashamed? The heart is ashamed, Hegel writes, "if its love is incomplete; it upbraids itself if there is some hostile power which hinders love's culmination."[51] It is the shame that, though I am with you under the apple tree, I am still Krzysztof, and you are Jadwiga, that we were born, and that we will die. That love will not burn us up completely, that something of us will remain: the ashes of the earth.

Love, then, is an attempt to return to the sources of our innocence, which in everyday life are buried deep—but they are there somewhere, always, so long as we are alive, no matter how much trouble we've gotten ourselves into or how heavy a stone time has placed on top of them. "And it is there," André Breton writes, "right in the depths of the human crucible, in this paradoxical region where the fusion of two beings who have really chosen each other renders to all things the lost colors of the times of ancient suns."[52]

Let us not forget that this innocence, this Paradise, is here and nowhere else—that these "ancient suns" still shine, that from these hidden sources a lava flows that destroys everything there is, that innocence is, for life amid its everyday obligations, a hostile force. That eternity is a disease. That love, even the happiest love, is tragic.

In love, we are innocent, like children. We return to our lost innocence: the myth of Paradise becomes intertwined with that other, equally ancient myth: the myth of childhood. In ancient myths, Carl Kerenyi tells us, the divine universe, at the moment of its first appearance, was presented in the form of a "divine child." Most often the name applied to this child was "Eros." There is therefore nothing odd in the fact that the closest relative of this divine child turns out to be another divine figure, Dionysus. "Dionysus," Kerenyi writes, "is *so close* to [the divine Primordial Child] that [. . .] he is the overtone to the groundtone."[53]

As we have seen, the connection between love and the return to innocence, the return to childhood, was already discovered long ago.

The metaphor of the child-Eros demonstrates again, clearly, that this return to innocence—this love—cannot be a program, whether intellectual or moral. It does not and cannot be about departing one state (ignorance, sin) for another (knowledge, bliss). True, love is an effort to remove oneself from the past and the future, an attempt to maintain a distance from what was and what will be—but who is really able to accomplish this? Who can tear himself away from what was, from the pleasure or pain that it never returns, or from the hope that things will be different, or that they will always be the same? Can one even want something like that, to find oneself in such a state? What would the object of this knowledge be?

No, the return to innocence is neither a goal of knowledge nor a program of action. Each of us, Gadamer observes,[54] the good and the wise as well as the others, "suffers" and "seeks"—and thus cannot cast off the burden of time, cannot take flight. It is only (Gadamer again) "the ease of the child, the easy forgetting, its timelessness, its arising in the there of the moment, its playing. . . ."[55] which does not need any outer world, which demonstrates to us what innocence means. The child, the child at play, is a metaphor for the complete liberation from time and with it a liberation from all obligations and expectations, from pain and compassion. Nietzsche calls this liberation *amor fati*.

It is only when he transforms us into "children of heaven" and in this way "relieves" us (of all guilt) and liberates us from time that Zarathustra fulfills his mission, Nietzsche tells us. This liberation is the place where "his torrential passion [will become] still."[56] When I have found, in any given moment of my life, the child at play. When I have understood, in other words, that the life I am living is more than just a potential object of knowledge, more than some morality.

7

Love, I have suggested, is the flare-up of a disease that defines and distinguishes the human being. It is a sickness of the heart, blood, and body, an illness that is both painful and sweet: one is sick with eternity, unto death.

And thus, at the same time, it is an inflammatory condition that defines our bodily presence in the world. It demonstrates what "body" means.

The "body" is, first of all, the name for the mutability of human life, for its ephemerality, its susceptibility to suffering, for our mortality. The hair falls out, the skin grows wrinkly, the muscles go slack, more and more often something here or there hurts, until finally all of this will disintegrate and I will no longer be Krzysztof Michalski as you have known me: this is the "body."

But that is not all. The "body" also signifies something else; our bodily presence in the world has yet another side, inextricable from the first. "Mutability" need not mean only disintegration, degeneration, or ephemerality. It can also mean the ability to transform, the ability to assume a new shape, even in an unlimited capacity. We have seen how early Christianity already familiarized us with this idea: the bodies of the hermits and saints, the bodies of virgins, were subject to a discipline that was to have redirected them away from disintegration and death, toward heaven. "Sainthood is transfigured physiology," Cioran writes. "Every bodily *function* becomes a movement towards the sky."[57]

Nietzsche seconds this: what the body does "above all else," he argues, is "to create beyond itself."[58] The goal of this transcendence, of this transformation, is not some higher form of development; the transformation that is the body has no definite goal. It has no limits: at each successive point, all that I am, every form I have taken thus far, is undermined. Our bodies, Nietzsche tells us, are ultimately a "bridge" to that which transcends every meaning of humanity, to that which is utterly unknown, completely alien—to the hidden "overman" slumbering within us.

In love, in that which occurs between two people beneath the apple tree, this meaning of "body" comes to light. For it is only then, in love, that each of us moves out beyond himself and casts himself into darkness, without regard for risk, without protection.

One notion of the radical transformation of the body is undoubtedly that of resurrection. I have already discussed this notion in connection with the notion of change as degeneration; resurrection could be understood as the arrest of such change, and therefore as the arrest of degeneration, disintegration, and passing. It is something like perfect embalming (preceded as necessary by several successful plastic surgeries or a couple of organ transplants). The outcome of this kind of resurrection is that the body is supposed to lose its vulnerability to the destructive power of time; it is supposed to turn into an infinitely hard, utterly transparent, indestructible diamond.

In what sense, however, can such a diamond still be called a "body"? Can my life, minus its passing and the pain connected with it, really still be called a "bodily" presence in the world?

But we can understand resurrection in still another way, not so much as a continuation of life (with certain corrections) as it is but rather as a rebirth, as being born into a new life. Wasn't just such an understanding the intent of the Christian reinterpretation of the Platonic ideal of the immortal soul? Being born into a new life—what D. H. Lawrence called "the fall into the future, like a waterfall that tumbles over the edge of the known world into the unknown."[59]

Where is this border, "the edge of the known world"? Where is this unknown country, this "land not of our birth"?

Clearly, it cannot be a concrete place. In this sense, it's nowhere. But at the same time, it is in every moment of my life, insofar as every moment of my life contains within itself an incurable discontinuity, a reference to what is radically alien, completely unknown, to what is in this sense a mystery. Insofar as every moment of life hides a wound that makes us sensitive to eternity. If this is so, then every moment of my life is also a resurrection, a rebirth into a new life, a life of possibilities unknown until now, in my "previous" life.

When is this more evident than as the bodies of Romeo and Juliet are tensed in (fruitless) effort, each to offer him- or herself to the other, and in so doing to achieve that impossible unity that surpasses both him and her, though it does not destroy them—to grasp this new, alien, and strange sweetness, which stops the breath, seals the lips, and robs one of speech? Love is a rebirth; here, in love, Romeo and Juliet cast off the entire ballast of their pasts, their guilt, their obligations, their clothes, and become innocent again, naked: they are children once more. In this sense love is the "place" (the moment, though not a second, minute, or month) of resurrection, the "place" of immortality, which is hidden, which detonates what is.

Our "corporeality," which comes to light in our love, is therefore an expression of the infinitely creative nature of human life. It is an expression of the fact that our lives are, at every step, ready to give birth to something that surpasses them, something that does not fit within them, that cannot be known.

The body is therefore not merely an expression of the transitory nature of our lives but also a visible sign of rebirth and, in this sense, of our immortality. The body is not a thing, destructible, in which we are enclosed. It is an effort to move out beyond ourselves, beyond what is. It is a stretching of the hand—as far as one can, till it hurts—toward eternity.

In this context, both the notion of pain and that of suffering take on new meaning: the pain of the human body is not only the pain of disintegration, destruction, and decay. It is also the pain of birth, the painful birth of the new.

8

Despite appearances, isn't this notion of the body close to that of Christianity?

The story of the life and death of Jesus as recorded in the New Testament is supposed to tell us who we are: it is the story of the human condition. This story tries to convince us that the human condition cannot be understood without God. To help us in this understanding, God—so the story goes—became a man.

That is, a body.

"Behold my hands and my feet," the resurrected Christ says to the Apostles. "[H]andle me, and see; for a spirit hath not flesh and bones, as ye see me have" (Luke 24:39).

Here the body is what connects the carnal human to God incarnate.

In the New Testament, the incarnation of God is first of all a story about a love that demands that we cast aside everything there is. At the same time, it is a story about suffering greater than any guilt, about pain that does not stem from one's own past, about pain that opens a new world. Finally, it is a story about death, which is a step into darkness as well as a new beginning, about death accepted and integrated into one's own life, a death that shows what life really is, as Paul writes: "Always bearing about in the body the dying of the Lord Jesus, that the life also of Jesus might be made manifest in our body" (2 Cor. 4:10).

The tale of God's incarnation is the story of a child: a child who suffers, but without guilt; who loves, but is alien to everything that is ours; who dies, but rises from the dead, into a new life. The story of the child in us. Tadeusz Różewicz writes:

> I think of the small
> god bleeding
> in the white
> clothes of childhood
> of the thorn that tears
> our eyes mouth
> now
> and at the hour of our death[60]

9

And thus my presence in the world—my life—is irrevocably corporeal. The "body" is disintegration and death, but at the same time it is an effort, a stretching out of the hand until it hurts, toward the unknown, the new, the alien: toward eternity. From this it follows that love—the joining of two bodies, in ecstasy and pain—is an expression of the human condition. It brings to light who we really are.

Human life as a painful transformation; life pregnant with the new and unknown: is it odd, then, that in my account yet another metaphoric figure appears (anew), that of woman?

Wherever the "body" is the center of attention, "woman" immediately appears.

The corporeality of human life is expressed in the pain smoldering in each moment—for in every moment of my life, in my every gesture, in my every movement, a child is born in whom the world begins all over again. Every moment of one's life is the birthplace of something that had not been there before. It hurts.

This is pain of a particular kind. It does not arise from the past, from old misdeeds. It comes through no fault of one's own. It is therefore baseless. It is the pain of birth. Insofar as it knows this kind of pain, life is a "woman"—a birthmother.

Our lives are creative, radically creative: in what I do, a new world can appear at any moment. "[Y]et creativity requires suffering," Nietzsche notes. "Suffering signifies transformation, every birth contains death. To create, one must not only be a child, but also a birthmother."[61]

The suffering of giving birth, this "great pain"—Nietzsche writes in *The Gay Science*—"compels us [. . .] to descend into our ultimate depths and to put aside all trust [. . .]. I doubt that such pain makes us 'better'; but I know that it makes us more *profound*."[62] As a result of this pain, "[t]he trust in life is gone: life itself has become a *problem*. Yet one should not jump to the conclusion that this necessarily makes one gloomy. Even love of life is still possible, only one loves differently. It is the love for a woman that causes doubts in us."[63]

"Yes," Nietzsche declares, "life is a woman."[64]

"Life is a woman," then, also in the sense that we cannot be sure of her. That it is inherently problematic, that it's an unfathomable mystery. That we cannot have faith in it: each moment can make everything that has been till then lose its weight, its meaning, its reality. That, like a woman, it is changeable, deceptive, unreliable. Appearance, with yet another behind it. A labyrinth—with no way out. The truth about life is constantly slipping away, hidden behind an infinite line of masks, in the play of appearances. Or rather, life is precisely this slipping away, these masks, this play. This is the "truth" of life. And truth is therefore a woman.

> We no longer believe that truth remains truth when the veils are withdrawn [. . .]. Today we consider it a matter of decency not to wish to see everything naked, or to be present at everything, or to understand and "know" everything.
>
> "Is it true that God is present everywhere?" a little girl asked her mother; "I think that's indecent"—a hint for philosophers! One

should have more respect for the bashfulness with which nature has hidden behind riddles and iridescent uncertainties. Perhaps truth is a woman who has reasons for not letting us see her reasons?[65]

In the Bible, too, wisdom is a woman: Proverbs 9:1–5, Proverbs 1:20, Proverbs 8:1.

Life is corporeal, through the pain by which it is marked, the pain of a mother giving birth. It is the body in birth pangs, giving rise to the new, the body reaching out beyond itself, as far as possible, imbued with desire and longing, never to be sated. This pain, these pangs, this longing—they erode all certainty, they undermine all faith, they place everything there is in doubt, and it is because of them that the world becomes infinitely diverse. It disintegrates into endless colors, shades, meanings, and fragments, which can never be assembled into a single totality.

Life is, like a woman, mutable, alluring, a harbinger of the new.

Love: life par excellence.

The bearded monks, hermits, and saints of the Middle Ages were therefore not quite in error: it is true that inasmuch as life has anything to do with the body, woman plays one of the main roles within it. It is true that "a woman's body is fire," tempting us into it, to leap in and burn all that we have, all that we are. It is true that the works of woman are "birth and decay." But this fire, this temptation, these works—these are life itself.

The name that Plotinus imparted to love was therefore rather apt: "Aphrodite." The Heavenly Aphrodite: love, in which life as it is comes to light. The body, in pain that tears it asunder, gives birth to something that finds insufficient space within it, that surpasses it, that wounds and destroys it: eternity.

10

In love, life as it is comes to light. And yet it eludes concepts, it cannot be "perceived," it cannot be "known." What does this tell us about knowledge, about the concepts we use to grasp our lives and ourselves?

First of all, I am not talking here about two ways of accessing the essence of life, about an "emotion" (love) as distinct from "reason" (concepts). I am not appealing to you to love, and to throw out both sense and sensibility. I would like to show how a discussion of the concept of eternal love may lead to insight into the nature of concepts themselves—not to a resignation from reason in favor of love but to a concept of reason that does love justice: to a concept of rationality for which love is the source, not the antithesis.

In this context, what conclusions can we draw from the assertion that love exposes the chronic sickness of the world that is man, the disease of eternity? ("The earth has a skin," Zarathustra says, "and this skin has diseases. One of these diseases [. . .] is called 'man.'")[66]

Man is the eternity-disease, which means that the source of our humanity throbs with a particular kind of pain. Our humanity is constituted, is created, in suffering, in pain, in the pain of passing away and giving birth. This pain is therefore the ultimate tribunal before which our concepts must bear witness to their significance and to the meaning they have for us, to their validity for humanity. This pain is the ultimate criterion for the truth of our concepts. "[T]he real, incontestable truth, a truth marred by no external circumstance," writes Kafka, "is only physical pain."[67]

Love—true love—cannot escape pain. Nietzsche writes:

> We are not thinking frogs, nor objectifying and registering mechanisms with the innards removed: constantly, we have to give birth to our thoughts out of our pain and, like mothers, endow them with all we have of blood, heart, fire, pleasure, passion, agony, conscience, fate, and catastrophe.[68]

Consequently, our concepts are marked by our pain, the pain from which they arise. Suffering, and with it the body, is the precondition of the possibility of our knowledge. Our concepts contain our blood, our desires, our passions. They are alive. They are still—and always, though sometimes undetectably—warm, from the fire, from the flame of love that is burning somewhere in the depths of our lives. Origen wrote that our ability to orient ourselves among people and things—our identity ("soul")—results from the cooling of the originary fire of love. Knowledge is love cooled off.

Our concepts, still warm, will therefore never be ready, finished products. They can never be arranged into a pattern that will explain completely how things really are. They will always remain fluid, fragile, and temporary.

Insofar as our concepts arise from our pain, knowledge has no end.

"Knowledge is longing and desire," Nietzsche would write, "to know is to impregnate. Which means that, as creativity, all knowledge is ignorance. Complete knowledge of a thing would mean death, disgust, evil."[69]

If this is the case, then there can be no illusion that concepts, whatever they are, allow us to relieve the pain of our lives, that they will cure us of our eternity-disease. They won't. They themselves contain traces of this disease. Knowledge is not a treatment for this pain. It affords no real consolation. No logic or dialectic provides an answer to this pain.

Only love can. Or rather, one cannot live, one cannot comprehend, without love. Concepts do not suffice. There is no getting away from them, just as there is no escape from time, of which they are one expression. And yet there is also that gesture that constitutes me, that determines the meaning of my "I," beyond anything anyone can say about me, beyond all of my character traits, social roles, or particular signs: the gesture of moving out beyond everything, beyond myself, the sacrifice of myself as I have been till now. Without this gesture, my life would be unthinkable. Without the gesture that comes to light in love when I am facing you, naked, no longer Krzysztof—when I am facing you, I who am you, I in a sweet and painful effort, indifferent to all else, to be you.

IX

Our Insatiable Desire for More Future
On the Eternal Return of the Same

THAT EVENING IN ŻEROMSKI Park Joanna and I were playing hide-and-seek; I was lying on the moist earth, in the bushes, and didn't want to come out. Joanna walked up and down the paths for a long time, dusk was falling, and she was calling out: "Krzysztof! Krzysztof! Where are you?"

I remember this so well, but this was some time ago, not now. It will never be again. It's not coming back.

Or my father's hands, steady, reassuring. I held them, flying through the air, in a circle, like on a carousel. How I would like to return to that moment, to remember more of it: his face, what he was saying, the laughter we perhaps shared.

But I won't go back. I won't get a second chance. I won't remember anything else. "What thou lovest well," it turns out, does not remain.

People, events, and things slip out of our hands, they escape us irretrievably, never to return. They pass, become something that was, become the past. We will never succeed in getting back to them: something is in the way. All other hindrances, all other walls, can be broken down, whether by bulldozer, head, or dream. Not this. The past will not return. The river of time flows in only one direction.

Is there any more tangible proof of this than death? Nietzsche writes:

> Living among this jumble of little lanes, needs, and voices gives me a melancholy happiness: how much enjoyment, impatience, and desire, how much thirsty life and drunkenness of life comes to light every moment! And yet silence will soon descend on all these noisy, living, life-thirsty people. How his shadow stands even now behind everyone, as his dark fellow traveler! It is always like the last moment before the departure of an emigrants' ship: people have more to say to each other than ever, the hour is late, and the ocean and its desolate silence are waiting impatiently behind all of this noise—so covetous and certain of their prey. And all and everyone of them suppose that the heretofore was little or nothing while the near future is everything; and that is the reason

for all of this haste, this clamor, this outshouting and overreach-
ing each other. Everyone wants to be the first in this future—and
yet death and deathly silence alone are certain and common to all
in this future.[1]

And Emily Dickinson:

> We never know we go when we are going—
> We jest and shut the Door—
> Fate—following—behind us bolts it—
> And we accost no more—[2]

We will all eventually go to a place from which there is no return. We
will all eventually become an irretrievable, no longer mutable *past*. That
which no longer is.

2

But maybe not? Maybe this irreversible succession of moments marching
toward nothingness is merely an illusion? Maybe it isn't the ultimate reality? How we wish we could believe that! Passing away, irretrievably passing
away, is so painful, and we (though not all of us, and not always) so wish we
could add one more moment to those we already have behind us, and another, and another, that the words of prophets, philosophers, and poets who
demonstrate the unreality of time are greeted by our grateful enthusiasm.
To annul the irretrievability of time, to soothe that pain, to bring hope and
solace: this, many have believed, is what we demand of wisdom.
   Sometimes, as for the Greeks, the contemplation of nature seemed to
show the way to meeting this demand. The regular movement of the stars,
always the same, and always the same behavior of animals, fleeing, hunting, being hunted. The changeless cycle of life, day and night, birth and
death, and again from the beginning, day and night, birth—nature seems
to lack time, or at least to lack irreversible time: after the future (night), the
past (day) comes back to us, now the past, now the future, night and day,
day and night, undeviating.
   What might it mean, Schopenhauer would ask (rhetorically) in the
nineteenth century, that this gray cat I happen to be looking at, and which
happens to be playing in the yard, is another cat from the one that was
playing somewhere else fifteen years ago? And Czesław Miłosz:

> Tiger cubs grow up, learn to hunt, have their own families, while
> old tigers die or are killed—deaths, the manner of which we can

scarcely imagine—and this is repeated innumerable times, and the deer they have caught for lunch also fall innumerable times, and all this is happening in a *now* that knows neither past, nor future.[3]

Nature, this argument suggests, does not know irreversible time, does not know a past that has been lost forever. It is always the same, infinitely repeated gestures, forms, and figures, a ritual dance in which nothing new can happen. "In nature there is nothing new under the sun," Hegel writes. "Changes in the world of nature—infinitely varied as these might be—reflect nothing more than an eternally repeated cycle."[4]

In this view, death is also such a gesture, such a form, and not a onetime, irreversible occurrence: the seed dies in the ground in order to give birth to a new tree. To engage in this dance, to feel in one's movements, in one's muscles, beneath one's skin, our inseparable togetherness, a oneness with nature often obscured by dreams of human exceptionality—this is tantamount to breaking the chain of time that binds us to nothingness, to finding a cure for the pain of passing, for our fear of nothingness. Schopenhauer writes that one can "justly console himself for his own death and for that of his friends by looking back on the immortal life of nature, which he himself is."[5]

One instantiation of this position is the concept of the eternal return of the same: time is a circle, the world is constantly returning to where it began. This concept had already appeared as a myth in the ancient religious imaginations of various cultures of the Near East, as well as in ancient Israel. Noah rejoices, "While the earth remaineth, seedtime and harvest, and cold and heat, and summer and winter, and day and night shall not cease" (Gen. 8:22). The future will no longer bring anything new, neither surprises nor any new catastrophes: "the future," Gerhard von Rad explains regarding this passage, "(though the term is not really appropriate) is the extension of the present."[6] And Mircea Eliade writes: "[A]s reinterpreted by Greek speculation, [the myth of eternal return] has the meaning of a supreme attempt toward the 'staticization' of becoming, toward annulling the irreversibility of time. If all moments and all situations of the cosmos are repeated *ad infinitum*, their evanescence is, in the last analysis, patent; *sub specie infinitatis*, all moments and all situations remain stationary."[7]

Understood in this way, the concept of the eternal return of the same took hold in European thought with astonishing staying power through subsequent centuries. It appeared, among other places, in the works of Plato, Epicurus, the Stoics. In the eighteenth century, David Hume subjected it to a sarcastic critique, writing in *Dialogues Concerning Natural Religion* that it struck him as "the most absurd system that has yet been proposed."[8] This did not help much: a few decades later Schopenhauer would write: "We can compare time to an endlessly revolving sphere; the half that is always sinking would be the past, and the half that is always rising would be the future."[9] The apex of this circle, Schopenhauer concludes, is the present: immobile, always the same. Consequently, "time is like an irresistible stream, and the present like a rock on which the stream breaks, but which it does not carry away."[10] Like Plato, Epicurus, and Marcus Aurelius before him, Schopenhauer—ignoring Hume's critique—believes that when we regard time as the irreversible succession of moments, when we regard the difference between past and future as absolute, as irremediable, we are merely skimming the surface of phenomena. Looking better, deeper, we would see that the difference between past and future is relative, not absolute, that at the foundation of things everything simply is, everything lasts.

Moments pass only from the vantage point of my current experience—only insofar as (Schopenhauer argues) I fail to extricate myself from the "here and now," insofar as I fail to look upon this moment from a distance. If I do manage just that, when I look upon what I am experiencing from a bird's-eye view—from the perspective of time as a whole—I will see that there is nothing special in the moment I am now experiencing, that it is not unrepeatable, but that it is like others and therefore *repeatable*. And thus it does not pass, it does not fade into nothingness once and for all. I will then understand that "to pass" means essentially the same thing as "to return."

Which is reassuring.

The traces of this tradition—of the belief in the eternal return of all things, which brings us solace—can be found in the New Testament as well. For example, in the Acts of the Apostles, where we are told of Christ, "Whom the heaven must receive until the times of restitution of all things, which God hath spoken by the mouth of all his holy prophets since the world began" (Acts 3:21). Origen later develops this theme as follows:

> For the end is always like the beginning: and, therefore, as there is one end to all things, so ought we to understand that there was one beginning; and as there is one end to many things, so there spring from one beginning many differences and varieties, which again, through the goodness of God, and by subjection to Christ, and through the unity of the holy spirit, are recalled to one end, which is like unto the beginning.[11]

Yet it is already in the Old Testament that we also find a different concept of time: the angry and fearful words of the prophets bear witness to the kind of deep fissure that is to divide the history of Israel into the known "before" and the radically new "after," to what von Rad calls the "wall of fire"—God's judgment—which interrupts the continuity of time and opens the future. It is even more difficult to reconcile the argument of the eternal return of all things with history as told in the New Testament. How are we to reconcile the view that everything is eternally returning to where it has been with a belief in the history of God who was, in a particular time and place, incarnated as the son of a carpenter? With the belief that the life of this man-God, from his birth until his death some thirty-three years later, radically changes the history of the world, opening it to the kinds of possibilities that had never been there before? With this story's claim to change my life as well, two thousand years later, to open before me, too, entirely new, unparalleled, and unforeseeable possibilities?

If everything goes back to where it has already been, if time is like the current of a river that splits against the rock of what actually is—the eternal present—then Christ's death on the cross as described in the New Testament is a symbol, an archetype, a sign of something that always is. It ceases to be an unrepeatable, entirely unique, tragic event. It ceases to be the tragedy of a certain young Jew, Jesus, in his solitary agony, wracked with both fear and hope: at that time, in that one, unrepeatable moment, which changed the world into another, one that was completely different. To understand this event—this life, this death—means (if we think that everything is infinitely returning) to discover an immutable, eternal truth within its account, that "this is how gods behave." A zoologist has a similar understanding of the behavior of amoebas in various situations. But does understanding that "Jesus will lay in agony until the end of the world" amount to the same thing as understanding some universally valid proposition ("two and two make four," "a body immersed in fluid displaces its own weight in fluid") and applying it to one's own circumstance? Does that death—Christ's death on the cross—actually relate to me, to my life, based on the application of some general truth to my particular case? Is this why understanding *his* death will not allow *me* to go back to sleep, as it was for Pascal?

Thus we find nothing odd in the fact that the belief in the eternal return of the same met serious opposition in the Christian tradition. In *City of God*, Augustine writes:

> [H]eaven forbid that correct faith should believe that [. . .] the same ages and the same temporal events recur in rotation. According to this theory, just as Plato, for example, taught his disciples at Athens in the fourth century, in the school called the Academy, so in innumerable centuries of the past, separated by immensely wide and yet finite intervals, the same Plato, the same city, the same school, the same disciples have appeared time after

time, and are to reappear time after time in innumerable centuries in the future. Heaven forbid, I repeat, that we should believe this. For "Christ died once for all for our sins"; and "in rising from the dead" he is never to die again.[12]

"Whoever venerates [. . .] the apocatastasis," the second Council of Constantinople declares in concord with Saint Augustine, using the technical term for eternal return, "be he anathema. [. . .] Whoever says [. . .] that the end will be the true measure of the beginning, be he anathema."[13]

If we understand Christ's death and resurrection as unrepeatable events, as events within an unrepeatable, individual, absolutely unique life, then time's cyclicality is impossible. It is through that death and resurrection that the past is divided from the future: the hard, irreducible reality of that difference stands before our very eyes. If, then, the story of Jesus is to concern me (and this, after all, is Christianity's claim, that this is a story about me), then it has to concern me in the unrepeatable time of my life, from my birth at one point to my death at another. Today, and not some other time. This is not about me as an example of a given species, as the representative of a given nation or social class, of one or another manner or way of behaving.

And yet: can Christianity do without subjecting to doubt the reality of this difference, the difference between past and future? Can it dispense with the concept of eternity that we learn, or so it would seem, simply by looking at nature? And if it cannot, can these two concepts of time be reconciled: time as an eternal "now" beyond all passing, and time as irreversible passing, the time that is painfully and irremediably snuffing out my life, bit by bit, that limits my freedom, time that I cannot overcome? The time of Paradise, what Saint Hieronymus calls "the immoveable rock," that time that destroys nothing, that shatters nothing, that goes nowhere, time whose every moment is full, time that lacks nothing, has lost nothing, time in which there is no difference between past and future, versus the time of Paradise lost, time that destroys everything immersed within it, time in which what has been will not return, time that flows toward death, time permeated with nothingness, the time we know from our own experience.

3

Understanding what links these seemingly conflicting, or even mutually exclusive, concepts—eternity and passing, Paradise and its loss—this is the task Nietzsche posed to himself in the story of Zarathustra. Zarathustra, *the teacher of eternal return*. It is not by accident that the words and metaphors in this text so often echo the biblical story of Jesus: Zarathustra's story is an attempt to interpret that earlier one.

Zarathustra's story begins just as the thirty-year-old Zarathustra is leaving his homeland and going to the mountains to seek solitude. After ten years in the mountains, he decides to return to the valley, to people. He reveals his intention in his conversation with the sun. Just as the sun shares its light with mankind and nature, Zarathustra, Nietzsche tells us, wants to share his wisdom with others.

What purpose does this comparison serve?

First of all, the sun shares its light differently from the way Krzysztof Mroszkiewicz shared with us the roll he'd brought to school for lunch that day; the sun cannot choose to share its light or not: doing so is not one option among many. The sun shines (and thus shares its light) the same way that rain falls. In Nietzsche's metaphorical narrative, the sun is like a volcano that is always active, like milk that doesn't stop boiling over; this sun is excess, a constant movement beyond oneself. Consequently, the sun is not self-sufficient: it needs something or someone with whom to share, to whom to give its light. It needs someone like us: "But we [. . .] took your overflow from you," Zarathustra, standing in the sunlight with his animals, says to the sun.[14]

So, too, does the wisdom that Zarathustra has accumulated in his ten years in the mountains require someone with whom Zarathustra might share it: "Behold, I am weary of my wisdom, like a bee that has gathered too much honey; I need hands outstretched to receive it."[15] The comparison with the sun draws this image more precisely: there is, this comparison seems to say, always too much wisdom, it always needs hands outstretched toward it. Wisdom that has been accumulated but not imparted to others is like sunlight that does not shine, like rain that does not fall, like a square circle. Wisdom, like sunlight, is excess, an unrestrained moving out beyond oneself, a volcano that is always active, milk that is constantly boiling over, "the cup that wants to overflow."[16]

The comparison with the sun also tells us something else about wisdom. Zarathustra addresses the sun as "you quiet eye."[17] Whose eye? A bit later, Zarathustra encounters dancing maidens in the woods and sings them a song for their dance: "Into your eyes I looked recently, O life."[18] Thus the sun is the eye of life. The metaphor of wisdom, of sunlight, is a metaphor for life. The wisdom of Zarathustra we are discussing here is not, therefore, a collection of valid propositions, nor is it knowing how to arrive at them. It is a characterization of his life, and not just of his mind or consciousness. Zarathustra's wisdom rests in what he does, not primarily in what he thinks. It is his life's secret nerve, the essence of his vitality.

The narrative about Zarathustra is a narrative about the meaning of life.

One more thing. Nietzsche writes that "Zarathustra wants to become man again" when Zarathustra decides to descend from the mountains to share his wisdom with people, without whom he cannot live.[19] The "cup that wants to overflow" is therefore a metaphor for Zarathustra's becoming human. Zarathustra becomes a human being, his life becomes a human life. Accordingly, Zarathustra's humanization also tells us something about human life: just as Zarathustra, overflowing with wisdom, needs human hands outstretched toward him, mankind, human life, is a human hand reaching toward something that it is not (Zarathustra). In the context of Zarathustra's narrative and his descent from the mountains, the life of man turns out to be fundamentally incomplete, inadequate, unwhole; it extends beyond itself, not just in the sense that no stage of that life is final but also in that it reaches out—ever, necessarily, in every act—beyond what is human. The metaphor of the sun suggests that human life cannot be understood without the light of that which is no longer human, which marks it, necessarily. "Bless the cup that wants to overflow," Zarathustra says to the sun, "that the water may flow from it golden and carry everywhere the reflection of your delight."[20]

The story of Jesus and his meetings, conversations, and sermons also begins in earnest, according to Luke, in the thirtieth year of its hero's life: "Now Jesus Himself began His ministry at about thirty years of age" (Luke 3:23). Like Zarathustra, Christ then seeks solitude, Zarathustra in the mountains, Christ in the desert. Christ, too, returns to be among the people and share his Good News: "Then Jesus returned in the power of the Spirit to Galilee, and news of him went out through all the surrounding region" (Luke 4:14). The wisdom of God, like the wisdom of Zarathustra, is like an overflowing cup: "My cup runs over" (Ps. 23:5). In this way, he, too, assumes a human form, and God becomes man. And like Nietzsche, Matthew, Mark, Luke, and John do not tell us of a theologian's path toward the discovery of a doctrine, or of the amazingly swift development of its hero's intellectual gifts. Jesus' wisdom, too, consisted in how he lived; it is an indispensable aspect of his life. Removed from the context of his life, it would be nothing more than a collection of empty words. Telling us in this way about God become man, the Evangelists want to show a man in whom God is present, to show human life as an effort to overcome its own humanity, an effort—perhaps in vain but still inscribed in every moment of our lives—to cross out beyond ourselves, beyond what one is and can be, toward God. Just as with Nietzsche's story of Zarathustra, who came down from the mountains in order to "become man."

4

To life as a cup running over, to life as divinity humanized, to human life marked by the effort to move out beyond everything human, to life flooded in a sunlight that is not human—to this irreducible aspect of human life Nietzsche applies the term *overman*.

Let's consider it more closely.

Zarathustra's first speech to those with whom he wishes to share his wisdom starts with the words: "*I teach you the overman.*"[21] And immediately afterward he adds, "Man is something that shall be overcome."[22]

What does this mean?

Perhaps we should begin with the opposite of the *overman*, which we already know in the story of Zarathustra as the concept of the *last man*. Recall that the *last man* is man lacking nothing, free of shortcomings, free of pathologies. The last man does not get sick ("Becoming sick [is] sinful") and does not die ("the last man lives longest").[23] He does not love, if love means risking everything one has, if it is a fire in which all virtue and all reason, every happiness known till now, are lost (though he gladly loves if love is just pleasure, without pain: "What is love? [. . .] asks the last man, and he blinks").[24] The last man knows no differences that cannot be reconciled, and thus he knows no battle more important than life: "One still quarrels, but one is soon reconciled—else it might spoil the digestion."[25] The last man, then, is also someone who knows no fear of the utterly incomprehensible, the alien, the mysterious, the night. Of death: "A little poison now and then: that makes for agreeable dreams."[26] He is boundlessly judicious and utterly virtuous—so judicious and virtuous that, because of this, he can evade all dangers. He is someone who, thanks to his good judgment and virtue, has found happiness—unperturbed peace, undisturbed sleep: "'We have invented happiness,' say the last men, and they blink."[27] Seeking this ideal is tantamount, you may recall Zarathustra saying, to looking for "[g]ood sleep [. . .] and opiate virtues for it."[28]

In short, for Nietzsche the last man is the ideal of man, whose basis is man as he is.

Zarathustra exhorts his listeners to cast this ideal aside: "What is the greatest experience you can have? It is the hour of the great contempt. The hour in which your happiness, too, arouses your disgust, and even your reason and your virtue."[29] Man as he is—his happiness, his judgment, his virtue—should be overcome:

> The most concerned ask today: "How is man to be preserved?" But Zarathustra is the first and only one to ask: "How is man to be overcome?"
>
> I have the overman at heart, *that* is my first and only concern—and *not* man: not the neighbor, not the poorest, not the most ailing, not the best.
>
> O my brothers, what I can love in man is that he is an overture and a going under.[30]

And again: "I love him who wants to create over and beyond himself and thus perishes."[31]

The point here is thus not to idealize man as he is, not to nurture certain of his characteristics and jettison others. It is not only man as he is today who must be overcome, or else man as he was yesterday, not a particular form of man, but all of his forms. In "teaching the overman" Zarathustra tries to show us what man is, what he is capable of, man not only as this or that, not the reasoned animal or the being capable of laughter, not just some thing that, like one's lawn, can be cut, watered, made right. Man is, first of all, the constant overcoming of oneself, a question that remains open without end or limit. Consequently, the life of man is boundlessly risky, a game for everything, a game in which everything is at stake: *happiness* (such as we have achieved), *reason* (such as we have yet attained), *virtue* (such as we have managed to realize). It is a game for humanity, whose meaning must always be won anew. Man, Zarathustra argues, contains within himself an irremovable potential for total destruction and, by the same token, for radical change, dynamite that can blow up what is and open a path to the new. He is like a *dark cloud*, from which *lightning* could appear at any moment.

It is to this, the possibility of human life, that the term "overman" refers.

"Behold," Zarathustra tells the people in the marketplace, "I am a herald of the lightning [. . .]; but this lightning is called *overman*."[32]

We can see that, in speaking of the overman, Zarathustra does not mean the next (and possibly last) stage of human development. The overman is not the "blond beast," the Stakhanovite, the man of the bright future, the American of today. Nor is the overman a higher level of evolution, a species other than Homo sapiens, something into which man could evolve if only he were to behave as prescribed. He is not an angel. Nietzsche writes in *Daybreak*:

> However high mankind may have evolved—and perhaps at the end it will stand even lower than at the beginning!—it cannot pass over into a higher order, as little as the ant and the earwig can at the end of its "earthly course" rise up to kinship with God and eternal life. The becoming drags the has-been along behind it: why should an exception to this eternal spectacle be made on behalf of some little star or for any little species upon it! Away with such sentimentalities![33]

Zarathustra thus calls upon us to cast aside the ideal of the last man not in favor of another, competing ideal. This is not the point of the opposition between these two concepts. The overman is not an ideal, not the correction of man as he is now. It is true that Nietzsche uses this term to characterize the life of man as incomplete, inadequate, unwhole—but not in relation to something or someone that man (at least for now) is not. On the contrary, the term "overman" describes man as he is, it characterizes the life of man as such, the human condition: the overman is the meaning of human life.

It is only the poets who, Nietzsche jeers in *Zarathustra*, are always lifted "higher—specifically, to the realm of the clouds: upon these we [poets] place our motley bastards and call them gods and overmen."[34] The overman is not this "motley bastard" in the clouds, nor does the name apply to anything or anyone at all (like "monkey" or "Homo sapiens"). The overman, Zarathustra tells us, is a *bridge*: it is the possibility, hidden within each of our lives, that will not allow it to settle down, that pushes it out of every situation it finds itself in. It is a bridge to something that outgrows us, that moves out past our concepts. It is a bridge whose presence shapes our entire life, every moment, as Holland is shaped by its maritime border. It is not merely an instant in this life, whether the future, a high point, or the end—but this life as a whole. It is, as Zarathustra would say, "a bridge and not an end."[35]

Stanisław Brzozowski provides the following critique of certain of Nietzsche's interpreters:

> It seems to them that the overman is simply supposed to be the rise of a new species. What they don't know is that it is everywhere a constant presence and reality, that all creation is always and everywhere synonymous with the call to move beyond man![36]

Accordingly, the prefix *over-* in *overman*, as evoked in the call to "move beyond man," does not refer to some order that man encounters and has to adapt to, to a hierarchy in which man has his own place beside other species ("beings," "creatures") higher up or lower down. This *over-* defines human life as an effort to make of it something that outgrows it; it testifies to the fact that life cannot be just "mine," Krzysztof Michalski's (and therefore the life of someone I know, perhaps loosely or incompletely, but someone I know nonetheless), it cannot merely belong to "us," whatever we understand this "us" to be. That this life, "mine," "ours," is always, regardless of how much we determine it or how much we know about it, something more than me or us. That, accordingly, it has this irreducible, alien, *dark* side, in the face of which knowledge, all knowledge, fails, a side that cannot be known.

We should note that in this context the word "dark" takes on an additional meaning. "Darkness" here does not mean just a lack of knowledge. It is rather an excess, not a lack, the excess that life itself is, the excess of meaning, past everything we know and can know. From the vantage point of every individual moment, the darkness of life is darkness we could call deep, bottomless, mysterious, overcrowded with meaning, dense.

It is precisely this other, dark side of human life—life as a constant effort to move out beyond every form it has attained, life as ceaseless and unlimited risk—it is precisely this fundamental nature of human life that the ideal of the *last man* tries to conceal, cover up, and negate. The ideal of the *last man* turns out to be an attempt to ensnare human life in the spider web of *reason, virtue*, to reach unperturbed *happiness*, so as to snuff out, as we have seen, the *illness* within it, the reckless *love*, the irreconcilable *difference*, the unfathomable *mystery*. To triumph over *death*. Thus relieved of its dark aspects, life becomes quiet, safe, transparent (and thus rational), forever, infinitely, eternally. But such an ideal of life—"eternal life"—is, Zarathustra asserts in heralding the *overman*, the opposite of life as it is, and in this sense it is death: "Everywhere the voice of those who preach death is heard [. . .]. Or 'eternal life'—that is the same to me."[37]

Life, the concept of the overman suggests, is something else. Life cannot be "eternal" in the sense of "and so on," "endlessly," "infinitely," because life is the constant disruption of continuity, because to live is to overcome, perpetually, every form of life, every situation that determines it. In this sense, every finitude. Life is the cup that "overflows," but this does not mean simply that every moment is followed by some other moment, and another, and another. Each successive moment of life is this "overflowing cup," water bursting its banks, a volcano erupting. Hegel may have had something similar in mind when, after Schiller, he wrote of human life that "from the chalice of this realm of spirits / foams forth for Him his own infinitude."[38]

To love life then means, as Zarathustra tells us, to be prepared to cast off every form, every situation, in which I may find myself. Not to cling to life as I know it, tightly, at all costs, trying merely to cleanse it of everything that is uncomfortable, painful, dark, and unexpected. "Your love of life shall be love of your highest hope; and your highest hope shall be the highest thought of life [. . .]. [A]nd it is: man is something that shall be overcome."[39]

I love life when, as Konstanty Ildefons Gałczyński prays in the poem "Notes from My Failed Parisian Memoirs," I know how "to depart immediately and abandon my property, my wife, and my child." To liberate myself from what I know, from humanity as it is. To cast myself into darkness, into the alien, the new.

It is no surprise that, from the last man's point of view, the love of life that the concept of the overman manifests is a disturbance of normalcy, the subversion of reason: a *disease*. "All signs of the overman," Nietzsche notes, "appear in man as symptoms of a disease or madness."[40]

This disease—life that outgrows each successive form, every figure of my humanity—hurts. Of necessity, essentially, and not by accident. It is not possible to remove everything but joy from life, which is constantly overcoming itself; such a life cannot simply be pleasurable. The cup of life is full of bitterness. It is full of bitterness because life grows into each of its successive forms and adapts to them, is rooted in them, it nests there—and at the same time it obliterates them, it must abandon them, it must move on. It is the bitterness that comes of the fragility of all forms, the bitterness that leads to a desire that can never be satisfied, the desire to move out beyond what is, the *desire for the overman.*

"Bitterness lies in the cup of even the best love; thus it arouses longing for the overman."[41]

How much this *longing for the overman* differs from the striving toward the ideal of the *last man*! Its object is not a state that I would like to—that I am supposed to—attain. This longing does not have an object distinct from itself, just as the *love for the overman* has no object. (Juliusz Słowacki writes, "He loved nothing, he longed for nothing, / And yet he felt love and longing.")[42] The *desire for the overman* is inscribed in the very act of life: it defines life, it is life itself, its constant disquiet, which cannot be quieted. From the point of view of a person who aspires to the ideal of the eternal, quiet life (the last man), such desire, such longing, is utterly incomprehensible: "What is longing [. . .] asks the last man, and he blinks."[43]

The overman: the internal tension of human life, the tension between what is and the dark, the unknown, the alien, the new: that which outgrows life. Life overcoming itself, life shattered from within. This is where the bitterness comes from, the desire, the pain. A superhuman bitterness, superhuman desire, superhuman pain, for it cannot be made more palatable, it cannot be extinguished, cannot be relieved. There is no treatment for it, for this bitterness, this desire, this pain—they do not arise from any lack that I might identify and remove. While they permeate my life, they are not "mine," not the same way as "my" pain at the dentist or "my" longing for home: they are not from my world, the world of my own. They are "not of this world." It is in precisely this sense that they are "superhuman"—"divine."

This "superhuman," "divine" bitterness, this pain "not of this world," has another side. The unmasterable disquiet of human life, its constant effort to move out beyond itself, into the unknown, this inhuman *disease*, this "being-sick-from-overman" that leaves a trail of unidentifiable bitterness in every moment we live through—all this simultaneously creates a distance from what is, it liberates from every situation, from all conditions, from everything that binds us, from all roots. This bitterness of departure from all that had been mine is thus, at the same time, the joy of liberation, the sweetness of freedom. In *Philosophy in the Tragic Age of the Greeks*,

Nietzsche writes that "bitter and sweet are attached to each other and in-terlocked at any given moment."[44]

"Behold, I am weary of my wisdom, like a bee that has gathered too much honey," Zarathustra tells the sun before descending to the valley.[45] Zarathustra's wisdom, his nerve, the engine, the heart of his life, and thus of every human life, is like honey. Elsewhere, Nietzsche writes, "Honey, says Heraclitus, is at the same time bitter and sweet."[46]

In "teaching the overman," Zarathustra tries to convince us that our lives entail a peculiar sweetness and bitterness, a specific joy and pain, without which life would die. These afford mankind "a happiness that hu-manity has not known so far," Nietzsche writes in *The Gay Science*.[47] Not the happiness of undisturbed peace to which the *last man* aspires—a hap-piness that comes of dreams fulfilled or expectations met, from games won, desires satisfied—but a happiness that comes from the fact that life as I am living it is not mine alone, that it is also something more, that it shines with some no-longer-human, superhuman luster: "the happiness of a god [. . .] that, like the sun in the evening, continuously bestows its ex-haustive riches, pouring them into the sea, feeling richest, as the sun does, only when even the poorest fisherman is still rowing with golden oars! This godlike feeling would then be called—humaneness."[48]

Gold, the color of the sun setting into the sea, is in Nietzsche's eyes a metaphorical vision of the no-longer-human, the superhuman, in a human being. What is "divine" in him or her. Without this, without this *golden luster*—without the "overman," without this kind of "divinity"—human life cannot be understood.

But at the same time it is also Zarathustra, the one who tells those gath-ered on the square about the overman, who a moment earlier announces the *death of God*! Zarathustra, as you may recall, then encounters the holy man who, disillusioned with people, flees to the woods in order to dance and sing and give praise to God in solitude. And yet, Zarathustra thinks upon seeing this, there is no God, *God is dead*, God is gone. The holy man is therefore not holy at all: he's a poor old fool, lost in the woods with his own illusions. "God died: now *we* want the overman to live," Zarathustra says to himself.[49]

Could it be, then, that these two stories—the one about the speeches and adventures of Zarathustra, the other about the words and deeds of Jesus—here part ways?

Yes, most definitely—if in the words of the Gospels we seek a forecast for something that is about to happen, for some future, ideal state (the Kingdom of God), in which the undesirable aspects of human existence will vanish (at least for some), a state that is attainable only if you behave one way and not another, for example, by praising God in song and dance, like the holy man Zarathustra encounters in the woods. If the *Kingdom of*

God is a goal toward which one may—must!—strive, and which can be attained (under certain conditions), then to live happily for millions of years, without end. If the promise of the Kingdom of God is the promise of peace and security, admittedly not right away but later, and perhaps quite soon. If it is a vision of the happy ending that soothes us even today, allowing us to sleep peacefully, for God, this "Good Lord," like the salesman at the candy store around the corner who, with a good-natured smile, sold my daughters sweets—this "Good Lord," as Nietzsche writes in *Daybreak*, "arranges everything in a manner that will in the end be best for us."[50] ("[A] god who cures a cold at the right time," Nietzsche would write in *The Antichrist*, "or who bids us enter a coach at the very moment a violent rainstorm begins [. . .]. A god as servant, as mailman, as calendar man.")[51] If, in the words of Jesus, diseases, conflicts more important than life, the discomfort of ignorance, pain, and death—if all of these are merely transitory, if they are solely a lack, a pathology, an obstacle on the road to future *happiness* and an obstacle that can be removed, once and for all, by acting *virtuously* and *rationally*. If, therefore, in the warm light of the Gospels thus understood, the bitterness of human life becomes accidental, unnecessary, and its sweetness is no longer, like the honey of Heraclitus, also bitter. If the human condition is like a car that, damaged in an accident, Jesus promises to repair—assuming that we behave ourselves—and make like new, and never to break down again.

Doesn't this interpretation of Jesus' teachings recall the vision of the last man, the modern dream of eternal peace and security?

Perhaps, however, it is rather Heidegger who has it right: "There is no security for Christian life."[52]

Nietzsche's argument is similar. Jesus, he maintains, does not announce any future state at all, does not give people some goal that they must now achieve. The Kingdom of God is already here, it's real right now.

> The Kingdom of Heaven is a condition of the heart [. . .]: not something "above the earth." The Kingdom of God does not "come" chronologically-historically, on a certain day in the calendar, something that might be here one day but not the day before: it is an "inward change in the individual," something that comes at every moment and at every moment has not yet arrived—[53]

And elsewhere in Nietzsche's notebooks: "*Blessedness* is not a promise: it's already here."[54]

Here we can hear an echo of the Gospel of Luke: "And when he was demanded of the Pharisees, when the kingdom of God should come, he answered them and said, The kingdom of God cometh not with observation: Neither shall they say, Lo here! or, Lo there! for, behold, the kingdom of God is within you" (Luke 17:20–21).

"The Kingdom of God," Nietzsche argues, is therefore not an ideal state of things that one might eventually attain but is rather inscribed in the life of mankind, in the lives of each and every one of us, in every moment, every corner of this life, "as the lightning, that lighteneth out of the one part under heaven, shineth unto the other part under heaven" (Luke 17:24). Jesus' mission depends precisely on opening our eyes to this lightning. "[T]he word 'son,'" Nietzsche would write in *The Antichrist*, "expresses the *entry* into the over-all feeling of the transfiguration of all things (blessedness); the word 'father' expresses *this feeling itself*, the feeling of eternity, the feeling of perfection."[55]

Somewhat later, D. H. Lawrence would conjure a similar image: "[T]he Father, through the Son wasting himself in a moment of consciousness, consciousness of His own infinitude and gloriousness, [. . .] a Spark of Joy thrown off from the Fire to die ruddy in mid-darkness, a Snip of Flame, the Holy Ghost, the Revelation. And so, the eternal Trinity."[56]

What does this new "sensitivity," this "state of the heart," this "Kingdom of God" mean? "If any man come to me," Jesus says to his crowd of followers, "and hate not his father, and mother, and wife, and children, and brethren, and sisters, yea, and his own life also, he cannot be my disciple" (Luke 14:26). Thus we are not dealing with the selection of certain (good) characteristics and the elimination of others (the bad ones) from life as we live it; the point is not to improve life as it is. We are not dealing with a heart sensitive to good and evil, to the possibility of betterment, but rather with the willingness to throw everything away, with a heart open to "something that comes at every moment and at every moment has not yet arrived."

The Kingdom of God so understood does not exclude the unpleasant, "negative" aspects of our lives, the diseases, irresolvable conflicts, ignorance, pain, and death. It does not shield us from risk. It does not drain the bitterness from the flavor of life; it is only the *last men* who take the sweetness of life for icing and God for the candy man. On the contrary, the Kingdom of God lends life its bitterness, or rather, it produces a specific, "heavenly" bitterness, that essential additive to the sweetness of "blessedness." For one cannot enter the Kingdom of God without fear and trembling. How else could I deal with the prospect of throwing away everything I hold dear?

This is why, as Słowacki writes, "you tremble when God glitters with man."[57] And William James declares, though Nietzsche might well have said the same:

> Let us then resolutely turn our backs on the once-born and their sky-blue optimistic gospel; let us not simply cry out, in spite of all appearances, "Hurrah for the Universe!—God's in his Heaven, all's right with the world." Let us see rather whether pity, pain,

and fear, and the sentiment of human helplessness may not open a profounder view and put into our hands a more complicated key to the meaning of the situation.[58]

If, then, it is possible to find God anywhere—this is how I read Nietzsche's interpretation of Jesus—it is in human life, and not in a cloud. By fleeing from people into the woods, the holy man whom Zarathustra encounters has deprived himself of the one possibility of meeting God: among people. "And they did not know how to love their God," Zarathustra says regarding the holy man and those like him, "except by crucifying man."[59] It is then, when "love of God" tears God's presence from human life (as the holy man whom Zarathustra meets in the woods has done), that God dies as well.

The Kingdom of God announced by Jesus is, according to this interpretation, an aspect of human life, much like the *overman*. It is, as Nietzsche writes, "the seductive flash of gold on the belly of the serpent *vita*."[60]

5

The next concept that Nietzsche uses to characterize life—a concept introduced in the second book of *Zarathustra*, the first having been devoted to the *overman*—is that of the *will to power*: "Where I found the living, there I found will to power."[61]

What does this mean? What is this *will to power*?

The will to power stands for Nietzsche first of all in opposition to the "will to live," to the desire to prolong life as we know it, to continue: "Only where there is life is there also will: not will to life, but [. . .] will to power."[62] The striving after continuation, though it certainly happens, is, Nietzsche argues, inessential to life; the point of living is not to go on living, not to prolong what already is, for "where there is perishing and a falling of leaves, behold, there life sacrifices itself—for power."[63] The fall: death and destruction, and thus the disruption of continuity, are not simply a negation, the opposite of life, but, Nietzsche maintains, belong to life itself, are constitutive of it. Life, by its very nature, opposes itself: it sacrifices, risks, destroys every form of itself. This self-opposition is what life really means.

"Loving life is very nearly the opposite of loving a long life," Nietzsche notes at the end of 1882.[64]

It is to this fundamental discontinuity of life that the term "will to power" refers.

This does not mean merely that there are matters for which it's worth sacrificing one's life (i.e., "power," "authority"), and that it's difficult to understand human life (as opposed to, say, that of an amoeba) without taking into account this readiness for sacrifice. Nietzsche has something greater in mind. In the expression "will to power," "power" does not signify some object of the will, something one wants. The point here is not that man essentially wants "power" (authority, strength, might) more than he wants a continuation of his life. Likewise, the term "will" in the expression "will to power" has no separate meaning; what is meant here is not a pre-disposition that might be turned in another direction, a "will" that could just as well "want" something else. The term "will to power" refers there-fore neither to the (undeniable) fact that people always either want or don't want something (as opposed to their thinking or sleeping), nor to the fact that they want different things at different times. In Nietzsche's usage, the *will to power* is a set expression; taken separately, its individual components have no independent meaning. It is an expression that characterizes human life as a whole, as *power*.

In other words, in describing life as a *will to power*, Nietzsche asserts that life does not adapt to the world but rather creates it: "what you have called world, that shall be created only by you: your reason, your image, your will, your love shall thus be realized."[65]

"Will" and *will to power* are thus completely different concepts: the *will to power* is not some form of "will." "Will," as a predisposition toward one thing or another, assumes the world is to a certain extent ready-made, di-versified in this way but not that (into what I want, and what I don't). Whereas, from the point of view of the *will to power*, the world is a field of unlimited creativity. It is entirely plastic, boundlessly open to change, fluid.

Nietzsche occasionally uses the word *Kraft* (force, strength) in the same meaning as the expression *will to power*. In *Twilight of the Idols*, he defines it thus: "Excess of strength alone is the proof of strength."[66] Which I take to mean that *strength* (*the will to power*) cannot be measured. It has no ex-ternal measure, no scale to which it can be fitted. Life understood as *force*, as *will to power*, is life that cannot be delimited, neither by that which is nor by that which can or should be. In this sense, it is "excess." Defined by the *will to power*, life is always something more than it is in any given mo-ment: it is excess. It is creative. Life is *force*, it is the *will to power*, because it always moves out beyond itself, creating one new form after another, none of which can become its ultimate form.

And it is for this reason that life is "unfathomable," that it "boils over," that it "flows."

Insofar as life is the *will to power*, it cannot be understood in reference to what it is, neither from the vantage of a more or less successful adaptation to the world as we find it nor in regard to a goal that could be achieved. Life, as the *will to power*, can be understood only in reference to itself, as a creative power unbounded by external barriers.

Darwin, by interpreting life as a competition for the best adaptation to the world as it is, a game whose stakes are survival itself, was therefore incorrect, as far as Nietzsche was concerned. "[T]he total appearance of life," Nietzsche writes in *Twilight of the Idols*, "is not the extremity, not starvation [in the sense of limitation from without, of external pressure], but rather riches, profusion, even absurd squandering"—and therefore creativity that cannot be locked into any fixed shape, creativity that exceeds every form it creates for itself.[67]

The Stoics, for Nietzsche, were wrong as well, though in a different way. For them, too, the measure of life was located beyond it: life, they taught, should be adapted to the world as it is, to the nature of things. "I find this way of thinking repulsive," Nietzsche notes. "[Stoicism] is finally forced to say: everything will be as it happens, and I'd have it no other way."[68] This attitude is especially evident in their understanding of pain, anxiety, and passion; the Stoics teach that they must be avoided, and they tell us how. Meanwhile, pain, anxiety, and passion, Nietzsche argues, are not products of the uncomfortable circumstance life has found itself in for one reason or another, whether due to divine providence or natural law, but are an expression of life as it truly is. They are an indispensable, constitutive element of a life that flows out beyond each of its successive forms, of a life that destroys whatever shape it has been given in order to create a new one.

The *will to power* is life that, at every step, moves out beyond itself, that is constantly sacrificing every form it has held until now; it is a life full of endogenous pain, anxiety, and passion, the "earthquake," the "terrible teacher of the great contempt, who preaches 'away with you!' to the very faces of cities and empires," in order to make room for what is as yet unknown, unforeseen, new. It is unbounded creativity.[69]

As we have seen, in the world of Nietzsche's concepts the term "will to power" performs a function similar to that of the term "overman": it characterizes life, life in its entirety, as a continuous movement beyond itself, as an uninterrupted overcoming of each of its forms.

What do we gain from using this new concept?

For starters, let's consider the following question: in declaring, through Zarathustra's lips, that "life is the will to power," is Nietzsche suggesting the discovery of some universal feature, some universal structure of life?[70] Does Zarathustra's claim that "life is the will to power" have a status similar to that of other propositions, such as "all cows are blue" or "two and two make four"?

No, that's not the point. If all forms of life are symptoms of the *will to power*, then concepts are as well. "Thoughts are forces," as Nietzsche once noted.[71] "In knowledge too," Zarathustra says, "I feel only my will's joy in begetting and becoming."[72] "Knowledge," Nietzsche would write in the margin, "is lust and thirst: knowledge is procreation."[73] Knowledge creates. Consequently, knowledge cannot be completed, by its very nature, and not because mankind, its subject, doesn't get there or cannot mature to that level. "All knowledge, as creativity, has no end."[74] In other words, "As creativity, all knowledge is non-knowledge."[75] As "power," as "creativity," knowledge contains within itself the potential to create something that does not yet exist, something new, and therefore something unknown, inexpressible. "Our greatest danger," Nietzsche notes while working on *Zarathustra*, "is faith in the possibility of total knowledge of creativity's limits."[76] It is evidence of life's weakness, its fatigue, a shadow of death.

The connection between knowledge and life thus excludes, Nietzsche concludes, the possibility of total knowledge. To this extent, the ultimate and universal structure of life (if this is how we were to understand the *will to power*) is a nonsensical notion. The phrase "will to power," as the term is used by Nietzsche, cannot therefore refer directly to the world and how it is ordered but first of all characterizes our concepts (as well as Zarathustra's wisdom): as an expression of life, as creative, and, because of this, temporary—as fragile.

And yet, is knowledge possible without some faith in the possibility of total knowledge?

No, of course not. Nietzsche would agree with me. When Nietzsche writes, "As creativity, all knowledge is non-knowledge," he uses the term "knowledge" the same way we usually do: I "know" that to get home I have to turn right, then left; I "know" that two and two make four. I "know" means here: I'm convinced that "things are the way I know them to be." This conviction, regardless of whether I'm right or wrong, is a necessary component of the meaning of my "knowledge." Knowledge strives toward an ultimate determination, it presupposes a claim to universal and unconditional validity, as well as to the possibility of satisfying that claim, the possibility that things are as it declares them to be. Without that possibility, knowledge is meaningless. Without the belief that—often, in principle, at least from time to time—things are the way I think they are, I couldn't reasonably formulate any assertion. My orientation in the world would be utterly impossible. How could I live (other than in an insane asylum), were I not convinced that I am Krzysztof Michalski (regardless of how wrong I may be about myself) and not a triangle, or an angel, or a wagtail?

If not for other reasons then, it is certainly as my own—as a condition of my orientation in the world, a condition of the possibility of my life—that knowledge contains within itself the claim to be *total knowledge*. Insofar as knowledge is anyone's, mine, Zarathustra's (wisdom), it strives to be definitive, certain, closed. As mine, as somebody's, knowledge is necessarily bound up with *faith in the possibility of total knowledge*, and by the same token (according to Nietzsche) it testifies to the exhaustion and weakening of creativity, snuffing out life. As somebody's, knowledge, even the wisdom of Zarathustra, cannot be released from the shadow of death.

Though it may be that I understand this word "mine" too narrowly here. It may be that, sometimes, when I say "my" or "mine," we can hear something more than a reference to Krzysztof Michalski, to me as I know myself. This is what a certain Johannes wrote to his Cordelia (Kierkegaard, in *The Seducer's Diary*):

> *My Cordelia,*
> "My"—what does the word designate? Not what belongs to me, but what I belong to, what contains my whole being, which is mine insofar as I belong to it. After all, my God is not the God who belongs to me, but the God to whom I belong, and the same when I say my native land, my home, my calling, my longing, my hope. If there had been no immortality before, then the thought that I am yours would break through nature's usual course.
> *Your Johannes*[77]

To the maidens he meets in the forest, Zarathustra sings, bringing them to dance, about himself, about his own life, and about his own wisdom. About his wisdom, which knows what life is like: wild, because it cannot be reined in by any form, locked into any given formula; creative, because it is a will, a force that shatters any obstacle. The wise Zarathustra, it would seem, already understood life, had found its truth, had caught it in the web of his concepts (*will to power*); his wisdom had come so close to the truth, to life, that there is no longer any easy way of separating it from himself: "is it my fault that the two [my wisdom and my life] look so similar?"[78]

Similar, yet not identical. For in the end life, after all, will evade Zarathustra's wisdom, just as it will escape the knowledge held by any of us. Because that knowledge is mine, just as Zarathustra's wisdom is his, and life is indeed mine, but not completely, not quite: it is also something more, it is neither mine, nor his. Life overflows each of its forms, it overcomes any shape that can be given to it. It also overcomes me, as well as Zarathustra, insofar as he is me. Zarathustra, like me, so long as he lives, is marking the horizon of his life through his knowledge, through his concepts; he is making his nest, his home. But for life, for the force that life is, for the *will to power*, this horizon is not a limit, not a barrier, not a border. Life, in every moment of living, is more. Everything I am, everything that the word "I" contains, can burst at any moment like a soap bubble, and one day it will. Then I will die. This perspective is inextricably bound to my knowledge, to my concepts, and it gives them a bitter taste: it makes them painful.

Knowledge I cannot live without, a testament to my weakness, which casts the shadow of death on my life—and the life churning within that knowledge, a force overflowing the banks of every form, thereby slipping out from all concepts, a force that is dark with the excess of potential meanings, that is unknowable: *the will to power.*

"KNOWING and BEING are opposite, antagonistic states," writes D. H. Lawrence. "The more you KNOW, exactly, the less you *are.* The more you *are,* in being, the less you KNOW. This is the great cross of man, his dualism. The blood-self, and the nerve-brain self."[79]

No surprise, then, that, face-to-face with life, Zarathustra's wisdom, as close as it is to life, garners sadness, a premonition of separation:

> The sun has set long ago [. . .]; the meadow is moist, a chill comes from the woods. Something unknown is around me and looks thoughtful. What? Are you still alive, Zarathustra?
>
> Why? What for? By what? Whither? Where? How? Is it not folly still to be alive?
>
> Alas, my friends, it is the evening that asks thus through me. Forgive me my sadness.[80]

Why? What for? Whither? Where? These are wise questions, questions that, if they are not answered, make it difficult to live: to live, one must want this or that, reach for a goal, choose a path. But life, every life, is also something more than a collection of such answers. Life is also essentially stupid. It will not—it cannot—answer the questions *Why? What for? Whither?* These questions will never exhaust life: there is always too much of it. In every moment of living, life is something more than itself, and thus it cannot have an ultimate goal, an external point of reference. Only fatigue—*evening*—infuses us with (illusory) hope that we will reach its bottom. Life itself, life as it is—the *will to power*—wants nothing, is going nowhere. To put it another way, all it wants is itself: it is the will to will, and nothing more.

Somewhere out beyond all my concepts lies the unfamiliar, *dark* side of life. It is from there that the shadow of death falls on my knowledge, as well as on Zarathustra's wisdom; this is where despair and the longing that time entails originate. And yet that is not all: this dark zone, mine and not-mine, this ever-present excess of meaning among my concepts, which can never be translated into propositions, into an additional bit of knowledge, into a description of what is (beyond what we already know)—all this places my life beyond myself, beyond what I know about myself and my world, and thus also beyond (my) sadness in departing this world, beyond the cares, beyond my worry about everything I am to leave behind.

The concept *will to power*, then, does not describe life in the same way as the term "sky-blue" describes the sky. The *will to power* characterizes our lives, or rather moving out past our concepts, past what we know and can know about it. It points to the internal tension of human knowledge, its ambivalent connection to its source, the unknown, dark, constantly new life.

Thus it is no surprise that Nietzsche opposes his concept of *will to power* to Schopenhauer's concept of "will," as the common denominator for all phenomena. One of the "excesses and vices" of Schopenhauer, who "allowed himself to be seduced and corrupted by the vain urge to be the unriddler of the world," is, as Nietzsche writes in *The Gay Science*, "the unprovable doctrine of the *One Will*"—and thus the assertion that there exists something like a "will" that is identical in every context, a unity hidden within the diversity of life, the discovery of which allows us to arrange the puzzle of the world into a universal order.[81]

How could one prove the existence of such a thing? How could we prove the existence of an "I" completely independent of what I do, of a will that is entirely independent of what I want, an identical being (a substance, a subject) utterly independent of the circumstance in which this being finds itself, in which I find myself? It is not possible. Such concepts contradict (Nietzsche says) the very nature of concepts: they are supposedly independent from life, and yet concepts arise from life, are the expression of life. What I do, the situation I find myself in—that is, this life and no other—is the condition of the possibility of all understanding, of all concepts.

Against Schopenhauer, Nietzsche asserts that there is no universal, identical "will." "The metaphor of 'weak' will," he notes in 1888, "can be misleading. For there is no will, so it can be neither strong nor weak."[82] "There is no will": this does not mean that we cannot find something like a (universal and identical) will in the world, in the same way as we cannot find centaurs or grasshoppers (if one does not know where to find them). No: the very concept of such a "will," the concept of a common denominator to which we can reduce the diversity of life (for example, a universal and identical "will"), is impossible.

The *will to power* is not, then, such a common denominator. It does not reduce the diversity of life. It does not reduce the diversity of the situations in which life (mine, yours, Zarathustra's) can find itself. It does not gather all of these situations into some kind of system; it does not bind them to each other. The claim that "life is the will to power" does not mean that, regardless of what distinguishes one situation from another, life "wants only one thing" in them all. Rather, it means the opposite. It means that no such concept exists or can exist: one "meaning," one "content," which links all the moments and all the facts of life into a single whole. Life, Nietzsche wants to convince us with the help of the concept *will to power*, is in every situation pregnant with the unknown, with the radically alien. It is therefore necessarily diverse, or perhaps better: the very concept of life contains an irremovable diversity, a diversity with no prospect of unity. This is the difference between that which is, in any given moment, and the unknown, the alien, the possible—the irremediable rift in life, the fact that in every moment life is the excess that cannot be accommodated in any concept, any structure, any form. "Internal" diversification: not from the point of view of an object that disintegrates or is created in life (such as a common denominator?), nor from the point of view of a goal that life is allegedly pursuing. This is a difference of another kind than that between yellow and white or between the complete happiness of mankind and the stage where we currently find ourselves; it is a diversity that supposes no heretofore extant identity (yellow, white, happiness and the way toward it) but precedes all identity, or is rather an element of every identity, is inscribed within every identity. Because every identity—every form, every structure, every concept—has this other, *dark* side that slips out from knowledge, an opening toward the alien, toward the unexpected.

Life—life itself, the *will to power*—is irremediably diverse, and thus it heals no wounds, smooths no antagonisms, affords no peace: "For that will which is the will to power must will something higher than any reconciliation."[83] Since our concepts bear witness to a life that is always *overcoming* itself, it becomes necessary to understand them in the context of the *struggle* that leads to this triumph and to discern in them the instruments of same, to see them as "weapons," to hear in them "clattering signs that life must overcome itself again and again."[84]

"I must be struggle," Life says to Zarathustra.[85]

Nietzsche has one more name for what we are discussing here: *appearance*. Life is basically, essentially—so he writes—appearance. Not in the sense that it seems to be "X" when it is (actually) "Y" but because no form it takes is solely what it is, because no truth about it is or can be the "whole" truth, that the very concept of "the whole truth" is, in reference to life, nonsense. In *The Gay Science*, Nietzsche writes: "What is 'appearance' for me now? Certainly not the opposite of some essence: what could I say about any essence except to name the attributes of its appearance! Certainly not a dead mask that one could place on an unknown *x* or remove from it! Appearance is for me that which lives and is effective."[86]

This is why, as we have seen, a metaphor for life that often appears in Zarathustra's sermons is that of a woman. Woman is, in Nietzsche's eyes, the play of appearances, the shimmer of light on the gently undulating sea, dresses, blouses, stockings, ribbons. Powder and lipstick. There, but also not there. A smile, a promise, temptation—and nothing left in the hand but air: "But perhaps this is the most powerful magic of life: it is covered by a veil interwoven with gold, a veil of beautiful possibilities, sparkling with promise, resistance, bashfulness, mockery, pity, and seduction. Yes, life is a woman."[87]

There is no "real" life hidden beneath this *golden veil of possibility*, just as beneath the play of feminine appearances—the lipstick, the clothes, the smiles, the tears—there is no "truth" about the woman (a naked lady). This veil, this play—this is already it, this is life itself: femininity. If "truth" stands in opposition to "appearance," then it is also in opposition to life, the enemy of femininity. In *Beyond Good and Evil*, Nietzsche writes:

> But she does not *want* truth: what is truth to woman? From the beginning, nothing has been more alien, repugnant, and hostile to woman than truth—her great art is the lie, her highest concern is mere appearance and beauty. Let us men confess it: we love and honor precisely *this* art and *this* instinct in woman—we who have a hard time and for our relief like to associate with beings under whose hands, eyes, and tender follies our seriousness, our gravity and profundity almost appear to us like folly.[88]

The point here is not that women lie and that life, too, is full of deceptions and appearances. *Woman* is, in this context, a metaphor for irremediable diversity: woman, who can never be permanently bound in a given form, understood unambiguously, conceptualized, fixed to the burden of what is. Like woman, life is also "light," also "stupid." "Lying" and "appearance" are, in this usage, the means by which the world manifests itself in our lives, such that every form thereof contains, and veils, this other, dark side—it can never be what it seems, and nothing more.

This being the case—if life is the *will to power*, and there is no truth in the face of which life would be rendered powerless; if life cannot be accommodated by any structure, and the burden of what is will never rid it of its lightness—then, Zarathustra declares, "Willing [i.e., the will to power] liberates."[89] Life as *will to power* is absolutely free. "Will—that is the name of the liberator and joy-bringer; thus I taught you, my friends."[90]

Which certainly does not mean that human will is not supposed to know any limits and that all is permitted. "*What I warn against*," Nietzsche notes, "the libertinage, the principle of '*laisser aller*,' should not be confused with the will to power (—which is the counterprinciple)."[91] "Will," in this context, is the *will to power*, and thus not a human capacity separate from "reason" or "feeling," identical in different situations and therefore independent of them. The *freedom* we have in mind here is rather another way of characterizing the kind of excess that life itself is, at every moment: its immanent *lightness*, the fact that life is a *force*, a power with no limits, a creative power.

Understood in this way, the free, creative life, the will to power—so wrote Stanisław Brzozowski, following in Nietzsche's footsteps a bit later—is "an absolute beginning, [. . .] the rise of something [. . .] that cannot be derived from any concept [. . .]—[it] is the source of all truth, good, beauty, reality."[92]

Doesn't this interpretation of life presuppose that there is no God? Doesn't it suggest that availing oneself of this potential for freedom, of this creative quality of life, requires us to remove the restrictive binds of so-called external (divine?) rules, the burden of obligations and objectives that have been imposed on life: the *death of God*?

Indeed, Zarathustra says, "Away from God and gods this will has lured me; what could one create if gods existed?"[93] What would be left of creativity if there existed a God who fixed the framework within which human life had to be situated, to which it was supposed to adapt? If the burden of the obligations God has imposed on us would not allow us to depart from what is, if it bound us, through responsibility and guilt, to what we have already done? And doesn't Jesus, as he is described in the Gospels, present just such a framework? Doesn't he announce these kinds of obligations, at the same time promising to sympathize with those who fail to meet them? Doesn't he exhort his listeners to understand his words—and to adapt their lives to them?

Perhaps, however, the Nietzschean interpretation of life as the *will to power* implies not only a critique of Christianity but also a unique reading of the biblical story of Jesus. God's presence in human life is not, as this reading would have it, something like a set order that determines what's up, what's down, what's true or false, good or bad. The words of Jesus are not meant primarily to convince his audience of how things are: "And my speech and my preaching was not with enticing words of man's wisdom, but in demonstration of the Spirit and of power: That your faith should not stand in the wisdom of men, but in the power of God" (1 Cor. 2:4–5). And elsewhere in the same letter: "For the kingdom of God is not in word, but in power" (1 Cor. 4:20). The words of Paul, like those of Christ, whose messenger Paul wishes to be, strive (according to this interpretation) to change reality, and not just our perception of it. They are a force that aims to transform the life they address, to liberate the heretofore unrealized possibilities within it. God's words are supposed to allow my life—for it is also to me that they are addressed—to overcome the burden of the factual, the burden of my condition until now. They open it to the unexpected, they give rise to its capacity for the future—its *lightness*. To understand these words, to assimilate this message, means to tear oneself away from everything that is: to discover the anxiety hidden in the depths of my life, the impatience of the caged bird, which longs to fly off God-knows-where, so long as it's somewhere else, into free space—the impatience with life as it is, which compelled Paul to go to the Corinthians and the Thessalonians—"For this cause, when I could no longer forbear" (1 Thess. 3:5)—and to share his impatience with his listeners. Impatience, anxiety, and at the same time anguish, suffering—because, after all, it isn't easy, it's not always easy to tear oneself away from what is. But then the joy that is unknown to the life we have had till now—not the joy that comes from achieving a goal, from fulfilling one's dreams, from a sudden surprise, but the joy of my liberation from everything that has been mine, the joy of the lightness of life, unearthly freedom, the "joy of the Holy Spirit." "And you became followers of us," Paul writes to the Thessalonians, "and of the Lord, having received the word in much affliction, with joy of the Holy Ghost" (1 Thess. 1:6).

"For the word of God is quick," Paul writes to the Hebrews, "and powerful, and stronger than any two-edged sword, piercing even to the dividing asunder of soul and spirit, and of the joints and marrow" (Heb. 4:12). The word of God is a force, dynamite that blasts apart life as it is. This is the very basis of God's love for man, a love that has little to do with pity, with sympathy that accepts the world as we find it. "For the love of Christ constraineth us" (2 Cor. 5:14)—it drives us from the place where each of us happens to be, whether we are rich, poor, happy, or sad. That we might not remain as we are, that we might find ourselves "beside ourselves" (2 Cor. 5:13). It opens us to the unknown, the new, the terrifying, the blessed—to the *Kingdom of God.*

Zarathustra speaks similarly of the will to power: "But my fervent will to create impels me ever again toward man; thus is the hammer impelled toward the stone."[94] Similarly, God said to Jeremiah, "Is not my word like as a fire [. . .] and like a hammer that breaketh the rock in pieces?" (Jer. 23:29). This is precisely how Zarathustra understands his love for mankind ("*I love people*," Zarathustra tells the hermit as the book opens): it is the kind of love we mean, Nietzsche writes, when we speak of "great love," a love in which the human being crosses beyond itself and everything human, everything that has been human till now. A love that moves beyond accepting what one finds and, in this way, beyond all pity and all forgiveness: "all great love is even above all its pity; for it still wants to create the beloved."[95]

6

And so, Nietzsche argues, we—we people—are free, utterly free. The *will to power* is a concept that indicates the fundamental, inalienable *freedom* of human life, of a life that is constantly, ceaselessly shattering each of its forms in turn. Life, my life, knows no bounds—although we are each individually capable of one thing and not another, too weak, too stupid, inherently burdened: we do encounter such limits. Deep down, Nietzsche says, our possibilities are unlimited—somewhere deep in "me," deep in my "soul," at the core of our "lives," we are utterly free, creative without limit—despite the fact that in our daily lives the world as it is weighs upon our lives and thoughts.

If this is so, however, if the essence of human life is the *will to power*—which means that life surpasses, necessarily, all possible bounds—if human life is creative and cannot be enclosed within any concept, if our lives are the source of the meaning of all reality, then how are we to understand the fact—so hard, so difficult to bear—that I will never return to my father's arms, that I will never see my dead friend again?

What am I to do with this, with a moment to which I cannot return? What am I to do with the past? In *Physics*, Aristotle says that "time wastes things away, and that all things grow old through time."[96] How do we reconcile this with unbounded human freedom? Zarathustra says to the people:

> Willing liberates; but what is it that puts even the liberator himself in fetters? "It was"—that is the name of the will's gnashing of teeth [. . .]. Powerless against what has been done, he is an angry spectator of all that is past. The will cannot will backwards; [. . .] he cannot break time.[97]

Perhaps, then, in the end we aren't free at all? Perhaps this so-called freedom of ours is nothing more than the freedom of a horse in its paddock, a tiger in its cage? Maybe it's only freedom within the framework of an irremovable barrier—the past, now lost forever?

Either I am completely free, or what has been will never be again, and the past is an insurmountable barrier.

Is it really the case, however, that what has been will never return? Maybe the past can come back, maybe there's some way of turning it back our way? Maybe, then, the difference between past and future is not final: maybe it can be effaced, maybe it can be negated?

This is the ultimate task that Nietzsche assigns to Zarathustra: to prove that the past is not some boulder that can never be rolled back—"to re-create all 'it was'" so that it is no longer an insurmountable barrier, a burden one cannot cast off, once and for all, "[t]o redeem what is past in man" so that it can return again.[98]

To overcome death.

But how? The answer is supposed to be Zarathustra's *abysmal thought*, the thought in which the most important threads of his sermons run together, the thought to which the concept *will to power* leads: the thought of the *eternal return of the same*. This is Nietzsche's central thought, which organizes his conceptual universe.

It seems, then, that Nietzsche would link up here with the long tradition of the concept I discussed earlier and would say, following Schopenhauer (whom Nietzsche after all regarded, at least for a certain time, as his teacher): "We can compare time to an endlessly revolving sphere": what is, the *present*, is a *rock*, not subject to the passage of time.[99]

But no: Nietzsche's answer is diametrically opposite. So let's take a closer look.

It is not a direct response. Rather, it is hidden—not by chance, I believe—in a series of Zarathustra's metaphorical stories and conversations. Zarathustra introduces it as he is telling the sailors on a ship about a puzzling vision he had had some time before.

The protagonists of this vision are Zarathustra himself and his opponent: "half dwarf, half mole, lame, making lame, dripping lead into my ear, leaden thoughts into my brain," Zarathustra describes him to us.[100] Zarathustra and the dwarf are climbing up a mountain and sparring with each other. Their argument intensifies until Zarathustra brings it to a head: "Dwarf! It is you or I!" he says.[101] What separates them so dramatically? "[Y]ou do not know my abysmal thought. *That* you could not bear," Zarathustra tells the dwarf.[102] Zarathustra clearly believes that it is his *abysmal thought* that constitutes the difference between himself and the dwarf.

Just then, a surprising sight presents itself to the climbers: a gate that marks the meeting place of two paths. Each of these paths starts from the gate and moves in a different direction; both disappear into infinity. Over the gate there is an inscription: "the moment." We might expect, then, that it is this vision, the vision of the gate/moment, as well as Zarathustra's conversation with the dwarf about what it might signify (which he relays to the sailors), that is supposed to explain to us this *abysmal thought* of Zarathustra's, the abysmal thought that separates him so dramatically from the dwarf.

The two paths that meet at the gate/moment are, as Zarathustra explains to the sailors, the past and the future. They do not just meet, "they offend each other face to face [. . .], these paths contradict each other."[103] Which means: they differ. Here, in this *moment*, their difference comes to the fore. It is here, in this *moment*, that the past differs from the future.

It is also from this point, from this *moment*, from the moment of their meeting, that the past and the future run infinitely in opposite directions. Does this mean, Zarathustra asks the dwarf, that, having left this particular *moment* ("now"), the past and future will never meet again? Is the difference between them therefore irremovable, the past irretrievable, time irreversible?

No, the dwarf answers, not at all: time is a circle, everything comes back to the same place.

If this is true, if the dwarf is correct, then the distinction between past and future is not final: the past is not an insurmountable barrier. The dwarf would then have found the answer we have been looking for, the perspective in which the difference between past and future disappears: he who succeeds in understanding that time is the eternal return of the same, that what has been will be again, has no need to fear time's destructive power.

Zarathustra, however, is not satisfied with the dwarf's answer. He rejects it. In fact, he rejects it angrily, as if he'd wanted to say: "Time's a circle? Everything that has been will be again? What nonsense!" Nevertheless, immediately following this angry response, Zarathustra repeats what the dwarf had just said, in a sequence of (seemingly) rhetorical questions:

> Must not whatever *can* happen have happened [. . .]? [. . .] And if everything has been there before—what do you think, dwarf, of this moment? Must not this gateway too have been there before? [. . .] And this slow spider, which crawls in the moonlight, and this moonlight itself, and I and you in the gateway, whispering together, whispering of eternal things—must not all of us have been there before?[104]

Wasn't all of this there already, and mustn't it keep returning eternally?

But then maybe the dwarf was right after all?

Here Zarathustra's conversation with the dwarf breaks off unexpectedly. There is a change of scene: "Where was the dwarf gone now? And the gateway? [. . .] Was I dreaming, then? Was I waking up?"[105] Zarathustra now sees before him (so he tells the sailors)—in a dream? in waking life?— a young shepherd, "writhing, gagging, in spasms, his face distorted, and a heavy black snake hung out of his mouth."[106] He tries to help the shepherd, to pull the snake from his mouth, but cannot. So he screams—or, rather, something screams within him—"Bite! Bite its head off! Bite!"[107] The shepherd heeds his advice, bites off the snake's head, spits it out far from himself, and laughs an uncomfortable, uncanny laugh: "Never yet on earth has a human being laughed as he laughed!"[108]

"Oh, my brothers," Zarathustra says regarding his vision, "now a thirst gnaws at me, a longing that never grows still [. . .] for this laughter [. . .]; oh, how do I bear to go on living!"[109]

Zarathustra's narrative ends here.

How are we to understand the scene with the shepherd and the snake? A couple of pages later (in the passage entitled "The Convalescent"), Zarathustra interprets it himself in his conversation with the animals that accompany him on his journey, a snake and an eagle. Yet another dramatic scene precedes this conversation: Zarathustra's attempt, as he tells it, to bring forward the *ultimate depth* of his life, the *abyss* opening within his life (again, we may surmise, we're talking about Zarathustra's *abysmal thought*). He has now nearly succeeded, it seems to Zarathustra—"My abyss speaks, I have turned my ultimate depth inside out into the light"—and yet at the last minute his attempt fails, and Zarathustra casts aside with disgust what he has brought to light.[110]

For the animals observing Zarathustra, this entire attempt to bring his abysmal thought to the fore looks like an attack of serious illness; Zarathustra is unable to recover for some time. When he finally does show signs of life again, the animals try to help him return to health, to the old life, and lure him with promises of the world lying before him: "O Zarathustra[:] Step out of your cave: the world awaits you like a garden."[111] The order of the world, the order that brings us to health, that offers consolation and peace, is (the animals say) the eternal return of all things: "Everything goes, everything comes back, eternally rolls the wheel of being. Everything dies, everything blossoms again; eternally runs the year of being. [. . .] In every Now, being begins [. . .]. The center is everywhere. Bent is the path of eternity."[112]

But this time, too—much as had happened in the earlier conversation with the dwarf, who had said something similar—Zarathustra reacts angrily, and now ironically as well:

> "O you buffoons and barrel organs!" Zarathustra replied and smiled again. "How well you know what had to be fulfilled in seven days [the seven days of his illness], and how that monster crawled down my throat and suffocated me. But I bit off its head and spewed it out. And you, have you already made a hurdy-gurdy song of this? But now I lie here, still weary of this biting and spewing, still sick from my own redemption. *And you watched all this?*"[113]

Zarathustra's reaction here is precisely the aforementioned commentary to the earlier scene: the shepherd struggling with the snake, from the dream Zarathustra had told to the sailors, turns out here to have been Zarathustra himself. The violent attack of illness in the scene with the animals is that other, dramatic struggle of Zarathustra with the snake as seen from outside, from the perspective of the animals observing him. If this is the case, then the struggle of the shepherd-Zarathustra with the snake must also have been about his attempt to bring to light Zarathustra's *abysmal thought*. As was the first of these scenes, Zarathustra's conversation with the dwarf in front of the gateway/*moment*. All three scenes, it turns out, share the same theme: Zarathustra's *abysmal thought* and the context in which he presents it, the *moment*.

The sequence of the three scenes (Zarathustra with the dwarf before the gate; the shepherd and the snake; Zarathustra and his animals) now becomes, I believe, more decipherable. Zarathustra responds disapprovingly to the efforts of the animals, which wish to comfort him with a vision of the eternal wheel of existence ("O you buffoons and barrel organs!"), for the animals, as he accuses them, only "watched" his struggles. They cannot, therefore, understand what those struggles are about. We can surmise, then, where Zarathustra's rejection of the dwarf's words comes from in the first scene, when the dwarf, at the *vision* of the gateway/*moment*, declares that time is a circle: the dwarf, like the animals a little later on, is only *looking at the moment*. But the *moment* cannot be seen in the same way as one can see and describe a gate. The *moment*, Zarathustra's reaction suggests, can be understood only by someone struggling, as the shepherd/Zarathustra struggles with the snake/illness, and not by someone who, like the dwarf (and Zarathustra) before the gateway, or like the animals observing Zarathustra's illness, merely "watched all this."

Which explains why Zarathustra's conversation with the dwarf before the gate breaks off so suddenly and why the scene changes from the first to the second. So long as Zarathustra and the dwarf are wrestling with each other over what they *see* (the gateway/*moment*), as they are in the first scene, the difference between them cannot be properly understood, and their argument cannot be resolved. From the observer's perspective the *moment* cannot be grasped, so that consequently neither Zarathustra's *abysmal thought* nor the difference between Zarathustra and the dwarf can be explained.

Zarathustra does not agree with the dwarf, not because the dwarf's statement was incorrect or had to be corrected but because the *sight* of the gateway/*moment*, with the paths of the past and future running from it, is not a good basis for understanding his *abysmal thought*. This thought is supposed to be (as we learn in the scene with the animals) the abyss opening from the depths of life—Zarathustra's life, yours and mine—"[m]y abyss," "my ultimate depth."[114] To understand this abyss, it is not enough to look at it as at a view from the window: one must actually stand above it. One must bear the risk—deep, abysmal risk—oneself. One must fight, suffer, and enjoy for oneself.

It is not, therefore, primarily the words (of the dwarf) that stand correction but the situation in which they are said. This is why there is a change of scene: in the next, Zarathustra is no longer an observer but becomes, in the figure of the shepherd struggling with the snake, a participant.

Only then—only for the participant, for someone who struggles and suffers, who experiences and acts—does the *moment* become comprehensible and the difference between the past and the future assume its meaning. It is not a spectacle that I could view from some distance. The *moment* is the "place" where the past and the future meet, the "place" where the difference between the past and the future arises, the difference we call "time"; it is in what I am doing, in what is happening to me, that the future is separated from the past. It is here, in my life, that this differentiation occurs. My life is an "earthquake" that destroys what is, that turns it into a "past," but that also "reveal[s] new wells," the wells of the future.[115]

In other words, the moment I am now in, the moment in which I act and experience something, is necessarily open, open to the future, saturated with the future as an integral feature of the present. The word "future" in this context does not signify something "that is about to happen," the instances that follow the one I am now living through. The "future" is now primarily a feature of the very moment in which I find myself: it is its open nature. In other words, it is an excess of meaning that makes the moment in which I find myself something that cannot be, in any respect, "seen."

Now it becomes clear why the *moment* we have been speaking of is not "some" moment, not one moment among many. There cannot be two moments in which I am now—such an assertion would make no sense—and thus such a *moment* is also not "one": the distinction between the singular and the plural does not make sense here.

But in what sense, then, can what has been come back again? In what sense can the future be identical to the past? We have been expecting an answer to this question from Zarathustra's *abysmal thought*. The aforementioned scenes suggest that the perspective of the *moment* is a necessary condition for understanding this thought. However, since such a *moment* cannot be grasped from a distance, since it cannot be "observed," then what does it mean that it "returns"? In what sense can the *moment* "repeat" itself?

When I say that in a given musical composition a certain sound repeats itself, a motif in a melody, a word in a text, I mean the very same sound, the very same motif, the very same word, which appears again. But how can we say of the *moment* that it is "the very same" if the *moment* is defined by the fact that, being incurably open, it can never be completely defined? How can I assert that that other, subsequent moment is actually exactly the same as the one I'm in now if I cannot observe them and thus compare them? And, finally, what does the "very same" moment mean—what does "repetition" mean—since, in relation to the moment we're talking about, there's no point in using the singular and the plural?

It seems, then, that the "moment" can be considered repeatable only under the condition that it can, in some sense, be closed and defined, and consequently "observed," the way the dwarf does, the way the animals do.

Only insofar as this "moment" is, as in the eyes of the dwarf and the animals, a unit of time, delimited front and back: "this slow spider, which crawls in the moonlight, and this moonlight itself, and I and you in the gateway, whispering together, whispering of eternal things." Insofar as it is one of many—infinitely many—"moments" on the time line, an instant preceded by an infinite number of earlier—and in this sense "past"—instants, and itself preceding an infinite number of subsequent, "future" instants. Only then, it would seem, can one speak reasonably of the "moment's repeatability." But this would not be the *moment* I am writing in now, indefinable, inevitably open to the future.

The instant, the very one that has just passed, can return—only (it would seem) when we succeed in closing the moment's opening toward the future. (Zarathustra refers to this operation as "crucifixion": "they sacrifice the future.")[116] This is precisely what the dwarf does, and the animals as well, when they tell Zarathustra about the *eternal return of the same*, as if they were describing some kind of spectacle, the sunset, some storm outside the window.

To put it another way: When I see the world as a spectacle—like someone who, counting everyone present, forgets to count himself (the metaphor is Heidegger's)—the difference between past and future disappears, and the world (and I in it) becomes a sequence of events recurring as if on a wheel, ever anew, endlessly. This is the dwarf's point of view, the animals' perspective, and this is why time to them seems to be a wheel, the eternal return of all things. "If I were to determine that time's direction (forwards or backwards)," Nietzsche notes in 1888, "is logically indifferent [which is exactly what I do when I leave myself out of the equation], I would take the head—the moment I find myself in—for the tail."[117]

Either the world, the landscape upon which the dwarf and the animals are gazing, is the *wheel of existence*, which "is eternally turning" (But then what does it mean that what returns is the "past"? Then what could the "future" mean? Why would we have to call this wheel "time"?)—or else the past really does differ from the future, and time is real (Only then in what sense could we speak of its repetition?).

We cannot see the past or the future as though they were the blueness of the sky or the whiteness of snow. When we look at the world as if it were the street outside our window—as the dwarf does, as the animals do—time bursts and breaks into little pieces: the spider in the moonlight, us in the doorway. Pieces that are no longer time. Has this already happened? Is it about to happen? We cannot know. What I see, is; it is merely an illusion that we see everything in its passing. The words "past" and "future" are meaningless here. The difference between "was" and "will be" is unrecognizable. Time, the difference between past and future, is no longer real.

And yet Zarathustra teaches us that the difference is real. Time is real. The burden and pain of the past are real. As are the risk of the future, the joy of creation.

The dwarf's proposal, and that of the animals, as to how we should understand the identity of past and future, as to how we should understand *the eternal return of the same*, is therefore unacceptable to Zarathustra. Sure, Zarathustra wants to discover the unity of time but not at the expense of denying its reality. He wants to understand the identity of past and future but at the same time the difference between them as well. *The eternal return of the same* and, simultaneously, *time* itself. To understand the unity of past and future, as well as their difference: this is the task he has assigned himself.

"And this is all my creating and striving," Zarathustra says, "that I carry together into One what is fragment": that I show you, my listeners, how all these pieces, these fragments, these remnants of shattered time, belong together—that I show you that they are a unity after all, that they are parts of a whole—the unity, the whole, of time.[118]

In describing the *moment* in the three scenes I have interpreted above—in describing the context in which his *abysmal thought* might be comprehensible—Nietzsche has in mind precisely this kind of unity, this kind of whole. He has in mind the unity, the connection, the *nexus* of past and future—but of the past and future not in the sense of past or future instants, not in the sense of "yesterday" or "tomorrow," but as an aspect of each individual instant. For every instant, every *moment*, "leaves," "passes," precisely because, at the same time and by the same token, it "becomes," because it is "a new beginning." For how else could we understand "passing," if not in connection to "becoming," if not as the other side of the eruption of heretofore unknown possibilities? The *earth shakes* (everything that is, is fragile, impermanent: it passes), and, simultaneously, *new wells* drive forth (everything begins anew). This connection, the unity of "passing" and "becoming," is the precondition of their difference.

"Passing" and "becoming" (and in this sense "past" and "future") are not two successive events, one following the other. No, Nietzsche argues, "passing" and "becoming" are an indivisible unity. Everything passes precisely because everything begins anew. Precisely because the "future" is, first of all, an aspect of every instant, of every moment, the "past" characterizes it as well. And it is only because of this that the pieces of time can be arranged in a sequence from "was" to "will be," first one, then the other, yesterday this "spider by the light of the moon," tomorrow, perhaps, that "laughter."

"Everything," Nietzsche notes, "has two faces, one that of passing, the other of becoming."[119]

Accordingly, neither passing nor becoming is a local, delimited change—these falling leaves, that growing hair. This change has no limits, nor can it. The "change" from "was" to "will be" cannot be reduced to anything that happens to some object, to this one, not that one. Nor to any objective content. Everything passes, and not just the body, which withers, as opposed to diamonds, which are forever. Everything also begins anew. Everything—not this, as opposed to that—this word, "everything," has no objective meaning in this context. In other words, "passing" and "becoming" are not the same kind of qualification as "blue" or "square." There's no sense in saying that "everything" is blue, and "passing" and "becoming" are not characteristics of a given object. There is no "something" here that is changing, no "something" that is becoming, no common denominator, no single objective meaning, no identical content.

In this sense, the *moment*—the unity of passing and becoming—is also the totality, what is for Nietzsche the one possible, all-encompassing totality.

When I speak of "passing" and "becoming," I therefore cannot mean a process like a fire, building a house, or the return of the same note in a musical canon. "Passing" and "becoming" characterize the way in which the world—the whole world, "everything"—is manifest. Heidegger spoke of "being" in this sense: the way in which something exists as opposed to "something that is." "To be," as I understand Nietzsche's argument, amounts to "passing" and, at the same time, "becoming."

"The world," Nietzsche notes in the spring of 1888, "becomes, it passes, but it never started to become, and it will never cease to pass."[120] Which means: the "world is" only insofar as it is simultaneously becoming and passing.

Let us note that this is not the same as to say that "the world is changing" or that it "constantly creates new forms." "Let us beware of thinking," Nietzsche writes in *The Gay Science*, "that the world eternally creates new things."[121] The "world," after all, is hardly "something": it is not a thing, not an object. It is not "something" that could change, grow bigger or smaller, or gain "new" qualities. "World" characterizes the way something that is, is. When Nietzsche writes about the "constantly creative character of all events" (in a note from the early 1880s), he therefore does not mean that something new is constantly added to what already is.[122] Hardly: *all* things pass and arise. This is how they *are*. Nothing that is is forever, and thus it "is" not, but "passes." In this sense—and in this sense alone—everything is "open to the new." It "is" not, but "becomes." These are two sides of the same thing.

The "world" is the totality of everything (the only possible totality), it is everything as a whole, and given the fact that everything is arranged into precisely this kind of whole, everything passes and becomes. This is why another word that Nietzsche uses for this whole—another word for "world"—is *force; the force of unvarying magnitude*[123]—not unvarying in the same sense as when I say that Leszek is unvaryingly shorter than myself but insofar as it makes no sense to speak of this force in terms of lesser or greater. "Infinitely new becoming is a self-contradiction," Nietzsche notes in 1881: "it would demand infinitely *growing* force."[124] Hölderlin would write:

> For the world of all worlds, the all in all which always *is*, only *presents* itself [. . .] in the decline [. . .] or, more generically, [. . .] in the beginning of time and world [. . .]. [. . .] *This decline or transition* [. . .] is felt in the parts of the existing world so that at precisely that moment and to precisely that extent that existence dissolves, the newly-entering, the youthful, the potential is also felt. For how could dissolution be felt without union; if, then, existence shall be felt and is felt in its dissolution, then the *unexhausted* and *inexhaustible* of the *relations* and *forces* must be felt more by dissolution than *vice versa*.[125]

The *moment*: the unity of past and future, past and future—time—as a whole. In this sense: eternity. Not an endless succession of instants but the "place," the "moment" of time where past and future are two sides of the same thing. (E. M. Cioran writes, "When speaking of life, you say *moments*; of eternity, *moment*.")[126] Understood in this way, eternity is not the opposite of time but its aspect, its necessary dimension. Its horizon. Necessary, because without it time—the difference between past and future, and thus accordingly of passing and becoming—would be impossible. Without this unity that difference would be incomprehensible. Without it, time would disintegrate into disparate pieces, among which we would search in vain for the past, present, or future.

"But perhaps time itself is rooted in eternity and forms part of it?" Nicholas Berdyaev would ask.[127]

The meaning that Nietzsche imparts to the term "appearance" ("life is an appearance") now becomes, I think, even more understandable. As Ryszard Przybylski writes in reference to Shelley, "eternity transforms being into appearance."[128] No moment of life simply "is" but "becomes" and "passes" simultaneously: it is the unity of "becoming" and "passing"— eternity. It is for precisely this reason that it is always also something else, something more than it is, and in this sense it is *appearance*, not because something is hidden behind it, some "essence," some "truth," some "reality." It is thanks to eternity—this connection, this unity of past and future—that none of life's forms is final, that life is a *riddle* with no ultimate solution. It shimmers like the sea in the sun. It comes as no surprise that the sea and the sun are Nietzsche's favorite metaphors.

We can also now see better why life *is a woman*, what it means that life—like "the sun of womanhood sending out its rays in an infinite multiplicity" (Kierkegaard)—is the irremediable diversity of passing and becoming, the diversity that makes all forms of life fragile and therefore pregnant with the unknown.[129] A diversity that is possible thanks to the fact that it is simultaneously a unity, that it is a whole, the unity and whole of the moment, the unity and the whole of eternity. "When I have seen and seen again," Kierkegaard continues, though the life-woman might just as easily say this in conversation with Zarathustra, "observed and observed again, the multiplicity of this world, [. . .] then I fold up the fan, then what is scattered gathers itself together into a unity, the parts into a whole."[130]

Let us not forget that all these words—"moment" and, in this regard, "eternity," as well as "time," "past," and "future"—acquire meaning only in the context of what I do, in the context of my life. The *moment*—Nietzsche convinced us of this in his stories about Zarathustra's adventures with the dwarf, the snake, and the animals—can be understood only by a participant, not by an observer. Time is me; eternity is me, my life. My life, its every step, undermines everything that is; it sets off the *earthquake* and uncovers *new wells*. This creative human activity unveils the fragility of everything that seems to be (whereas it is passing away and becoming). It is my life that connects "today" and "sometime"—"Where would future and past dwell closer together than in you?" Zarathustra asks Life—and thereby plants an explosive charge beneath that which is; it is my life that opens the future and thus pushes what is into the past.[131] This is why Zarathustra says in his conversation with Life, "I called you [. . .] 'umbilical cord of time.'"[132] Eternity is the engine of my life. "I taught them," Zarathustra tells us about his mission, "to work on the future and to redeem with their creation all that *has been*."[133]

Which means: he has taught the people to be themselves, he has taught them to live. Eternity—that link between passing and becoming, the link between past and future—is "mine" or "yours" not in the way that pants or a pen can be but as the body is, as the heart is: intimately, inextricably, forever, so long as I am alive. Eternity is intertwined with everything I do and think; it co-creates the meaning of life. Without it, my life would be incomprehensible. This is where its color (gold), imperceptible to the eye, comes from, as well as its incomparable flavor (bittersweet): the color, the flavor, of life, in which the world comes to the fore.

My life separates past and future from one another, and at the same time it binds them together. (Human life, Plotinus once wrote, is the way that unity can also entail variety.)[134] Eternity is its hidden current, its inextinguishable fire—its vitality, which shatters any form it may attain.

Consequently, Nietzsche notes: "*Non alia, sed haec vita aeterna.*"[135] The eternal life is not some other place, sometime, some other time, which awaits us as soon as this one, the one we know, is over. "*This life,*" Nietzsche notes elsewhere, "*this is your eternal life!*"[136]

It is precisely in being permeated with eternity that life is the *will to power*, that it is *force*: it is stronger than any form it might assume, and thus it flows, passes, becomes. This is why no instant in my life is as it is, identical with itself, like a chair or a triangle: each instant passes, each becomes, by itself. Every moment of life leads by itself beyond itself. To put it more metaphorically, every moment, a new beginning, "wants, desires the next," not some situation, one particular instant or another, but precisely this connection between end and beginning, past and future, passing and becoming, this *moment*, infinitely. "O my soul," Zarathustra says to Life, "how could you not crave eternity?"[137]

We are not speaking here about the desire—and what could be more natural?—that my life will never end, that it should go on, "and so on," "without end." Not about what Hegel calls the "spurious infinite," which results from crossing successive limits. The endless, insatiable desire for moments to come—the ever-so-painful fact that time is me—is an expression of the intrinsic nature of each individual moment of my life, of its internal fissure, its rupture, the very saturation with eternity that makes it impossible to quiet—like a bitch in heat—to keep it as it is, to continue. "[T]he Infinite," Hegel wrote, referring to the true infinite and not the "spurious" kind, "is a self-determination based on self-reference, an assertion of its own, internal determination."[138] It is precisely this "internal determination," the intrinsic nature of life in its every moment—eternity—that makes time flow, that makes life "go on," without end.

The instants I have lived through do not follow one after another, one might also say, like pearls on a string. Today does not simply replace yesterday. "'Yesterday' has died into the 'today,'" Plutarch writes, "and the 'today' is dying into the 'tomorrow.'"[139] Death, the passage of a single instant of the day, is a birth, the becoming of another. Each of them, each instant, thus already contains this passage within itself, this reference to the other: each instant already "is" the other as well, and thus it "passes," it "becomes"—it is not. Each instant is the beginning and the end in one.

Like a point on a wheel. Thus the metaphor for time—for Zarathustra, as it once had been for Heraclitus—is the wheel. Because, as Heraclitus says, "In the case of the circle['s circumference] beginning and end are common."[140] Nietzsche notes, "Man is a new force [*sic!*], the first movement, the self-propelled wheel."[141] In a fragment cited earlier Zarathustra says to Life, "I gave you new names [. . .]; I called you [. . .] 'umbilical cord of time.'"[142] And he adds (in a note to this fragment), "eternal will."[143] And "return": insofar as it is like the point on a wheel, insofar as it is a beginning and an end in one, insofar as it thus destroys and begins everything anew of its own accord, every *moment* of life is reproduction, repetition—*return*. Not accidentally, but necessarily: it is constant return, always anew—*eternal return*. Not the repetition of some content, of some form, of one situation or another, but always anew, infinitely, on an unending time line.

"The self-propelled wheel." Not a merry-go-round, as the animals wanted. What is, passes; of its own accord it changes into the past, for at the same time the future sprouts up within it, a future that splits it apart, that bursts it from within. The life of man is a *wheel*, it is *eternal return*, insofar as in every moment it ends and begins again—not because the events in this life are a repetition of something that has already happened and will keep happening infinitely many times, not because it is sealed up in some unit of time and keeps coming back to the same place, like the horse on a merry-go-round.

Comparing two or more states of things, two or more instants, will not allow us to understand *the eternal return of the same*. Neither will observing some process that is independent of me. *The eternal return of the same* is something that is happening to me at this very moment, at this moment of my life. The dwarf and the animals, for whom the world is a spectacle, a merry-go-round that never stops, cannot understand this.

As we can see, Zarathustra and Nietzsche understand *the eternal return of the same* quite differently from the animals and, earlier, the dwarf. But Zarathustra not only rejects their interpretation but does so, as we saw in the first scene with the dwarf, angrily, and later with horror and revulsion as well: "Had I ever seen so much nausea and pale dread on one face?" Zarathustra says at the sight of the shepherd, the snake wrapped around his throat.[144] Then, a moment later: "'Bite! Bite its head off! Bite!' Thus it cried out of me—my dread, [. . .] my nausea, [. . .] cried out of me."[145] Zarathustra reacts in the same way, with horror and disgust, to what he sees in his fever-dream: "Nausea, nausea, nausea—woe unto me!"[146] From Zarathustra's point of view, then, this is not a common mistake but a revolting and dangerous attack. Zarathustra and the dwarf do not merely differ from one another but do so dramatically.

Where does this disgust, this horror, this drama come from?

Zarathustra's opposition to the dwarf does not stem, as we now know, from intellectual disagreement: it's not about the dwarf (and, later, the animals) saying "A," whereas Zarathustra thinks, "No, it's not 'A' but 'B.'" Sure, the dwarf does say that "time is a circle," but Zarathustra does not say, "No, time is not a circle"; he does not contradict the dwarf's view. On the contrary, Zarathustra also believes, as we have seen, that time is a circle. This is also the case in his exchange with the animals. In both instances, it is not the content that provokes Zarathustra's objection but the fact that the animals—and, before them, the dwarf—*watched* what they speak about (the world, time, the moment, eternal return). "By looking at life one begins to forget it," Zarathustra could have said, as Cioran did.[147]

Only what are they supposed to do if they want to learn how things are? If they want to learn the truth? How else, if not by creating some distance, by finding a perspective from which one could see things as they are, independent of me, of my pain, of my joy? Two and two are four, the Earth revolves around the sun, grass is green, the bench is hard: that's how it is, or it's not. What do my sufferings or joys have to do with it? How does what I do enter into it? And this being the case, I should, insofar as it is within my power, disregard all of it (my sufferings, my joys). Only then will I *see* how things are. The animals' and the dwarf's having *watched* what happens is, or so it would seem, a metaphor for an ideal cognitive attitude, a metaphor for knowledge.

Knowledge, we might also say, presupposes that something is the case—or isn't. Without this presupposition, the notion of "knowledge" makes no sense. It is for precisely this reason that knowledge requires a "view" detached from what I do, divorced from the variable course of my life, a view exactly like that of the dwarf looking at the gate, of the animals watching Zarathustra struggle with his illness. If this is so, however, then the world that Zarathustra is telling the sailors about cannot be an object of knowledge, it cannot be grasped with concepts: the "world" that actually "is" not, the "world" in the sense of "everything," in the sense of *everything in everything*, the passing and becoming of everything. We can comprehend passing and becoming only "from outside," only from the perspective of something that is not itself becoming or passing away. That is not "living." That "is." "We can understand *becoming*," Nietzsche notes, "only as the passage from one lasting, 'dead' state to another lasting, 'dead' state."[148] And thus: we cannot comprehend it at all. The "world"—passing, becoming—is unknowable.

Hölderlin's "earthly fire" always burns something, destroys something; passing and becoming are "heavenly fire": nothing of the kind can be found here. In the "real" process of disintegration there is always something that disintegrates (the aging body, the burning house). Passing is an "ideal" disintegration (Hölderlin's distinction as well); no object disintegrates here. Which is why, Hölderlin says, "the idealistic dissolution differs from the so-called real one [. . .] in that, due to the ignorance of its beginning and end point, the dissolution has to appear inevitably as a real nothing, so that all existence, hence particular, appears as totality."[149]

Knowledge informs us about what is. We know what is. Passing and becoming "is" not. In this sense, it is "nothing." It is incomprehensible.

The dwarf and the animals think that among the seemingly chaotic diversity of phenomena they can identify the lasting, unchanging structure that lends the chaos a kind of order, that turns the jungle into a garden: the wheel of time, *the eternal return of the same*. This structure, they believe, makes passing and becoming—and thus time, the succession of instants—comprehensible. But they are mistaken. Not in the sense that they confuse "A" and "B," that they make some error that Zarathustra later corrects. The animals and the dwarf are mistaken in the same sense as knowledge in general is "mistaken." They are mistaken because they assume, as knowledge assumes, that the "world" (passing, becoming) can be comprehended as one might comprehend the properties of a triangle or the physics of evaporation, whereas the "world" is not comprehensible in this way. Passing and becoming cannot be comprehended; they escape our concepts. They escape conceptual knowledge. Chasing after them with our concepts, we only grasp emptiness, only nothing. "A world in a state of becoming," Nietzsche notes, "could not, in a strict sense, be 'comprehended' or 'known.'"[150]

"And he who grasps too much / lets eternity pass him by," Rilke writes.[151]

Knowledge, then, is "false"; it is always "mistaken." And yet we have to know, if we are to live. We need stability, identity, being. A house, a homeland, a woman. A bench to sit on. Knowledge, cognition, is an expression of this need, evidence of this necessity. The lives we live are, at any given moment, infested with concepts that tell us how things are. Knowledge's claim to truth expresses the necessary condition of life; it is life's self-affirmation. Life, Nietzsche will say, is "[a] will to the thinkability of all beings."[152] The "error" of the dwarf and the animals, like the "error" upon which knowledge rests, is therefore uncorrectable. It's not that the dwarf and the animals are making a mistake that they could just as well not make.

Consequently, every concept, any knowledge, contains within itself an internal tension, a tension that cannot be abolished. It assumes that there "is" something that can be known, and by so doing it negates life (which passes and becomes, but "is" not) and is simultaneously the necessary expression of that life.

Nietzsche, we may recall, calls the negation of life *nihilism*. The tension that bursts knowledge from within means that any knowledge is essentially *nihilistic*. *Nihilism*, the contradiction of life, lies at the basis of knowing anything. Everything we know—not just one view or another, one or another fragment of knowledge—is imbued with *nihilism*, based in *nihilism*, arises from *nihilism*, flows from negation, from the contradiction of life.

The words "negation" and "contradiction" may be misleading in this context. For they may suggest that some kind of logic connects "knowledge" with "life," that there exists a point of view that would allow us to catch the tension between them in a net of concepts, to understand them, to grasp them. And, as a result, to release the tension, to reconcile both sides. This is precisely how Hegel understood the opposition between knowledge and reality: whoever discovers their dialectical connection will understand, Hegel argues, what unites them, and thus he will reconcile them. "The two worlds [the world of knowledge and the world of reality] are reconciled," Hegel writes, "and heaven is transplanted to earth below."[153] And elsewhere: "To recognize reason as the rose in the cross of the present and thereby to enjoy the present, this is the rational insight which *reconciles* us to actuality, the reconciliation which philosophy affords."[154] From this point of view, any negation or contradiction, any kind of malfunction, weakness, or sickness of knowledge—and with it any pain, any misery—turns out to have been necessary and, at the same time, transitory: it turns out to have been a path toward the ultimate reconciliation of knowledge and reality. Marx, in similar fashion, sees in every conflict, in any opposition between thought and reality—and consequently in the suffering that arises from it—only a passing pathology along the way toward their definitive reconciliation. "Evil and suffering, in [Marx's] eyes," writes Kołakowski, "had no meaning except as instruments of liberation."[155]

Whereas no logic can take hold, and thus relieve, the tension between knowledge and life that Nietzsche talks about. This tension neither grows nor fades; there cannot be more or less of it. Without it, knowledge is unthinkable. In Zarathustra's stories and speeches, this tension—*nihilism*—is presented figuratively as a *struggle* (as the shepherd's with the snake) or as a *sickness* (as Zarathustra's, watched by the animals). But unlike in Hegel and Marx, the *struggle* will never end, and the *sickness* can never be cured.

This peculiar character of the relation between knowledge and life is expressed in Zarathustra's narrative, I believe, through the metaphors of *anger, horror,* and *nausea.* Unlike such negative phenomena as suffering or exploitation in the eyes of Hegel and Marx, this *anger,* this *horror,* this *nausea* are not temporary. They are a metaphorical expression of a confrontation with no possibility of mediation, evidence of a discord that will never end in reconciliation. The confrontation with *nihilism* will not end —the metaphors of *anger, horror,* and *nausea* suggest—in a moment of mutual understanding, in an instant of recognizing some common rationality within them. The parties to this conflict cannot be set straight, cannot be arranged into a sensible pattern. There are no intermediaries here, no bridges, no common denominator. This confrontation cannot be translated into ideas, or understood and thereby settled, neutralized, or "liberated into concepts," as Hegel would wish.

On the other hand, while they cannot be reduced to concepts, the metaphors of *nausea, horror,* and *anger* do nevertheless tell us something about them: they tell us something about concepts in general and about their connection to life. They tell us that concepts are necessarily inadequate, that life—passing, becoming—cannot be accommodated within them, that they are thus fragile, that they burst from within, of their own accord. That they therefore cannot serve as a solid foundation, that they do not secure the ground beneath our feet. The metaphor of *nausea* that Zarathustra feels therefore has yet another meaning: it can also mean the "seasickness" of someone who's just had an abyss open up beneath his feet, of someone who, like Zarathustra, no longer knows, "What is above? What is below?" Nausea is therefore just as much evidence of having lost all orientation, evidence of the lack of any point of reference, and thus also of gravity. Someone who has no orientation, no point of reference, no gravity, becomes light, free "as a bird." (But, after all, he is not a bird, and he is used to some ground beneath his feet. Thus the nausea.)

Nausea, in Nietzsche's lexicon, is then not merely a metaphor of uncompromising, though futile, opposition or negation. This *nausea* also testifies to our capacity for unlimited freedom, for liberation, which comes to the fore in the inadequacy of concepts. This *nausea*, this contempt, Zarathustra tells his listeners, "is the greatest experience you can have."[156] *Nausea* from life as it is, from everything that organizes it, that orders it, that gives it weight, that makes it comprehensible; *nausea from happiness* (which comes from achieving some goal), *nausea from virtue, nausea from reason. Nausea*—not a logical response, not opposition in the name of a higher ideal or another, better reality: "nausea itself creates wings."[157]

Insofar, therefore, as knowledge not only tells us how things are but also demonstrates its own weakness, its own sickness, a sickness whose symptom is nausea—it is not merely a negation but also an affirmation of life. It is not an affirmation of some content, assent to life "as it is" or could be. It is not a discreet act that evinces someone's (my) relation to "life" (as if "life" were similar to weather or to my Aunt Kazia's poor manners) but life itself, ceaselessly evading knowledge, overflowing from all concepts. In this sickness, in this bursting of knowledge, life comes to the fore, not as this or that, not as some as yet unknown content, as a still-hidden reality, but as the suspension of all meaning, as a new beginning, as creativity. As a chance to move out into open space, into the open fields. In this sense, knowledge, corroded by nihilism and negating life, is at the same time its affirmation.

Knowledge and life, in this context, are thus not two different or opposite series of aspects, qualities, or characterizations: one here, the other there, life here, knowledge there. Hardly: life is manifest in this very *nausea*, in this *horror*, in the fragility of concepts, a fragility they themselves indicate, in *anxiety* that does not allow us to reconcile ourselves to any of the conditions of our life, in the inhuman joy of liberation—and in this way only. In the sickness of life, in its internal struggle. In its *nihilism*.

"Life" is not some separate (in relation to knowledge) unity, a separate object, a form of being, something that "is" somewhere over there, albeit just out of reach. Thus when I write that "knowledge is essential for life," I do not mean an essence, the structure or internal mechanism of some object or being (as when I talk about the properties of a triangle or causes of rain). Knowledge is "necessary" for life because life is the horizon of our concepts made manifest only through them: as their opening to something that does not fit within them, as a fissure that cannot be described conceptually and (thus) sealed up.

The affirmation of life that Nietzsche traces in the pathology of knowledge, in its bursting from within, in its lack of solid foundations, cannot, of course, be "mine." I, Krzysztof Michalski, am not its subject. The suspension of all meaning, the new beginning, unbridled creativity—all these lead out beyond everything that determines me as myself and as a human being, beyond everything that is mine and that is human. In this way, knowledge also opens superhuman possibilities that outgrow man and are unknown to him. (This is what Gadamer calls "a message from elsewhere.")[158] The metaphorical figure for this kind of affirmation in Nietzsche's writing is, as we know, the *overman*. Another is the *child*, "a new beginning, a game, a self-propelled wheel, a first movement, a sacred 'Yes.'"[159]

From this, from the superhuman affirmation of life—and not from satisfaction in having reached a goal, nor from the joy of defeating an enemy—arises the laughter of the shepherd/Zarathustra after his struggle with the snake. A laughter that liberates from everything I had taken for my own, from everything I know as human: "How this laughter shattered my windows!" Zarathustra complains. "How it tore out my entrails and cut through my heart!"[160] An inhuman laughter: "Never yet on earth has a human being laughed as he laughed!"[161] And it is for precisely this, for this laughter—for a freedom that exceeds everything human—that "[m]y longing [. . .] gnaws at me" and makes life as it is, life as I lead it, however it is, impossible to bear: "oh, how do I bear to go on living!"[162] It makes life's happiness, its reason, its virtue, somewhere deep down, *nauseating*.

Nausea, horror, laughter, longing: these are Nietzsche's metaphors for the immanent tension of knowledge: its connection to life, which cannot be grasped by any concept, any logic. *Nausea, horror, laughter*—not just these concepts or the words that name them. Words, Nietzsche maintains, are inadequate: words tell us what is, how it is—this is this, that is something else. They tell us how we are. They express some content, and in so doing they determine, they grind into the ground, they burden: "Are not all words made for the grave and heavy? Are not all words lies to those who are light?"[163] Words lie about *lightness*, insofar as they essentially point to this or that, insofar as they point to what is and thereby contradict the unearthly *lightness* of life that is hidden behind all content, the *lightness* that introduces anxiety into knowledge and makes all concepts fragile. Thus there are no words that Zarathustra could find to respond to the dwarf, there before the gateway, no words to express his *abysmal thought*. It is no wonder that Zarathustra's story suddenly breaks off.

"Then it spoke to me without voice," Zarathustra later says about his exchange with Life. "'You know it, Zarathustra?'"[164] What can Zarathustra say to this question? "It," after all—his *abysmal thought, the eternal return of the same*—is unknowable. It cannot be put into words. In what way, then, can this silence, this *lightness*, the *new beginning*, the *eternal return*— the *abysmal thought* that Zarathustra seeks—be thought, be understood?

First of all, in seeking an answer to this question, Nietzsche cannot do without metaphor. Metaphors refer words to something beyond their meaning; they indicate the excess of meaning hidden within them. It is precisely this function that words serve in the story of Zarathustra: they do not merely mean what they mean but also, through this metaphorical excess of meaning, refer us back to the circumstance in which they are uttered, to something that happens, to something that someone does. That someone is me, or rather, it is my life, that which is happening with me, the only context in which this answer makes sense. (In other words, I have to find myself in Zarathustra if his story is to become meaningful.) But I, this story suggests, am also something more than just myself: this is Zarathustra, "the advocate of life," "the advocate of the circle," the advocate of a superhuman effort that exceeds human possibilities.[165]

Nor is it by accident that Zarathustra's answer assumes the form of a narrative, a narrative about his words but also about his adventures. The narration is not merely an illustration of a thought that could just as well have been expressed otherwise. Rather, it is the only form of expression appropriate here. There is no conclusion that gives the entire story its meaning: the redemption that closes the story of sin, the emancipation of humanity that concludes a history driven forward by the alienation of man, the happy ending that ties the story together ("and they lived happily ever after"), or the ultimate catastrophe. The story of Zarathustra's meetings and speeches does not close with a couple or a dozen sentences (ostensibly) explaining his *abysmal thought*; it does not end with a solution to the riddle of eternal return. Zarathustra's story doesn't end at all, just as it never begins. ("No stranger to me is this wanderer," says the holy man whom Zarathustra meets at the beginning of the book, "many years ago he passed this way.")[166] It neither ends nor begins because its every moment— every *moment* of the human life it narrates—"passes" and "becomes" at the same time; each one is essentially open, unconcluded.

This is why Zarathustra says that his *abysmal thought*, his thought of the *eternal return*, demands *courage*. *Courage*—that concept which has already been invoked many times—is one of Nietzsche's meta-concepts (like *over-man* or *will to power*), a concept that refers to the limit of knowledge, impossible to mark, the concept of knowledge's irremediable openness, its incompletability. The concept whose function is to refer the *abysmal thought* to the context of my life, the sole context in which this "thought" can be understood: if, in every moment of my life, everything ends and everything begins again, then no progress of knowledge, no accumulation of knowledge, even if it is infinite, can save me from the step into darkness that each successive instant entails or can protect me from risk, from unbounded risk. Zarathustra's story, this concept of courage suggests, can therefore be "whole" only in the same sense as my life is "whole": insofar as in its every moment the whole life "passes" and "becomes," insofar as in every moment its whole meaning is questioned. Insofar as its every moment is, in this sense, a return, *the return of the same.*

Not even death is a limit on this risk: it is not, in its meaning, an indisputable fact—the courage inherent in life, writes Nietzsche, is stronger than death. It is this courage that says, "Was *that* life? [. . .] Well then! Once more!"[167]

It is for precisely this reason, as we already know, that Zarathustra chooses sailors as the audience for his stories: "To you, the bold searchers [. . .] drunk with riddles, glad of the twilight [. . .] to you alone I tell the riddle that I *saw*."[168] The sailors represent courage, they are willing to face risk. This is why, Zarathustra argues, they are a more receptive audience to what he has to tell them: "Zarathustra was a friend of all who [. . .] do not like to live without danger."[169]

It is this whole story, a story without beginning or end—or, rather, a story whose every moment is a beginning and an end at the same time—that is Zarathustra's answer to Life's question ("You know that, O Zarathustra?"), Nietzsche's answer to the question of what it means "to think *the abysmal thought*," to what "understanding" could mean in this context. A story that must become my own to make any sense. A story whose every moment, precisely as beginning and end, undermines all meaning constituted so far, everything that I am, my entire "I," and in this way severs its connections to what has happened before and will happen after, thereby earning the right to be called "eternity." "How does the instant become a gate to eternity?" Cioran asks. "Eternity can be attained only if there are no connections [. . .]. [. . .] The experience of eternity is void of life."[170] This is a story that, as a result, cannot be summarized, a story without a moral, without a purpose.

The *abysmal thought*, then, is not an individual thought about something, like the one about a body immersed in water, or that other one about Mary and what we did that day. *Thinking the abysmal thought*—Zarathustra's *abysmal thought*—does not mean adding another piece to the knowledge one already has. The concept of *eternal recurrence*—Nietzsche's *abysmal thought*—is not a concept like every other. It is not knowledge about something. It is rather the self-limitation of knowledge, a fissure within it, the sudden opening of an empty space, which comes to the fore in "horror, nausea, laughter," as Nietzsche noted during the winter of 1869–70.[171] It is rather a skepticism that cannot be expressed but metaphorically, a skepticism toward all knowledge, knowledge that cracks when it touches life, the manifestation—through life, and not through words or concepts—of an additional quality to all concepts, entirely independent of their content, a manifestation of their fragility, their trembling, their warmth, which testifies to the fire raging deep within them.

Nietzsche writes, "Zarathustra tells us the *mystery* that everything returns."[172] This does not mean that Zarathustra informs us of something we didn't know before. No, Zarathustra tells us the *eternal return* as a mystery. *Eternal return* is a mystery, a message that does not fit into concepts and habits we have assembled so far, in anything we know or can know. Zarathustra tells us this mystery, Nietzsche writes, "from the happy perspective of the overman," out of superhuman happiness.[173] Not from the perspective of a happy conclusion but from the vantage point of that inhuman affirmation of life, alien to all that is familiar, the affirmation inscribed in the constant, continuously renewed effort to overcome what is; in the unending conflict, in the conflict with no possibility of peaceful resolution.

How different is the affirmation of life—how different the vision of the world—that Hegel, Nietzsche's implied opponent, unfolds before us: "The essence of the universe, at first hidden and concealed, has no power to offer resistance to the courageous search for knowledge; it must open itself up before the seeker, set its riches and its depths before his eyes to give him pleasure."[174]

Is it strange, then, that Nietzsche's *abysmal thought*, thus understood, brings no solace? The efforts of the eagle and the snake to comfort the sick Zarathustra with their story of the eternal return of all things are condemned to fail. Their story is supposed to ease his pain, to quiet his anxiety, to cure him. Their *kind* words, words about the eternal return, like "rainbows and illusive bridges between things which are eternally apart," attempt to unite every moment into the order of what is, into the cosmos, into a garden, into hard reality. In vain, always in vain, because the unity of each moment is also an incurable fissure, because concepts of that which is are constantly undermined by "passing" and "becoming." Because our lives, our activities, constantly destroy (and thus they hurt) and simultaneously open new, heretofore unknown perspectives (and thus they disturb us). The animals try to heal this tear, this sickness of Zarathustra's. They try to join the past and future in the unity of some content, to discover some continuity within them, to show that they are not fundamentally different from one another, and thus deprive the *moment* in which Zarathustra now finds himself (suffering) of its open, dark, painful, unsettling nature. But this is not possible. The *abysmal thought* resolves no conflict, cures no sickness, joins no fragments that do not fit together. Life *is* the sickness, the sickness of *nihilism*; pain, nausea, and terror cannot be eliminated from it. It is for precisely this reason that Zarathustra calls himself not just the "advocate of life," "the advocate of the circle," but also "the advocate of suffering."[175]

The tale of Zarathustra brings no solace. It does not supply the reader with tools to remove suffering, anxiety, or nausea from his or her life, or even to make a life full of suffering, anxiety, and nausea bearable. Life—and this is the story's message—is unbearable. There is a thorn in life's side that cannot be removed; without it, the anxiety that we call life would not be possible, since it is because of this thorn that life goes on. This thorn is eternity.

The main figures of the story, Zarathustra and the dwarf, are now becoming, I hope, more understandable. As is the difference between them. They do not advocate accurate or inaccurate views; it is not their views that separate them. Nor are they the representatives of two distinct principles, of two objectively distinguishable tendencies. Certainly, the dwarf is a metaphor for the figure of knowledge, the "spirit of gravity," with thoughts "heavy as lead," who sits on Zarathustra's back and drags him down to the ground, to the "here and now," binding him to life as it is—a metaphor for knowledge which, like the heavy snake, bites at the throat of the shepherd/ Zarathustra and chokes him so as to take away his (inhuman) *lightness*, his freedom: life. And Zarathustra, that "dancing god," is a metaphor for life, a metaphor for its lightness, which liberates itself from all enclosure, from all definition, a metaphor for a life that never simply is. But life and knowledge, this *lightness* and this *gravity*, the dwarf and Zarathustra, cannot be understood separately; they are not independent concepts. They are comprehensible only in their interconnection, an interconnection that cannot be dissolved and that is itself not governed by any logic. Only in conflict, then, in struggle, without any possibility of mediation, without a common denominator, without the prospect of peace. "To understand" thus means "to participate": the conflict between Zarathustra and the dwarf is "understandable" only insofar as I succeed in translating it into my life, in inscribing it there—in living it. This conflict is the immanent, incurable rift of life, of my life, of life as I can know it, of a life that is as it is, gathered into some résumé, some meaning, measured with the rhythm of instants, this today, that yesterday, this other thing tomorrow. It is the disruption of that continuity. In every *moment*: not sometimes but always, and thus beyond time as a succession of instants, and in this sense eternally, the entire meaning of my life up till now gets suspended, "the clock of my life drew a breath."[176]

From the point of view of life as I live it, of life as it is, this is naturally a threat, a sickness, a madness. Zarathustra is a dangerous madman. But knowledge, too, is dangerous for life, as the dwarf is for Zarathustra. If things were as the dwarf would have them—if everything really did return to how it had been, if what is were like *rock* (everything: small and large, base and noble), if the past and future were not divided by an abyss, if they were united into some kind of continuity—then life, this ever-new beginning among the rubble of what has been, would have no room to take off, to breathe. This is where Zarathustra's *anger*, his *nausea*, his *horror* originate, as he opposes the dwarf and his interpretation of *eternal return*.

The danger that the dwarf and Zarathustra pose for one another is a danger that comes out of nowhere, an unknown, an undefined danger. There are no barbarians at the gate, no bacteria in the urine. In fact, there's nothing to know here, no logic: words fail. This is why, in his description of Zarathustra's argument with the dwarf, Nietzsche characterizes the opponents with the same words, and Zarathustra repeats what the dwarf had just said: for one as well as for the other, the point is *eternal return*. It is not just the dwarf who is the *spirit of gravity*, not only knowledge that *weighs* on us, but Zarathustra's *abysmal thought* is also a *burden*. "If this thought gained possession of you," Nietzsche writes, "[it] would lie upon your actions as the greatest weight."[177] This *burden*, Zarathustra goes on to warn, "would change you as you are or perhaps crush you."[178] *Change and crush*—but not like the news that Jadzia ended up marrying Kowalski, not because you learn something awful, not because of a particular content: the *abysmal thought* changes and crushes because it exposes all meaning to unlimited risk, because it is the unconditional courage that every moment, every step of my life, demands. Now it is the dwarf who symbolizes *lightness*. With his story, he wants to rob the moment of its weight; there is no risk here, he argues, since the future is like the past, the trees grow, airplanes land, Monday comes after Sunday, and so on, and again, and again. This is precisely why the "courage finally bade me stand still and speak: 'Dwarf! It is you or I!'"[179]

So it is not in words that we are to seek the difference between the dwarf and Zarathustra. It is not at all a difference between one thing and another but rather the internal diversity of life itself, "the life that itself cuts into life."[180]

The *dwarf* and *Zarathustra*, the *spirit of gravity* and the *dancing god*, the peace that knowledge brings and the risk of life: two human/inhuman figures bound together by an irresolvable conflict, empty so long as I do not inscribe them within my own life. The human condition.

Let's come back to the question from which we started: is liberation from time, liberation from the past, possible? Can we overturn the stone of time?

No, it's impossible; the stone of the past cannot be overturned. I will never play with Joanna as we once did in Żeromski Park, nor will my father hold me in his arms and spin me around. I am powerless against the past; I cannot make it come back. No, I cannot "will backwards," there is no "liberation from the river of time," my will "cannot break time."

My will. My, Krzysztof Michalski's, will. For me, as I am, there is no liberation from the river of time. The will cannot shatter time, it cannot force the past to return—insofar as it is someone's will, mine, yours, Basia's, somebody's. Insofar as the past I am talking about is a piece of time, that play way back when, or the Battle of Grunwald; insofar as "was" amounts to the same as "is," only with another date, as Cyprian Norwid wrote, "today, just further on"—insofar as I can "watch" it, "know" it. As a spectator of the past, I am powerless. My will is powerless. All I can do is "gnash my teeth": it will not return.

So why am I gnashing my teeth anyway? Why do I want what has been to be again? Nietzsche says that the *spirit of gravity* is to blame, the tendency, constitutive of life, to bind oneself to "here" and "now," to this home, that woman, this country. It is the fact that we understand the world through the prism of concepts that tell us how it is. *Nihilism*. It is thanks to *nihilism* that I am who I am: Krzysztof Michalski, a Pole, Homo sapiens. It is I, with everything that I have collected in my life so far, who wants (and how could I not?) to hold onto all of it and rebels against the fact that I cannot.

Exactly: I cannot. This is precisely what Zarathustra is to demonstrate through his wanderings and his speeches; that each successive moment, every step in our lives, undermines all of this puts all concepts in question, every "here," every "now." It replaces "is" with "passes" and "becomes." In this *infinitely small* (for where could we place its boundaries, given that there "is" nothing here, that everything "becomes" and "passes"?) *moment*, in this non-dimensional point that cannot be seen, that cannot be known, everything ends and arises again: it returns. "In your every action," Nietzsche notes, "all that has been runs together and is repeated."[181]

In this way, in my every action an opportunity for liberation from *the eternal river of things* opens up, an opportunity for liberation from the chain of events that shape my life. But this is not the liberation of myself as I am today; none of my features or characteristics, nothing that is mine, passes the test of passing. No content returns. And yet "something" in me does return. Or, rather, everything does. In every moment my entire life is placed under a question mark: I am born anew, I become a *child*, with no past, no worries about the future, no wish to hold on to anything that passes. This is why my identity will never be closed.

"I teach you," Zarathustra says, "liberation from the eternal river."[182] This does not mean that Zarathustra will show us how to stop this river. On the contrary, Zarathustra teaches us that this river cannot be stopped. He teaches that in every moment of life "being" means "passing" and "becoming." That every moment is therefore also the beginning and the end of everything: "the river is ever returning to itself."[183] It is here, in this return, in this eddy, in this moment, that we gain the opportunity to cast off the baggage of the past, to tear ourselves from the "here and now," from everything that has been mine. A chance at a new beginning. A chance at liberation from what is. "[Y]ou keep entering the same river as yourselves," Zarathustra says.[184] "The same river," because each of its moments, each moment of my life, is at the same time a beginning and an end, and in this sense it is "the same." "As yourselves," because in each of these moments I am born anew. Identity of content is not what Nietzsche has in mind; the river is not "the same" like the Vistula when it passes Krakow and when it passes Gdansk. I am not the same Krzysztof Michalski as I was yesterday when I enter that river today. It is not my reality that is liberated here. This is a liberation that concerns me as I can be.

The past—the park, the river, that yesterday—will not return. Despite this, however, the past is not an insurmountable barrier, not to the life within me that is constantly beginning all over again, not to the child born in each moment of my life, a child who does not feel the burden of passing and does not try to stop it. *To think the abysmal thought* is to grasp (let's say it again: with one's life, not with knowledge) human reality not as a ready-made result, not as something that is, but as the making of the unknown.

The *will to power*, after all, encounters no obstacles that it cannot overcome. Not even the past poses such an obstacle. Not even death. The life I live is free, boundlessly free: not even I, nor any form I can assume, am its limit, because each moment of this life is a beginning and an end at the same time, an eternity that destroys everything it encounters and thereby opens out to the new and unknown. Of course, Nietzsche wrote in one of his earliest works, *Philosophy in the Tragic Age of the Greeks*, "[m]an is necessity down to his last fibre, and totally 'unfree,' that is if one means by freedom the foolish demand to be able to change one's *essentia* arbitrarily, like a garment."[185] I cannot make a triangle sing or turn today back to yesterday. But my every gesture, my every motion, potentially undermines everything that is, suspends all meaning, and in so doing exposes me to unlimited risk and opens unlimited opportunities.

The fact that this is not all, that our lives are not merely creative, that we do not live as fire, is because, Nietzsche adds, "moist slime fills [our] souls," and it is only with great difficulty that they burn with eternity's flame.[186]

"I taught [the people]," Zarathustra says, "eternity and liberation from the river."[187]

Eternity: this *infinitely small moment*, like lightning, that interrupts the continuity of my story and burns what is, turning it into what has been. The infinitely small moment by which my life, over and over again, severs the continuity of time, the succession of instants, making them flow. The sickness of life. The source of an anxiety that cannot be explained within the succession of instants, that cannot be known. The source of the tragedy of human fate. The burning, golden, noonday sun, the moment of the shortest shadow, the smallest, least connection with what was before and what will be after. The silence between words, where, as the poet Jan Lechoń wrote, "the heart dies of fright" (for it loses everything it had had) and at the same time "trembles like a string, with happiness" (of a new birth). This is the moment when (Lechoń again) "time again the heart in love tears apart / The golden threads the heart itself incautiously weaved" and starts "to tremble [. . .] for eternity, like the stars."[188]

Eternity, Zarathustra will say, is "as the gleam of divine eyes."[189]

7

"Divine" eyes…. Once again we encounter the paradox we had been discussing earlier: Zarathustra, who had heralded the death of God, refers to divinity even when he is talking about his most important thought. The concept of eternity, the concept of *the eternal return of the same*, unites, as we have seen, the most important threads of Nietzsche's thought. It comes as no surprise, then, that this paradox makes another appearance here, and with particular bite.

This is not a secondary matter. Nietzsche, as we have seen, lives with biblical tales from his very earliest, almost adolescent work, through his last, written in madness. His texts are full of crypto-quotations from the Old and (predominantly) New Testaments and are saturated with biblical concepts and metaphors. His thinking is an unceasing debate with that other story, the story told by Matthew, Mark, Luke, John, and Paul: a wrestling with God.

Nietzsche was undoubtedly a critic of Christianity. He regarded certain of its forms—what he took for its dominant forms—as an expression of *nihilism*, as a symptom of the pathology of life. The concept of God was being used, he believed, to support and complement reason: "Wherever there is a hole in your reason, you immediately fill it with the simplest of stopgaps: its name is 'God.'"[190] Religion and Christianity, serving thus as an extension of reason, as an attempt to enclose life in categories that are independent of it, an attempt to discover its "truth," to discover how it "is," are nihilism. Such religion "places life's center of gravity not in life but in the 'beyond,'" Nietzsche writes in *The Antichrist*, and thus "one deprives life of its center of gravity altogether."[191] Which means that it deprives life of its character as unbridled possibility, it takes away the unlimited risk constantly confronting it and conceals the fact that the point of life is, at every step, that everything is at stake. "[W]ith the beyond," Nietzsche continues, "one *kills life*."[192]

We should not be misled by the zeal of this critique: its purpose is not to correct an error, to treat a pathology, or to set us on the right path. True, religion in this sense—the forms of Christianity that serve the function described here—is not necessary. *Nihilism*, Nietzsche believes, is. *Nihilism*, after all, is an irreducible part of the meaning of our lives: the claim to know "how life is," all this knowledge gathered together in our words and in our deeds, is the necessary point of departure for each new step, every reflection. This is why *nihilism* cannot be defeated once and for all—and at the same time every step in our lives is an effort to do so.

But the story of Jesus, according to Nietzsche, contains something more, not just fodder for a nihilistic interpretation of human life. In Nietzsche's eyes, this story also shows, as we have already seen, the radical lack of continuity in human life, its radical freedom, which breaks through all of the binds that grow with time. "Using the expression somewhat tolerantly," Nietzsche writes in *The Antichrist*, "one could call Jesus a 'free spirit'—he does not care for anything solid [laws, concepts, words]: the word kills, all that is solid kills."[193] Nietzsche believes that Paul translated Jesus' message into a doctrine, a collection of assertions about what is and, in so doing, imbued it with this stabilizing, nihilistic function.

Perhaps, however, Nietzsche reads Paul too one-sidedly. Perhaps in the letters of Paul, as in other texts from the New Testament, we can find proofs not only of difference but also of affinities between Zarathustra's story and that of Jesus, as well as of the visions of the human condition contained therein (as Heidegger and Giorgio Agamben attest). Traces of a similar understanding of the human condition: as being sick with eternity, sick with the Apocalypse that marks its every instant. Perhaps our analysis of the Nietzschean concept of eternity—of *the eternal return of the same*—could help in understanding these traces.

So let's have a closer look at them.

"We shall all be changed, in a moment, in the twinkling of an eye," Paul writes to the Corinthians (1 Cor. 15:51–52). What does he mean? Perhaps some (brief) moment in the future, a moment in which the Kingdom of God will come, the Messiah will come, our time will end, and we'll be saved. But what does "brief" mean here, or the "twinkling of an eye"? Couldn't it mean a time "briefer" than any instant we know, briefer than a year, a month, a second? And thus impossible to date? Time that cannot be measured, that cannot be defined?

If so, then what could the question "When?" mean, as in "When will this be?" It is not that we don't have an answer, that we do not know. If we are to understand it as a question of date, it makes no sense: "the twinkling of an eye," a "blink of the eyes of God," is not like rain or the Battle of Grunwald—it's not an event that begins here and ends there. It is a moment incommensurate with the time in which we live, with this succession of instants between yesterday and tomorrow.

In that case, doesn't this mean that we are speaking here about every instant? About time in general, and not just a piece of it? When, in his First Letter to the Corinthians, Paul writes, "But this I say, brethren, the time is short" (1 Cor. 7:29), he doesn't mean, perhaps, that we only have fifteen minutes, or ten years, left. Perhaps he is rather saying that time is always *brief*, that we never have time, that each and every instant is fractured and, in this way, open to the coming of the Kingdom of God, to the arrival of the Messiah. This fracture is then that "twinkling of an eye," the "moment" that cannot be grasped in the categories of temporal succession. "The day of the Lord," Paul would write to the Thessalonians, "so cometh as a thief in the night" (1 Thess. 5:2): suddenly, unexpectedly, nobody knows when. Any moment. Every moment must therefore be ready for this coming.

"Therefore let us not sleep, as others do," Paul continues, "but let us watch" (1 Thess. 5:6).

The future that I think Paul is speaking of thus characterizes every instant we live through. It is a future that in itself is not some "yesterday," some "today," one of many instants following one after another. It is a future that will not happen. This future—this fracture, this opening of each individual instant—undermines in "the blink of an eye" all of time to date and in this way "might gather together in one all things [. . .] both which are in heaven, and which are on earth" (Eph. 1:10). It gathers all of time that has been into a *single moment, a blink of an eye*, and opens it toward the radically other. This future is just as much the past, a past that isn't some "yesterday" but a quality of the very time I am living through, an aspect of the "now." A past that never was.

Future and past not as separate instants but as one and the same, "a single moment," "a blink of an eye": eternity. Eternity: the *change* of time inscribed in every instant of my life, the *blink of an eye* that gathers together my entire past and opens my entire future, a *change* that, Paul tries to convince us, Jesus (the Messiah, the Savior) introduces into our lives. Eternity: the touch of God.

In this sense, the kind of *change* announced by Paul, the Kingdom of God, is already here. The Messiah has already come. He's in every instant of my life. "What are the 'glad tidings?'" Nietzsche asks in *The Antichrist*. "True life, eternal life, has been found—it is not promised, it is here, it is *in you*."[194]

Our lives thus turn out to be something more than merely the story of a plumber or a postal clerk. "[Y]e are [. . .] the epistle of Christ," Paul writes to the Corinthians, though he means everyone who wishes to hear him, "written not with ink, but with the Spirit of the living God; not in tables of stone, but in fleshy tables of the heart" (2 Cor. 3:3).

The time of our lives is not an evenly measured succession of instants in which I am, the movement of a watch's hands, a river that I watch from outside (as the animals imagine it in Zarathustra's story). The real time of our lives is the time I myself am, time whose every moment contracts at the touch of God.

The "change" that we shall all undergo does not therefore occur in time, like the transition from antiquity to feudalism, or from capitalism to communism. The point is not that unending health and happiness will some-day take the place of death, disease, and suffering in our lives. The point is not that the present order will be replaced by another. This *change* does not create some other, new world. It is rather the unlimited potential for free-dom that, as Paul announces, the arrival of Christ brings into our lives, rendering them unlimited possibility. "Therefore if any man be in Christ, he is a new creature: old things are passed away; behold, all things are become new" (2 Cor. 5:17). The result of this divine touch, of this "gleam of divine eyes," is not some new content but just a transformation, a meta-morphosis: as a result, all things, all our connections and concepts, all our laws, turn out to be problematic and fragile. Transitory.

> But this I say, brethren, the time is short: it remaineth, that both they that have wives be as though they had none;
>
> And they that weep, as though they wept not; and they that rejoice, as though they rejoiced not; and they that buy, as though they possessed not;
>
> And they that use this world, as not abusing it: for the fashion of this world passeth away. (1 Cor. 7:29–31)

True, each of us is a child of his or her own time: we come from what has been, our past marks the horizon of the future before us. But that's not all. It is not just that each of us has his own past, his own future, his own time, but that we are also beyond it: we have no time. We come not just from our parents, our ancestors, earlier stages of evolution, but also from somewhere else: from beyond the continuum of instants, from beyond the reach of potential memory. An answer to the question "Who are we?" is not possible without referring to this sudden "change," to this "gleam of divine eyes" that undermines whatever meaning has been amassed till now and, in so doing, opens up a space where, as W. H. Auden wrote, "All journeys die here: wish and weight are lifted."[195] Maybe this is just what is meant by the word "paradise," not some "where," some "when," but a deep current, the hidden dimension of the time of our lives, thanks to which we are not merely children of time but also children of God. ("Everyone is the child of God," Nietzsche writes in *The Antichrist*, "Jesus definitely presumes nothing for himself alone.")[196] Children of God, without a past, unhindered by the succession of instants, free. "Except ye be [. . .] as little children, ye shall not enter the kingdom of heaven" (Matt. 18:3).

Can one want this? Can one want to become a child, without a past, without expectations of the future, beyond the succession of instants, as Gadamer asks rhetorically in his wonderful essay on Nietzsche? No, of course not. It's impossible. Like the sermons of Zarathustra, the words of Jesus related by Matthew do not suggest what to do, nor do they contain a plan of action. They point to the irremovable internal tension peculiar to human life, the constant struggle between what is, what each of us has become, and that absolute freedom that arises from the fracture of every instant, a freedom that does not allow me ever to be solely a father, a son, a Pole, a teacher, which does not allow me to be identical with myself. They uncover the impatience hidden beneath life's continuity, the anxiety buried beneath the events of the day, the impatience and anxiety brought about by the very fact that I am alive and not just by some reflection on this life, impatience and anxiety that do not allow me to remain in the same place, to take it easy, to be as I am. These words show that the life I am living is one that, as Paul wrote, "we could no longer forbear" (1 Thess. 3:1).

From the perspective of time as a succession of instants, from the perspective of my curriculum vitae, of my place in society, in the order of things, this *change* from the touch of God, this eternity, is a sickness. A fever. "I am come to send fire on the earth; and what will I, if it be already kindled? [. . .] Suppose ye that I am come to give peace on earth? I tell you, Nay; but rather division" (Luke 12:49, 51).

"The significance of Christianity," Berdyaev writes, "lies in its demonstration that eternity or the divine reality can break the chain of time, penetrate into and appear as the dominant force in it. [. . .] And yet it represents a constant struggle between the eternal and the temporal."[197]

Which does not mean a struggle between two orders, between two tendencies, two principles, one thing with another. Eternity—the kind of *change* that Jesus heralds in this interpretation—does not, in fact, open a separate sphere of meanings. It is rather the impossibility of stabilizing, the impossibility of enclosing any meaning within the context of human life. This is why, as Nietzsche writes in *The Antichrist*, the "concept, the *experience* of 'life' in the only way he [Jesus] knows it, resists any kind of word, formula, law, faith, dogma."[198] The struggle between eternity and time cannot be understood as a unity; it cannot be described or explicated; there is no logic here that would allow us to interpret any opposition—as Hegel does through the concept of negation—as a step toward ultimate unity. Nietzsche goes on to suggest that Jesus "never had any reason to negate 'the world'; the ecclesiastical concept of 'world' never occurred to him."[199]

If all of this is true, then the message of Jesus cannot be a doctrine or a theory. Jesus and Paul after him are not calling on us to accept certain theses. "There is no such thing as a content of faith," writes Agamben. "To believe in Jesus Messiah does not mean believing something about him."[200] Jesus does not lecture (God cannot be touched by reason, Pascal thought). He does not argue. For Jesus, Nietzsche writes, "the very idea is lacking that a faith, a 'truth,' might be proved by reasons."[201] He speaks in parable and metaphor ("And the disciples came, and said unto him, 'Why speakest thou unto them in parables?'"—Matt. 13:10). He wants to move us: "his proofs are [. . .] 'proofs of strength.'"[202] His presence is supposed to move us, to *change* human life.

To "understand" his message—as Paul wants of the Romans, the Corinthians, and the Thessalonians—that is, to find Christ's presence in human life, is not the same as to learn that two and two make four or to decode someone's DNA. It means to live "in a Christian way": *to keep watch*. An incomprehensible, insane task from the perspective of the rationality of life up to that point. Superhuman. For the presence of Christ, the touch of God, undermines everything I have been, and thus it brings to every instant of my life the hope of a new beginning, the hope of a return to absolute childhood. It demolishes the continuity and safety of my life. It demands unlimited courage. It shouldn't be surprising, then, that, as Ryszard Przybylski has observed, an especially popular image of Christian existence is sailing, and of the Christian, a sailor.

As a result of divine presence, Paul writes to the Romans, "the creature was made subject to vanity [i.e., passing], not willingly, but by reason of him who hath subjected the same in hope, because the creature itself also shall be delivered from the bondage of corruption [i.e., passing] into the glorious liberty of the children of God" (Rom. 8:20–21). This is why we sigh longingly for childhood. Not in words, not in concepts. That's not the same as wanting something, even very strongly. "[For] we know not what we should pray for as we ought" (Rom. 8:26). This sigh, this longing, cannot be expressed ("with groanings which cannot be uttered"—Rom. 8:26). It is the sigh, the longing, of life itself—not my life but of the life in me, the life whose continuity has been disrupted by God's touch, thereby opening it to unbounded, incomprehensible, and thus terrifying risk and, simultaneously, to joy—joy "in much affliction, with joy of the Holy Ghost" (1 Thess. 1:6)—to a sweetness I have not known till now.

"God, that little bee," Jarosław Iwaszkiewicz writes, "calls as no one calls," without words, somewhere within me.[203] It is this call that makes the life I am living too narrow, too small, something "I could no longer forbear."

Notes

Preface

1. Friedrich Nietzsche, *The Portable Nietzsche*, ed. and trans. Walter Kaufmann (New York: Penguin, 1982), p. 257.
2. Friedrich Nietzsche, *Werke: Kritische Gesamtausgabe*, ed. Giorgio Colli, Mazzino Montinari, et al. (Berlin: Walter de Gruyter, 1967–) (hereafter KGA), vol. 5.2, p. 411.
3. Friedrich Nietzsche, *Philosophy in the Tragic Age of the Greeks*, trans. Marianne Cowan (Washington, DC: Regnery Publishing, 1962), p. 62.

I. Nihilism

1. Friedrich Nietzsche, *The Will to Power*, trans. Walter Kaufmann and R. J. Hollingdale, ed. Walter Kaufmann (New York: Vintage, 1968), p. 9. Author's emphasis.
2. Ibid., p. 12. Author's emphasis.
3. Ibid., p. 13. Author's emphases.
4. Ibid., p. 20.
5. Leszek Kołakowski, "Rozumienie historyczne i zrozumiałość zdarzenia historycznego" [Historical understanding and the intelligibility of history], in *Kultura i fetysze: Zbiór rozpraw* (Warsaw: Państwowy Instytut Wydawniczy, 1967), pp. 221–39.
6. Nietzsche, *The Will to Power*, p. 376.
7. Ibid., p. 272.
8. Ibid., p. 267.
9. Ibid, p. 25.
10. Friedrich Nietzsche, *The Gay Science: With a Prelude of Rhymes and an Appendix of Songs*, trans. Walter Kaufmann (New York: Vintage, 1974), p. 328.
11. Stanisław Brzozowski, *Kultura i życie* [Culture and life] (Warsaw: Państwowy Instytut Wydawniczy, 1973), p. 630.
12. Nietzsche, KGW, vol. 7.2, p. 84.
13. Nietzsche, *The Portable Nietzsche*, p. 242.

II. Time Flows, the Child Plays

1. Friedrich Nietzsche, "On the Uses and Disadvantages of History for Life," in *Untimely Meditations*, ed. Daniel Breazeale, trans. R. J. Hollingdale (Cambridge: Cambridge University Press, 1997), p. 60.
2. Ibid., p. 61.
3. Ibid.

4. E. M. Cioran, *Tears and Saints*, trans. Ilinca Zarifopol-Johnston (Chicago: University of Chicago Press, 1995), p. 115. Author's emphasis.

5. Nietzsche, *The Portable Nietzsche*, p. 139.

6. Nietzsche, *Untimely Meditations*, p. 61.

7. Ibid., pp. 63–64.

8. Ibid., p. 62.

9. Friedrich Nietzsche, *The Basic Writings of Nietzsche*, ed. and trans. Walter Kaufmann (New York: Modern Library, 2000), p. 493.

10. Nietzsche, *Untimely Meditations*, p. 62.

11. Ibid., pp. 63–64.

12. Ibid., p. 91.

13. Michel Foucault, "Nietzsche, Genealogy, History," in *The Foucault Reader*, ed. Paul Rabinow (New York: Pantheon Books, 1984), p. 91.

14. Nietzsche, *Untimely Meditations*, p. 67.

15. Ibid., p. 121. Author's emphasis.

16. Ibid., p. 89.

17. Ibid., p. 92.

18. Ibid., p. 76.

19. Ibid., pp. 105–6.

20. Ibid., p. 98.

III. Good and Evil, Joy and Pain

1. Nietzsche, *The Will to Power*, pp. 375–76. Author's emphasis.

2. Nietzsche, *The Basic Writings of Nietzsche*, pp. 513–14.

3. Nietzsche, *The Gay Science*, pp. 281–82. Author's emphases.

4. Ibid., p. 174.

5. Nietzsche, *The Basic Writings of Nietzsche*, pp. 461–62, 473. Author's emphasis.

6. Ibid., p. 474.

7. Ibid., p. 483. Author's emphasis.

8. Ibid.

9. Ibid., pp. 476–77. Author's emphasis.

10. Ibid., p. 474

11. Ibid., p. 469. Author's emphases.

12. Ibid.

13. Blaise Pascal, *Pensées*, ed. and trans. Roger Ariew (Indianapolis: Hackett, 2005), p. 58.

14. Ibid., p. 33.

15. Ibid., p. 164.

16. Ibid., p. 66.

17. Ibid., p. 52.

18. Ibid., p. 141.

19. Saint Augustine, *Confessions*, trans. Henry Chadwick (Oxford: Oxford University Press, 2009), p. 199.

20. Pascal, *Pensées*, p. 236.

IV. Reason, Which Hurts

1. Nietzsche, *The Portable Nietzsche*, p. 264.
2. Ibid., p. 329.
3. Ibid.
4. Ibid., p. 278.
5. Nietzsche, KGA, vol. 6.4, p. 359.
6. Ibid., p. 329.
7. Nietzsche, KGA, vol. 5.2, p. 388.
8. Nietzsche, *The Portable Nietzsche*, p. 153.
9. Ibid., p. 159.
10. Ibid., p. 213.
11. Ibid., pp. 213–14.
12. Ibid., p. 150.
13. Ibid., p. 159.
14. Ibid., p. 196.
15. Ibid., pp. 216–17.
16. Heraclitus, *Fragments*, ed. and trans. T. M. Robinson (Toronto: University of Toronto Press, 1987), p. 37.
17. Nietzsche, *The Portable Nietzsche*, p. 265.
18. Ibid. Author's emphases.
19. Ibid., p. 215.
20. Ibid., p. 213.
21. Ibid., p. 216.
22. Ibid., p. 312.
23. Nietzsche, KGA, vol. 5.2, p. 420. Author's emphasis.
24. Nietzsche, *The Portable Nietzsche*, p. 326. Author's emphasis.
25. Ibid., p. 283.
26. Nietzsche, KGA, vol. 6.4, p. 375.
27. Nietzsche, *The Portable Nietzsche*, pp. 276, 278.
28. Ibid., p. 283.
29. Ibid., p. 276. Author's emphases.
30. Ibid.
31. Ibid., p. 277.
32. Ibid., p. 329.
33. Ibid., p. 278.
34. Ibid. Author's emphasis.
35. Ibid.
36. Ibid., p. 129.
37. Ibid., p. 277.
38. Ibid., p. 221.
39. Ibid., p. 338.
40. Ibid.
41. Ibid., p. 339.
42. Nietzsche, KGA, vol. 7.1, p. 114.
43. Ibid., p. 130.
44. Friedrich Nietzsche, *Daybreak: Thoughts on the Prejudices of Morality*, ed.

Maudemarie Clark and Brad Leiter (Cambridge: Cambridge University Press, 1997), p. 46. Author's emphasis.

V. The Time Is at Hand

1. Nietzsche, *The Will to Power*, p. 327.
2. Nietzsche, *The Gay Science*, p. 283. Author's emphasis.
3. "2 (Syriac Apocalypse of) Baruch (early Second Century A.D.)," trans. A.F.J. Klijn, in *The Old Testament Pseudoepigrapha*, vol. 1, *Apocalyptic Literature and Testaments*, ed. James H. Charlesworth (New York: Doubleday, 1983), p. 651.
4. Pascal, *Pensées*, p. 273.
5. Gerhard von Rad, *Theologie des alten Testaments* [Old Testament Theology] (Munich: C. Kaiser, 1993), p. 326.
6. Pascal, *Pensées*, pp. 22, 64.
7. Ibid., p. 50.
8. Ibid., p. 51.
9. Jacob Taubes, *The Political Theology of Paul*, trans. Dana Hollander (Stanford: Stanford University Press, 2004), p. 76.
10. Pascal, *Pensées*, p. 50.
11. Ibid., p. 62.
12. Martin Heidegger, "Die Zeit des Weltbildes" [The Age of the World Picture] in *Holzwege* (Frankfurt am Main: V. Klostermann, 1977), p. 83ff. The available English translation of this passage loses the sense of the original. See Martin Heidegger, *Off the Beaten Track*, ed. and trans. Julian Young and Kenneth Hynes (Cambridge: Cambridge University Press, 2002), p. 63.
13. Nietzsche, *The Will to Power*, p. 325.
14. Ibid., p. 461.
15. Nietzsche, *The Portable Nietzsche*, p. 242.
16. Nietzsche, *The Will to Power*, p. 326.
17. Nietzsche, *The Portable Nietzsche*, p. 197.
18. Ibid., p. 198.
19. Ibid., p. 199.
20. Ibid.
21. Ibid., p. 601. Author's emphasis.
22. Ibid., pp. 617–18.
23. Nietzsche, *The Gay Science*, p. 283.
24. Nietzsche, *The Will to Power*, p. 451.

VI. The Death of God

1. Plato, *The Works of Plato: The Benjamin Jowett Translation*, ed. Irwin Edman (New York: Modern Library, 1956), p. 117.
2. Saint Augustine, *Confessions*, p. 15. Augustine's quote is taken in turn from Psalm 78: "For he remembered that they were but flesh: a wind that passeth away, and cometh not again."

3. Plato, *The Works of Plato*, pp. 119, 121.

4. Jorge Luis Borges, *Selected Non-Fictions*, ed. Eliot Weinberger, trans. Esther Allen, Suzanne Jill Levine, and Eliot Weinberger (New York: Viking, 1999), p. 486.

5. Plato, *The Works of Plato*, p. 121.

6. Gustave Flaubert, *Madame Bovary*, trans. Geoffrey Wall (New York: Penguin, 2002), p. 310.

7. Plato, *The Works of Plato*, p. 122.

8. Michel de Montaigne, *The Complete Essays*, trans. M. A. Screech (New York: Penguin, 1993), p. 89ff.

9. Plato, *The Works of Plato*, p. 137.

10. Ibid., p. 143.

11. Ibid., p. 189.

12. Epicurus, *The Epicurus Reader: Selected Writings and Testimonia*, trans. and ed. Brad Inwood and L. P. Gerson (Indianapolis: Hackett, 1994), p. vii.

13. Plato, *The Works of Plato*, p. 111.

14. D. H. Lawrence, *Women in Love* (New York: Penguin, 2007), p. 194.

15. William Hazlitt, "On the Feeling of Immortality in Youth," in *The Collected Works of William Hazlitt*, ed. A. R. Waller and Arnold Glover, vol. 12 (London: J. M. Dent, 1904), p. 151.

16. Hans-Georg Gadamer, "Der Tod als Frage" [Death as Question] in *Gesammelte Werke*, vol. 4 (Tübingen: Mohr, 1987), p. 163.

17. Ibid., p. 170.

18. Emmanuel Levinas, *God, Death, and Time*, trans. Bettina Bergo (Stanford: Stanford University Press, 2000), p. 72.

19. Franz Kafka, *The Diaries of Franz Kafka*, ed. Max Brod, trans. Joseph Kresh, Martin Greenberg, and Hannah Arendt (New York: Schocken, 1976), p. 244.

20. Saint Augustine, *Confessions*, p. 74.

21. Plato, *The Works of Plato*, p. 181.

22. Nietzsche, *The Portable Nietzsche*, p. 608.

23. Quoted in Emmanuel Levinas, *Proper Names*, trans. Michael B. Smith (Stanford: Stanford University Press, 1996), p. 176 n. 16.

24. Saint Augustine, *Confessions*, p. 227.

25. Montaigne, *The Complete Essays*, p. 96.

26. Pascal, *Pensées*, p. 273.

27. Saint Augustine, *Confessions*, p. 141.

28. Levinas, *God, Death, and Time*, p. 193.

29. Nietzsche, *The Portable Nietzsche*, p. 142.

VII. Eternity's Flame

1. Saint Augustine, quoted in Peter Brown, *Augustine of Hippo: A Biography* (Berkeley: University of California Press, 2000), p. 242.

2. Plotinus, *The Enneads*, trans. Stephen MacKenna (New York: Penguin, 1991), p. 351.

3. Borges, *Selected Non-Fictions*, p. 135.

4. Nietzsche, KGA, vol. 5.2, p. 550.

5. Nietzsche, KGA, vol. 7.1, p. 5. Author's emphasis.
6. Nietzsche, KGA, vol. 6.4, p. 135.
7. Nietzsche, *The Portable Nietzsche*, p. 313.
8. Nietzsche, KGA, vol. 5.2.
9. Lawrence, *Women in Love*, p. 172.
10. Nietzsche, *The Portable Nietzsche*, p. 313. Author's emphases.
11. Friedrich Hölderlin, *The Death of Empedocles: A Mourning-Play*, trans. David Farrell Krell (Buffalo: SUNY Press, 2008), p. 101.
12. Ibid., p. 102.
13. Nietzsche, *The Portable Nietzsche*, p. 252.
14. Nietzsche, KGA, vol. 8.3, p. 167.
15. Nietzsche, KGA, vol. 8.3, p. 166ff.
16. Ibid, p. 166.
17. Ibid.
18. Nietzsche, KGA, vol. 7.3, p. 280ff.
19. Nietzsche, *The Portable Nietzsche*, p. 313.
20. Lawrence, *Women in Love*, p. 172.
21. Quoted in Brown, *Augustine of Hippo: A Biography*, p. 242.
22. Edmund Husserl, *The Phenomenology of Internal Time-Consciousness*, ed. Martin Heidegger, trans. James S. Churchill (Bloomington: Indiana University Press, 1964), p. 114.
23. Kołakowski, "Rozumienie historyczne i zrozumiałość zdarzenia historycznego."
24. Nietzsche, KGA, vol. 3.2, p. 317.
25. Nietzsche, KGA, vol. 5.2, p. 468.
26. Ibid., p. 402.
27. Ibid., p. 398.
28. Nietzsche, KGA, vol. 7.3, p. 285.
29. Nietzsche, KGA, vol. 5.2, p. 402.
30. Nietzsche, *The Portable Nietzsche*, p. 313.
31. Ibid.; Hölderlin, *The Death of Empedocles: A Mourning-Play*, p. 102.
32. Nietzsche, *The Portable Nietzsche*, p. 313.
33. Ibid.
34. Ibid. Author's emphasis.
35. Nietzsche, *The Gay Science*, p. 32.
36. Nietzsche, *The Portable Nietzsche*, p. 334.
37. Nietzsche, *The Basic Writings of Nietzsche*, p. 737.
38. Nietzsche, *The Portable Nietzsche*, p. 247.
39. Nietzsche, KGA, vol. 7.1, p. 382.
40. Aristotle, *The Basic Works of Aristotle*, ed. Richard McKeon, trans. C.D.C. Reeve (New York: Modern Library, 2001), p. 541.
41. Nietzsche, KGA, vol. 7.1, p. 433.
42. Nietzsche, *The Portable Nietzsche*, p. 211.
43. Nietzsche, KGA, vol. 7.1, p. 507.
44. Kafka, *The Diaries of Franz Kafka*, p. 392.
45. Nietzsche, *The Will to Power*, p. 262.

46. Ibid., p. 34.

47. Nietzsche, *The Portable Nietzsche*, p. 313.

48. Ibid., p. 274.

49. Jose Ortega y Gasset, "Tod und Auferstehung (1917)" [Death and Resurrection], in his *Gesammelte Werke*, vol. 1 (Stuttgart: Deutsche Verlagsanstalt, 1996), p. 100.

50. D. H. Lawrence, *Studies in Classic American Literature*, ed. Ezra Greenspan, Lindeth Vasey, and John Worthen (Cambridge: Cambridge University Press, 2003), p. 109.

51. G.W.F. Hegel, *Lectures on the History of Philosophy, 1825–26*, vol. 2, *Greek Philosophy*, ed. and trans. Robert F. Brown (Oxford: Oxford University Press, 2006), p. 80. Here, Hegel is quoting Plutarch, who is in turn quoting Heraclitus.

52. Heraclitus, *Fragments*, p. 25.

53. Seneca, *Dialogues and Essays*, trans. John Davie (Oxford: Oxford University Press, 2009), pp. 83–84.

54. Seneca, *Four Tragedies and Octavia*, trans. E. F. Watling (New York: Penguin, 1966), p. 275.

55. Origen, *Homilies 1–14 on Ezekiel*, trans. Thomas P. Scheck (Mahwah, NJ: Paulist Press, 2010), p. 43.

56. See Henry Chadwick, *The Church in Ancient Society: From Galilee to Gregory the Great* (Oxford: Oxford University Press, 2001), p. 516.

57. Hegel, *Lectures on the History of Philosophy*, 2:80.

58. Ibid., 2:78.

59. Martin Heidegger, "Heraklit: Der Anfang des Abendländischen Denkens (1943)" [Heraclitus: The Dawn of Western Thought], in *Gesamtausgabe*, vol. 55 (Frankfurt am Main: Klosterman, 1976–), p. 61.

60. Kathleen Freedman, trans., *Ancilla to the Pre-Socratic Philosophers*, ed. Hermann Diels (Cambridge, MA: Harvard University Press, 1948), p. 29.

61. Heidegger, "Heraklit," 55:64.

62. Nietzsche, KGA, vol. 5.2, p. 549.

63. Nietzsche, *The Portable Nietzsche*, p. 122.

64. Nietzsche, KGA, vol. 6.4, p. 157.

65. Nietzsche, *The Portable Nietzsche*, pp. 205, 638.

66. Ibid., p. 341.

67. Nietzsche, KGA, vol. 5.2, p. 504.

68. Nietzsche, *The Gay Science*, p. 117.

69. Nietzsche, KGA, vol. 6.4, p. 285.

70. Nietzsche, KGA, vol. 7.1.

71. Nietzsche, *The Portable Nietzsche*, p. 284.

72. Nietzsche, KGA, vol. 15, p. 194.

73. Nietzsche, *The Gay Science*, p. 36.

74. Nietzsche, KGA, vol. 6.4, p. 648.

75. Ibid.

76. Origen, *Spirit and Fire: A Thematic Anthology of His Writings*, ed. Hans Urs von Balthasar, trans. Robert J. Daly (Washington, DC: Catholic University of America Press, 1984), p. 326.

77. Nietzsche, KGA, vol. 7.1, p. 420.
78. Lawrence, *Studies in Classic American Literature*, p. 123.
79. Nietzsche, *The Gay Science*, p. 228.
80. Nietzsche, *The Portable Nietzsche*, p. 311.
81. Nietzsche, KGA, vol. 7.1, p. 637.
82. Franz Kafka, *Letters to Friends, Family, and Editors*, trans. Richard Winston and Clara Winston (New York: Schocken, 1977), p. 16.
83. Nietzsche, *The Portable Nietzsche*, p. 122.
84. Ibid., p. 126.
85. Nietzsche, KGA, vol. 7.1, p. 374.
86. Nietzsche, *The Portable Nietzsche*, p. 83.
87. Nietzsche, *Daybreak*, p. 105.
88. Nietzsche, *The Portable Nietzsche*, p. 123.
89. Nietzsche, KGA, vol. 6.4, p. 92.
90. Nietzsche, KGA, vol. 5.2, pp. 370–71.
91. Nietzsche, *The Portable Nietzsche*, p. 290.
92. Nietzsche, KGA, vol. 6.4, p. 445.
93. Borges, *Selected Non-Fictions*, p. 134.
94. Ibid., p. 332.
95. Stanisław Brzozowski, *Pamiętnik* [Memoirs] (Krakow: Wydawnictwo Literackie, 1985), p. 72.
96. Nietzsche, *The Portable Nietzsche*, p. 301.
97. Nietzsche, KGA, vol. 5.2, p. 400.
98. Nietzsche, *The Portable Nietzsche*, p. 238.
99. Nietzsche, *The Will to Power*, p. 310.
100. Origen, *Spirit and Fire*, pp. 329–30.
101. Lou Andreas-Salomé, *Friedrich Nietzsche in seinen Werken* [Friedrich Nietzsche in His Works] (Vienna: Verlag von Carl Konegen, 1894), pp. 120–21. An English translation of this work omits many significant passages: Lou Salomé, *Nietzsche*, ed. and trans. Siegfried Mandel (Urbana: University of Illinois Press, 2001).
102. Andreas-Salomé, *Friedrich Nietzsche in seinen Werken*, p. 19.
103. Nietzsche, KGA, vol. 5.2, p. 402.
104. Cioran, *Tears and Saints*, p. 14. Author's emphasis.
105. Piero Camporesi, *The Incorruptible Flesh: Bodily Mutilation and Mortification in Religion and Folklore*, trans. Tania Croft-Murray (Cambridge: Cambridge University Press, 1988), p. 36.
106. Nietzsche, KGA, vol. 7.1, p. 213.
107. Franz Kafka, *Nachgelassene Schriften und Fragmente* [Unpublished Writings and Fragments], ed. Malcolm Pasley, vol. 1 (Frankfurt: S. Fischer, 1993), p. 8.

VIII. Eternal Love

1. Plotinus, *Enneads*, trans. Stephen MacKenna, abridged and introduced by John Dillon (New York: Penguin, 1991), p. 174.
2. Rainer Maria Rilke, *Lay of the Love and Death of Cornet Christopher Rilke*, trans. M. D. Herter Norton (New York: W. W. Norton, 1959), pp. 51, 55.

3. Quoted in Caroline Walker Bynum, *The Resurrection of the Body in Western Christianity, 200–1336* (New York: Columbia University Press, 1995), p. 340.

4. Nietzsche, *The Gay Science*, p. 333.

5. Flaubert, *Madame Bovary*, p. 199.

6. Saint John of the Cross, *The Living Flame of Love by St. John of the Cross with His Letters, Poems and Minor Writings*, trans. David Lewis (New York: Cosimo, 2007), pp. 54–55.

7. Camporesi, *The Incorruptible Flesh*, pp. 157–58.

8. Quoted in Bynum, *The Resurrection of the Body in Western Christianity*, p. 340.

9. Plotinus, *Enneads*, pp. 176–77.

10. Quoted in Camporesi, *The Incorruptible Flesh*, p. 78.

11. Louis-Ferdinand Céline, *Journey to the End of the Night*, trans. Ralph Manheim (New York: New Directions, 2006), p. 109.

12. Quoted in Hans Urs von Balthazar, *Presence and Thought: An Essay on the Religious Philosophy of Gregory of Nyssa* (San Francisco: Ignatius Press, 1995), p. 73.

13. St. Gregory of Nazianus, *Of God and Man: The Theological Poetry of St. Gregory of Nazianus*, trans. Peter L. Gilbert (Crestwood, NY: St. Vladimir's Seminary Press, 2001), p. 134. Author's emphasis.

14. John Climacus, *The Ladder of Divine Ascent*, trans. Colm Luibheid and Norman Russell (Mahwah, NJ: Paulist Press, 1982), pp. 125, 123–24.

15. Porphyry, "On the Life of Plotinus and His Work," in Plotinus, *Enneads*, p. ciii.

16. Origen, "Fragment on Psalm 1.5," quoted in Bynum, *The Resurrection of the Body in Western Christianity*, p. 64.

17. James McKonkey Robinson, ed., *The Nag Hammadi Library in English*, 3rd ed. (New York: Brill, 1988), p. 235.

18. Benedicta Ward, ed., *The Desert Fathers: Sayings of the Early Christian Monks* (New York: Penguin Books, 2003), p. 31.

19. Ibid., pp. 39–40.

20. Quoted in *New Testament Apocrypha*, vol. 1, *Gospels and Related Writings*, ed. Wilhelm Schneemelcher, trans. R. McL. Wilson (Louisville: Westminster John Knox Press, 1991), p. 209.

21. Bynum, *The Resurrection of the Body in Western Christianity*, p. 224.

22. Quoted in Camporesi, *The Incorruptible Flesh*, p. 156.

23. Camporesi, *The Incorruptible Flesh*, p. 251.

24. Nietzsche, *The Portable Nietzsche*, p. 130.

25. Céline, *Journey to the End of the Night*, p. 207.

26. Nietzsche, *The Gay Science*, p. 333.

27. Ibid., p. 171.

28. Cioran, *Tears and Saints*, p. 118.

29. Saint John of the Cross, *The Living Flame of Love*, p. 9.

30. Ibid., p. 22.

31. Octavio Paz, *The Double Flame: Love and Eroticism*, trans. Helen Lane (Boston: Houghton Mifflin, 1995), p. 26.

32. Kafka, *Diaries*, p. 339.

33. Nietzsche, *The Portable Nietzsche*, p. 389.

34. Ibid.

35. Nietzsche, KGA, vol. 7.1, p. 88. Author's emphasis.

36. Michael Clanchy, ed., *The Letters of Abelard and Heloise*, rev. ed., trans. Betty Radice (New York: Penguin, 2004), p. 54.

37. Paz, *The Double Flame*, p. 159.

38. Cioran, *Tears and Saints*, p. 54.

39. Borges, *Selected Non-Fictions*, p. 135.

40. Emily Dickinson, *The Poems of Emily Dickinson*, ed. R. W. Franklin (Cambridge, MA: Harvard University Press, 1999), pp. 306–7.

41. Nietzsche, *The Portable Nietzsche*, p. 217.

42. Nietzsche, KGA, vol. 7.1, p. 221.

43. Paz, *The Double Flame*, pp. 114–15.

44. Nietzsche, *The Portable Nietzsche*, p. 235.

45. From Iwaszkiewicz's poem "Do Izoldy" [To Isolde].

46. Hans-Georg Gadamer, *Literature and Philosophy in Dialogue: Essays in German Literary Theory*, trans. Robert H. Paslick (Buffalo: State University of New York Press, 1994), pp. 38–42.

47. Bynum, *The Resurrection of the Body in Western Christianity*, p. 46.

48. Emmanuel Levinas, *Totality and Infinity: An Essay on Exteriority*, trans. Alphonso Lingis (Pittsburgh: Duquesne University Press, 1969), p. 34.

49. From Różewicz's poem "Nic" [Nothing].

50. Kafka, *Diaries*, p. 390.

51. Georg Wilhelm Friedrich Hegel, *The Hegel Reader*, ed. Stephen Houlgate (Oxford: Blackwell, 1998), p. 32.

52. André Breton, *Mad Love*, trans. Mary Ann Caws (Lincoln: University of Nebraska Press, 1987), p. 8.

53. C. G. Jung and C. Kerenyi, *Science of Mythology: Essays on the Myth of the Divine Child and the Mysteries of Eleusis*, trans. R.F.C. Hull (London: Routledge, 2005), p. 80. Author's emphasis.

54. Hans-Georg Gadamer, "The Drama of Zarathustra," trans. Thomas Heilke, in *Nietzsche's New Seas: Explorations in Philosophy, Aesthetics and Politics*, ed. Michael Allen Gillespie and Tracy B. Strong (Chicago: University of Chicago Press, 1988), p. 230.

55. Ibid., p. 231.

56. Nietzsche, *The Portable Nietzsche*, p. 230.

57. Cioran, *Tears and Saints*, p. 6. Author's emphasis.

58. Nietzsche, *The Portable Nietzsche*, p. 147.

59. D. H. Lawrence, *Study of Thomas Hardy and Other Essays*, ed. Bruce Steele (Cambridge: Cambridge University Press, 1985), p. 52.

60. From Różewicz's poem "Cierń" [Thorn].

61. Nietzsche, KGA, vol. 6.4, p. 134.

62. Nietzsche, *The Gay Science*, p. 36. Author's emphasis.

63. Ibid., pp. 36–37. Author's emphasis.

64. Ibid., p. 272.

65. Ibid., p. 38.

66. Nietzsche, *The Portable Nietzsche*, p. 242.

67. Kafka, *Diaries*, p. 410.

68. Nietzsche, *The Gay Science*, pp. 35–36.

69. Nietzsche, KGA, vol. 6.4, p. 135.

IX. Our Insatiable Desire for More Future: On the Eternal Return of the Same

1. Nietzsche, *The Gay Science*, pp. 224–25.
2. Dickinson, *The Poems of Emily Dickinson*, p. 573.
3. Czesław Miłosz, *Piesek przydrożny* (Krakow: Znak, 1997), p. 276. This passage is omitted from the English-language edition, *Road-Side Dog*.
4. G.W.F. Hegel, *Introduction to the Philosophy of History, with an Appendix from the Philosophy of Right*, trans. Leo Rauch (Indianapolis: Hackett, 1988), p. 57.
5. Arthur Schopenhauer, *The World as Will and Representation*, vol. 1, trans. E.F.J. Payne (Mineola, NY: Dover, 1969), p. 276.
6. Gerhard von Rad, *Old Testament Theology*, trans. David M. Stalker, vol. 2 (Louisville: Westminster John Knox Press, 2001), p. 102.
7. Mircea Eliade, *The Myth of the Eternal Return, Or: Cosmos and History*, trans. Willard R. Trask (Princeton: Princeton University Press, 1974), p. 123.
8. David Hume, *Dialogues Concerning Natural Religion*, 2nd ed., ed. Richard H. Popkin (Indianapolis: Hackett, 1998), p. 49.
9. Schopenhauer, *The World as Will and Representation*, 1:279.
10. Ibid., 1:280.
11. Origen, *Ante-Nicene Christian Library*, vol. 10, *The Writings of Origen*, ed. Alexander Roberts and James Donaldson (Edinburgh: T. & T. Clark, 1869), p. 55.
12. Saint Augustine, *City of God*, trans. Henry Bettenson (New York: Penguin, 1972), pp. 488–89.
13. Quoted in John Meyendorff, *Christ in Eastern Christian Thought* (Crestwood, NY: St. Vladimir's Seminary Press, 1975), p. 53.
14. Nietzsche, *The Portable Nietzsche*, p. 122.
15. Ibid.
16. Ibid.
17. Ibid.
18. Ibid., p. 336.
19. Ibid., p. 122.
20. Ibid.
21. Ibid., p. 124. Author's emphasis.
22. Ibid.
23. Ibid., p. 129.
24. Ibid.
25. Ibid., p. 130.
26. Ibid., pp. 129–30.
27. Ibid., p. 130.
28. Ibid., p. 142.
29. Ibid., p. 125.
30. Ibid., p. 399. Author's emphases.
31. Ibid., p. 177.
32. Ibid., p. 128. Author's emphasis.
33. Nietzsche, *Daybreak*, p. 32.
34. Nietzsche, *The Portable Nietzsche*, p. 240.
35. Ibid., p. 127.

36. Brzozowski, *Kultura i życie*, p. 643.

37. Nietzsche, *The Portable Nietzsche*, p. 158.

38. G.W.F. Hegel, *Phenomenology of Spirit*, trans. A. V. Miller (Oxford: Oxford University Press, 1979), p. 493.

39. Nietzsche, *The Portable Nietzsche*, p. 160.

40. Nietzsche, KGA, vol. 7.1, p. 221.

41. Nietzsche, *The Portable Nietzsche*, p. 183.

42. From Słowacki's epic *Poema Piasta Dantyszka, Herbu Leliwa, o Piekle* [The Poem of Dantyszek Piast, of the Leliwa Coat of Arms, on Hell].

43. Ibid., p. 129.

44. Nietzsche, *Philosophy in the Tragic Age of the Greeks*, p. 54.

45. Nietzsche, *The Portable Nietzsche*, p. 122.

46. Nietzsche, *Philosophy in the Tragic Age of the Greeks*, p. 54.

47. Nietzsche, *The Gay Science*, p. 268.

48. Ibid., pp. 268–69.

49. Nietzsche, *The Portable Nietzsche*, p. 399. Author's emphasis.

50. Nietzsche, *Daybreak*, p. 53.

51. Nietzsche, *The Portable Nietzsche*, p. 636.

52. Martin Heidegger, *The Phenomenology of Religious Life*, trans. Matthias Fritsch and Jennifer Anna Gosetti-Ferencei (Bloomington: Indiana University Press, 2004), p. 73.

53. Nietzsche, *The Will to Power*, pp. 98–99.

54. Nietzsche, KGA, vol. 8.2, p. 400. Author's emphasis.

55. Nietzsche, *The Portable Nietzsche*, p. 608. Author's emphases.

56. D. H. Lawrence, *Sons and Lovers* (New York: Penguin, 2006), pp. 470–71.

57. From Słowacki's poem "Odpowiedź na Psalmy Przyszłości" [Response to the Psalms of the Future].

58. William James, *Writings: 1902–1910* (New York: Library of America, 1987), p. 128.

59. Nietzsche, *The Portable Nietzsche*, p. 204.

60. Nietzsche, *The Will to Power*, p. 310.

61. Nietzsche, *The Portable Nietzsche*, p. 226.

62. Ibid., p. 227.

63. Ibid.

64. Nietzsche, KGA, vol. 7.1, p. 88.

65. Nietzsche, *The Portable Nietzsche*, p. 198.

66. Ibid., p. 465.

67. Ibid., p. 522.

68. Nietzsche, KGA, vol. 5.2, p. 550.

69. Nietzsche, *The Portable Nietzsche*, p. 301.

70. Nietzsche, KGA, vol. 8.1, p. 159.

71. Nietzsche, KGA, vol. 7.2, p. 156.

72. Nietzsche, *The Portable Nietzsche*, p. 199.

73. Nietzsche, KGA, vol. 6.4, p. 135.

74. Ibid.

75. Nietzsche, KGA, vol. 7.1, p. 215.

76. Nietzsche, KGA, vol. 6.4, p. 136.

77. Søren Kierkegaard, *The Seducer's Diary*, trans. Howard V. Hong (Princeton: Princeton University Press, 1997), p. 146.
78. Nietzsche, *The Portable Nietzsche*, p. 221.
79. Lawrence, *Studies in Classic American Literature*, p. 106. Author's emphases.
80. Nietzsche, *The Portable Nietzsche*, pp. 221–22.
81. Nietzsche, *The Gay Science*, p. 153. Author's emphasis.
82. Nietzsche, KGA, vol. 8.3, p. 186.
83. Nietzsche, *The Portable Nietzsche*, p. 253.
84. Ibid., p. 213.
85. Ibid., p. 227.
86. Nietzsche, *The Gay Science*, p. 116.
87. Ibid., p. 272.
88. Nietzsche, *The Basic Writings of Nietzsche*, p. 353. Author's emphases.
89. Nietzsche, *The Portable Nietzsche*, pp. 199, 251.
90. Ibid., p. 251.
91. Nietzsche, *The Will to Power*, p. 75. Author's emphases.
92. Brzozowski, *Kultura i życie*, p. 614.
93. Nietzsche, *The Portable Nietzsche*, p. 199.
94. Ibid.
95. Ibid., p. 202.
96. Aristotle, *The Basic Works*, p. 295.
97. Nietzsche, *The Portable Nietzsche*, p. 251.
98. Ibid., p. 310.
99. Schopenhauer, *The World as Will and Representation*, vol. 1, p. 279.
100. Nietzsche, *The Portable Nietzsche*, p. 268.
101. Ibid., p. 269.
102. Ibid. Author's emphasis.
103. Ibid., p. 270.
104. Ibid. Author's emphasis.
105. Ibid., p. 271.
106. Ibid.
107. Ibid.
108. Ibid., p. 272.
109. Ibid.
110. Ibid., p. 328.
111. Ibid.
112. Ibid., pp. 329–30.
113. Ibid., p. 330. Author's emphasis.
114. Ibid., p. 328.
115. Ibid., p. 323.
116. Ibid., p. 325.
117. Nietzsche, KGA, vol. 8.3, p. 167.
118. Nietzsche, *The Portable Nietzsche*, p. 251.
119. Nietzsche, KGA, vol. 7.1, p. 207.
120. Nietzsche, KGA, vol. 8.3, p. 166.
121. Nietzsche, *The Gay Science*, p. 168.
122. Nietzsche, KGA, vol. 7.1, p. 176.

123. Nietzsche, KGA, vol. 7.3, p. 280ff.

124. Nietzsche, KGA, vol. 5.2, p. 423. Author's emphasis.

125. Friedrich Hölderlin, *Essays and Letters on Theory*, ed. and trans. Thomas Pfau (Albany: State University of New York Press, 1988), p. 96. Author's emphases.

126. E. M. Cioran, *On the Heights of Despair*, trans. Ilinca Zarifopol-Johnston (Chicago: University of Chicago Press, 1992), p. 65. Author's emphases.

127. Nicholas Berdyaev, *The Meaning of History* (New Brunswick, NJ: Transaction Publishers, 2006), pp. 63–64.

128. Ryszard Przybylski, *Ogrody Romantyków* [The Gardens of the Romantics] (Krakow: Wydawnictwo Literackie, 1978), p. 128.

129. Kierkegaard, *The Seducer's Diary*, p. 176.

130. Ibid., p. 177.

131. Nietzsche, *The Portable Nietzsche*, p. 335.

132. Ibid., p. 334.

133. Ibid., p. 310. Author's emphasis.

134. Plotinus, *The Enneads*, p. 444.

135. Nietzsche, KGA, vol. 5.2, p. 550.

136. Ibid., p. 411. Author's emphasis.

137. Nietzsche, KGA, vol. 6.4, p. 521.

138. G.W.F. Hegel, *Werke in 20 Bänden*, vol. 4 (Frankfurt am Main: Suhrkamp, 1986), pp. 87–88.

139. Plutarch, *Plutarch's Morals: Theosophical Essays*, trans. C.W. King (London: George Bell and Sons, 1889), p. 191.

140. Heraclitus, *Fragments*, ed. and trans. T. M. Robinson (Toronto: University of Toronto Press, 1987), p. 61.

141. Nietzsche, KGA, vol. 7.1, p. 211.

142. Nietzsche, *The Portable Nietzsche*, p. 334.

143. Nietzsche, KGA, vol. 6.4.

144. Nietzsche, *The Portable Nietzsche*, p. 271.

145. Ibid.

146. Ibid., p. 328.

147. Cioran, *Tears and Saints*, p. 101.

148. Nietzsche, KGA, vol. 5.2, p. 397. Author's emphasis.

149. Hölderlin, *Essays and Letters on Theory*, p. 99.

150. Nietzsche, *The Will to Power*, p. 281.

151. Rainer Maria Rilke, "Nächtlicher Gang" [Night Walk], in his *Werke in Drei Banden*, vol. 2 (Weisbaden: Insel, 1966), p. 30.

152. Nietzsche, *The Portable Nietzsche*, p. 225.

153. Hegel, *Phenomenology of Spirit*, p. 355.

154. G.W.F. Hegel, *Outlines of the Philosophy of Right*, ed. Stephen Houlgate, trans. T. M. Knox (Oxford: Oxford University Press, 2008), p. 15. Author's emphasis.

155. Leszek Kołakowski, *Main Currents of Marxism*, trans. P. S. Falla (New York: Norton, 2005), p. 338.

156. Nietzsche, *The Portable Nietzsche*, p. 125.

157. Nietzsche, p. 317.

158. Hans-Georg Gadamer, "Nietzsche—der Antipode (1984)," in his *Gesammelte Werke*, vol. 4, p. 458.

159. Nietzsche, *The Portable Nietzsche*, p. 139.

160. Nietzsche, KGA, vol. 7.1, p. 472.

161. Nietzsche, *The Portable Nietzsche*, p. 272.

162. Ibid.

163. Ibid., p. 343.

164. Ibid., p. 257.

165. Ibid., p. 328.

166. Ibid., p. 122.

167. Ibid., p. 430. Author's emphasis.

168. Ibid., pp. 267–68. Author's emphasis.

169. Ibid., p. 267.

170. Cioran, *On the Heights of Despair*, pp. 64–65.

171. Nietzsche, KGA, vol. 3.3, p. 69.

172. Nietzsche, KGA, vol. 7.1, p. 627. Author's emphasis.

173. Ibid.

174. Quoted in Martin Heidegger, *Hegel's Phenomenology of Spirit*, trans. Parvis Emad and Kenneth Maly (Bloomington: Indiana University Press, 1988), p. 5.

175. Nietzsche, *The Portable Nietzsche*, p. 378.

176. Ibid., p. 257.

177. Nietzsche, *The Gay Science*, p. 274.

178. Ibid.

179. Nietzsche, *The Portable Nietzsche*, p. 269.

180. Ibid., p. 216.

181. Nietzsche, KGA, vol. 7.3, p. 98.

182. Nietzsche, KGA, vol. 7.1, p. 209.

183. Ibid.

184. Ibid.

185. Nietzsche, *Philosophy in the Tragic Age of the Greeks*, p. 63.

186. Ibid.

187. Nietzsche, KGA, vol. 7.1, p. 144.

188. From Lechoń's poem, "Na 'Boskiej Komedii' dedykacja" [On the Divine Comedy: A dedication].

189. Nietzsche, *The Portable Nietzsche*, p. 223.

190. Nietzsche, KGA, vol. 7.1, p. 447.

191. Nietzsche, *The Portable Nietzsche*, p. 618.

192. Ibid., p. 650. Author's emphasis.

193. Ibid., p. 605.

194. Ibid., p. 601. Author's emphasis.

195. W. H. Auden, *Collected Poems*, ed. Edward Mendelson (New York: Modern Library, 2007), p. 293.

196. Nietzsche, *The Portable Nietzsche*, p. 601.

197. Berdyaev, *The Meaning of History*, p. 67.

198. Nietzsche, *The Portable Nietzsche*, p. 605. Author's emphasis.

199. Ibid., p. 606.

200. Giorgio Agamben, *The Time That Remains: A Commentary on the Letter to the Romans*, trans. Patricia Dailey (Stanford: Stanford University Press, 2005), p. 136.

201. Nietzsche, *The Portable Nietzsche*, p. 606.

202. Ibid.

203. Jarosław Iwaszkiewicz, *Ciemne ścieżki* [Dark Paths] (Warsaw: Czytelnik, 1982), p. 43.

Index